D1522832

Revitalization: Explorations in World Christian Movements Pietist and Wesleyan Studies
Series Editor—J. Steven O'Malley

21. *E. Stanley Jones Had a Wife: The Life and Mission of Mabel Lossing Jones*, Kathryn Reese Hendershot, 2007.
22. *German Radical Pietism*, Hans Schneider, 2007.
23. *The Making of an American Church: Essays Commemorating the Jubilee Year of the Evangelical United Brethren Church*, Robert L. Frey, 2007.
24. *Foundation for Revival: Anthony Horneck (1641–1697), the Religious Societies, and the Construction of an Anglican Pietism*, Scott Thomas Kisker, 2008.
25. *Evangelical Hospitality: Catechetical Evangelism in the Early Church and Its Recovery for Today*, Tory K. Baucum, 2008.
26. *Catholic Spirit: Wesley, Whitefield, and the Quest for Evangelical Unity in Eighteenth-Century British Methodism*, James L. Schwenk, 2008.
27. *John Wesley's Ecclesiology: A Study in Its Sources and Development*, Gwang Seok Oh, 2008.
28. *The Rise of Korea Holiness Church in Relation to the American Holiness Movement: Wesley's "Scriptual Holiness" and the "Fourfold Gospel,"* Meesaeng Lee Choi, 2008.
29. *A Higher Moral and Spiritual Stand: Selected Writings of Milton Wright*, edited by Timothy S. G. Binkley, 2009.

Revitalization: Explorations in World Christian Movements

This volume is published in collaboration with the Center for the Study of World Christian Revitalization Movements, a cooperative initiative of Asbury Theological Seminary faculty. Building on the work of the previous Wesleyan / Holiness Studies Center at the Seminary, the Center provides a focus for research in the Wesleyan Holiness and other related Christian revitalization movements, both historical and contemporary, which have had a world impact. The research seeks to develop analytical models of these movements, including their biblical and theological assessment. Using an interdisciplinary approach, the Center bridges relevant discourses in several areas in order to gain insights for effective Christian mission globally. It recognizes the need for conducting research that combines insights from the history of evangelical renewal and revival movements with anthropological and religious studies literature on revitalization movements. It also networks with similar or related research and study centers around the world, in addition to sponsoring its own research projects.

Binkley's critical edition of the writings of Bishop Milton Wright bring to light previously unpublished documents which shed important light on the religious culture and times of Wilbur and Orville Wright, the Bishop's illustrious sons of aviation fame. The study is appropriate to the Series by demonstrating how Milton Wright was a significant participant in the nineteenth century holiness movement, drawing from the Pietist heritage of his United Brethren tradition. For this reason, its publication here is congruent with the mission of the Center for the Study of World Christian Revitalization Movements.

J. Steven O'Malley, Series Editor and Director
Center for the Study of World Christian Revitalization Movements

*Milton Wright, 1871, during his tenure as Editor of the
Religious Telescope. Image courtesy of Special Collections
and Archives, Wright State University, Dayton, Ohio.*

A Higher Moral and Spiritual Stand

Selected Writings of Milton Wright

Edited by
Timothy S. G. Binkley

*Revitalization: Explorations in
World Christian Movements*

Pietist and Wesleyan Studies, No. 29

The Scarecrow Press, Inc.
Lanham, Maryland • Toronto • Plymouth, UK
and
The Center for the Study of
World Christian Revitalization Movements
2009

SCARECROW PRESS, INC.

Published in the United States of America
by Scarecrow Press, Inc.
A wholly owned subsidiary of
The Rowman & Littlefield Publishing Group, Inc.
4501 Forbes Boulevard, Suite 200, Lanham, Maryland 20706
www.scarecrowpress.com

Estover Road
Plymouth PL6 7PY
United Kingdom

British Library Cataloguing in Publication Information Available

Library of Congress Cataloging-in-Publication Data
Wright, Milton, 1828–1917.
  [Selections. 2009]
  A higher moral and spiritual stand : selected writings of Milton Wright / edited by
Timothy S.G. Binkley.
      p. cm. — (Pietist and Wesleyan studies ; no. 29) (Revitalization: explorations in
world Christian movements)
  Includes bibliographical references and index.
    ISBN 978-0-8108-6060-5 (pbk. : alk. paper) — ISBN 978-0-8108-6309-5 (ebook)
  1. Church of the United Brethren in Christ (1800–1889) 2. Church of the United
Brethren in Christ (Old Constitution) I. Binkley, Timothy S. G., 1963– II. Title.
  BX9876.W75 2009
  289.9–dc22   2009002342

♾™ The paper used in this publication meets the minimum requirements of
American National Standard for Information Sciences—Permanence of
Paper for Printed Library Materials, ANSI/NISO Z39.48-1992.
Manufactured in the United States of America.

Contents

Illustrations

Editor's Foreword

This study illustrates how Milton Wright (1828-1917) brought together issues of personal faith and public morality in the context of his position as Bishop of the United Brethren in Christ. He brings the authority of that office to bear upon two important historical developments of his age. One was the broader holiness movement, with its concerns for sanctity of life, especially as it bore upon the issue of secret societies and their perceived detrimental influence in nineteenth century America. Another was the history of aviation, in view of his formative influence on his sons, Orville and Wilbur, of aviation fame. The portrait of Bishop Wright's life and ministry which emerges in the course of this study relies on writings of Wright which are first brought into published form in this study. Not only do they shed new light on the family of these aviation pioneers; they also contribute to the understanding of the role of a Pietist-based denomination, the Church of the United Brethren in Christ, in the formation of American culture. The study also shows how Wright was consciously ministering in the tradition of Philip William Otterbein (1726-1813), the principal founder of that denomination in the post-revolutionary War era.

Binkley's careful work in editing these texts results in a volume that will be a valued resource for scholars and all persons interested in American religious history in the late nineteenth and early twentieth centuries. It is with pleasure that we include it in the Series.

J. Steven O'Malley, Editor
Pietist and Wesleyan Studies Series

Preface

Milton Wright is generally remembered as the father of aviation pioneers Wilbur and Orville Wright. Here at United Theological Seminary, Bishop Wright is also remembered as one of the school's founding fathers. That distinction was down-played for several generations following the United Brethren schism of 1889. Today the seminary has reclaimed its relationship with the man who was the public voice of the United Brethren Church during America's tumultuous post-Civil War era.

In 2005 United Theological Seminary advanced the preservation of Milton Wright's publications by bringing its Archives and Center for the Evangelical United Brethren Heritage collections into a new, environmentally-controlled facility. A grant from the Aviation Heritage Foundation, made possible by the Wright Family Fund of the Dayton Foundation, financed the re-housing of the Wright era *Religious Telescope* volumes in acid-free boxes. The seminary also used Aviation Heritage Foundation funds to begin the inventory and transcription of Milton Wright's articles. Republication of the editorials in this book is an effort to preserve Bishop Wright's spiritual legacy by getting his writings back out in front of the public.

Milton Wright was a man of firmly-held convictions who shared them un-hesitatingly with others. Never complacent, he sought out ever larger audiences. As a capable educator, preacher, and professor of theology, Milton Wright im-pacted the lives of hundreds. In print, he was able to speak to tens of thousands.

The 1869 General Conference of the Church of the United Brethren in Christ elected Reverend Wright editor of its most widely-read periodical. Shortly thereafter, the Wright family moved to Dayton, Ohio, home of the United Brethren Publishing House.

After eight years of writing multiple weekly editorials for the *Religious Telescope*, Milton Wright was elected bishop. This ended his career at the Publishing House. The promotion increased his authority within the denomination while actually decreasing his public exposure.

In all, Milton Wright published nearly one thousand titled opinion pieces in the *Religious Telescope*. For this volume I have selected one hundred thirty-five editorials that reflect the depth of his thought and the breadth of his interests. The Prologue features two introductory articles penned by Wright to inaugurate his editorship. The Epilogue contains Wright's editorial farewell and a follow-up article by Assistant Editor W. O. Tobey describing their working relationship. In between the reader will find four topical chapters: theological writings, articles on Christian piety and public morality (inseparable matters to Wright), columns discussing United Brethren Church matters, and commentary on political and social issues in the United States. The articles in each chapter are arranged chronologically so that the reader may trace developments in Wright's attitudes and arguments.

In some of his columns, Wright acted as reporter and commentator; more often he wrote as a preacher and teacher. His language is Victorian, but not overly flowery. Modern readers may find his frequent use of the first person plural an oddity. This was a literary convention of the day reflecting the fact that, as Editor, Wright's opinions were the official stance of his paper, which was the "official organ" of the United Brethren Church. Through his editorials, Milton Wright spoke both to and for his denomination.

Another word about language use might be helpful at this point. Wright often railed against "professors of religion." By this he did not mean Christian college and seminary faculty members! Instead, the phrase referred to those who, in his opinion, were Christians in name only. In contrast, the Christianity that Wright advocated was personal, heart-felt, and life-changing.

In this volume I have attempted to reproduce Wright's work accurately. The punctuation, capitalization, italicized words and phrases, antiquated spellings (e.g. "indorse" for "endorse"), and biblical citation formatting are as found in his original columns.

Some have viewed Milton Wright as a cantankerous curmudgeon. Wright's *Religious Telescope* editorials demonstrate that he was not simply a naysayer. He actively promoted education, social justice, ethical behavior, and vital faith. Some of Wright's social views were quite ahead of his times. His advocacy on behalf of women and minorities was sincere even though it may sound patronizing to modern ears.

Milton Wright did not pretend to like every person, group, or cause. He publicly scorned those whom he disliked. He wrote off the worst of his enemies as unredeemable "errorists."

Today's readers will find statements that appeal and statements that offend in the pages that follow. Surely, Wright's original readers had similarly mixed reactions.

As editor of this volume, I am grateful for the assistance of many people who have supported the project. I would like to thank the Rev. Dr. G. Edwin Zeiders, UTS President 1999-2007, and Dr. Jason E. Vickers, Director of the Center for the Evangelical United Brethren Heritage, for their encouragement. Special thanks are due to Dr. J. Steven O'Malley, who authored the introductory essay, and to Dr. Sarah Blair, Rychie Breidenstein, Barbara Buttram, Caryn Dalton, Dr. Robert Frey, Michelle Grimm, Glenna Holdeman, Jeffrey A. Landis, Mary Kay Mabe, Janet McDermott, Matthew Querns, and Nancy Rohrer, who assisted with transcribing and proofreading. I am grateful to the Wright State University Special Collections and Archives for granting permission to reprint several images from the Wright Brothers Collection in this volume. Finally, I wish to thank Steve Wright, Amanda Wright Lane, and the Aviation Heritage Foundation for their generous financial support.

Through the *Religious Telescope*, Milton Wright challenged Christians, denominations, and the United States of America to take "a higher moral and spiritual stand."[1] May this book help new generations to remember Bishop Wright and his great cause.

Dayton, Ohio

Note

1. Phrase quoted from the February 9, 1876 editorial "Our Centennial Celebration" which is reprinted in Chapter 3.

Advertisement for the Religious Telescope, 1893. Image courtesy of the Center for the Evangelical United Brethren Heritage, United Theological Seminary, Dayton, Ohio.

Introduction

Bishop Milton Wright and His World

By J. Steven O'Malley

Milton Wright was a child of the western frontier. Born in Rush County, Indiana, on November 17, 1828, he hailed from Puritan roots. He was reared in the Jacksonian era, which favored the common person over those with birthright privilege. That sentiment would have ramifications for the sides he took on the divisive issues of his day. It meant he would become an ardent opponent of slavery, and an equally ardent opponent of secret societies, which he perceived as threats to advancing the interests of the common person. In this perception he found company in the cause of the American Antislavery Society, established under the auspices of the holiness reforms emanating from Oberlin College in Ohio, as well as the Anti-masonic Party, that was organized in the year of Milton's birth, whose opposition to secret societies rested on the perception that it represented an autocratic elite.[1]

Like slavery, anti-masonry was viewed by Christian populists like Wright as contravening the egalitarian ideals of the western frontier. In this milieu, Wright's identity emerges as an agrarian-based social reformer, who links a radical, non-conformative approach to personal and social ethics with a universal view of truth, devoted to assimilating the interests and goals of religion and science. This fusion would be as the antidote to the secularist bias of modernism. It is because of these polarities that Wright can be found opposing both bourgeois secret societies and evolutionary thought, while also encouraging his sons' mastery of the long resistant hurdle of humanly-controlled aeronautical flight.

1

Some understanding of how these polarities in Wright's life and thought were shaped would appear to provide a useful grounding for an insightful reading of the selections from his writings which appear in this volume. To achieve that result, our attention may be directed to three concerns. First, being a churchman, we might consider the ecclesial context for his thought. Second, what were the official roles that he occupied in the course of his ministry, including how did these provide context for the articulation of his life's vision? Third, how might we assess his agenda as social crusader, apologist, and controversialist, in light of his vision for a renewed Pentecost in nineteenth-century America? The comments which follow reflect previous research on Wright as a representative of the holiness movement of the nineteenth century, as well as an indebtedness to the seminal research of Daryl Elliott in the writings of Wright.[2]

The Ecclesial Context

Although they exercised godly piety in their home, the parents of Milton Wright had migrated to frontier Indiana without denominational allegiance. Young Milton heard Presbyterian and Methodist preachers who passed through their neighborhood, rejecting the former for their Calvinism and the latter for what he regarded as their tendency to seek "popularity."[3] It was through his encounter with a leading Indiana preacher of the United Brethren in Christ that he was drawn to investigate their beliefs and rules of discipline. Concluding that they were "respectable but not cursed with popularity,"[4] by which he apparently meant worldly conformity, he made a profession of Christ in conversion, and received baptism. Sensing a call to public ministry, Wright completed a probationary period as exhorter and licensed preacher, and then successfully negotiated a newly instituted three-year course of study. These steps resulted in his ordination and admission to the White River (Indiana) Conference of that denomination in 1856."[5]

The United Brethren matched his sentiments for multiple reasons. Their theology was broadly Arminian, and yet their polity seemed to conform more to democratic standards than did the Episcopal Methodists. Appointments were made by a stationing committee of preachers in conference, rather than solely by a bishop, and licensed lay preachers were granted full membership in their conferences. Preachers held membership in local congregations as well as in their annual conferences to which they reported. They were devoid of liturgical formality in observance of the "ordinances" of baptism and the Lord's Supper, and the former was administered without preference as to form. Their greater emphasis rested upon the importance of being an "unpartisan" fellowship, in which a partisan spirit was regarded as a cardinal sin. This commitment meant that their unity was derived from the sense of brotherhood lived out at the grassroots level. Features of that brotherhood included lay preaching, the recognition of women in ministry at an early date (1847), and, especially important for Milton, the strict prohibition of membership in secret societies, which Milton regarded as a violation of that trust.[6]

The basis for these distinctives may be traced to their origins in colonial Pennsylvania, where they emerged as among the earliest expressions of an indigenous American denomination. On Pentecost Sunday, 1767, a "new light" Mennonite farmer preacher named Martin Boehm (1725-1812) conducted what was then known as a "big meeting" (*"grosse Versammlung"*) in a Pennsylvania barn. Awakened by apparent contacts with the revival traced to George Whitefield in the Middle Colonies, Boehm's intent was to announce the gift of the new birth in Christ to seekers gathered from a variety of German sects. His intent was not to form a new sect but to influence his hearers to return to their home religious communities with the revitalization of the Spirit's baptism. They would then form a higher unity in Christ that transcended party and denominational lines.

Boehm's most notable auditor was Philip William Otterbein (1726-1813), a German Reformed pastor who publicly embraced the surprised Anabaptist preacher with the expression *"wir sind Brüder"* ("we are brethren"), thereby launching a revitalization movement, consisting of magisterial as well as radical Protestants, that would slowly emerge into a denominational entity after 1800. Their initial intent to manifest a renewed Pentecost, and thereby initiate a post-Christendom age of the Spirit in the New World, reflected radical Pietist themes imported from eighteenth century Germany into the religious diversity that represented colonial Pennsylvania.[7] In terms of polity, United Brethren blended a Presbyterian commitment to a single order of representative ministry (elder) with a modified Methodist episcopal polity, which restricted bishops to terms based on popular election.

Wright's Spirited Leadership in the United Brethren Church and Its Larger Import

The unitive impulse that defined the early United Brethren blended well with the egalitarian spirit and disdain for privilege and oligarchy that reigned on the western frontier of Indiana. Their preachers reached the state by 1808, and they would emerge as among of the six largest Protestant denominations in Indiana in the nineteenth century. Milton Wright would become a leader in this advance, and in its commitments to impacting all facets of society with the transformative message of Jesus Christ, grounded in the experience of personal conversion.

With a hunger for knowledge, Wright served as a public school teacher as well as lay preacher en route to his ordination. He completed his collegiate education while also serving as a teacher in the "preparatory department" at Hartsville College, founded in Indiana by the United Brethren in the early 1850s. After a successful tenure as a professor at this college, he became convinced he was being called to missionary service in the Oregon Territory. Thomas J. Connor, a preacher in the White River Conference, had organized and led a wag-onload of colonists to plant a United Brethren community in that far flung terri-tory in 1853. Four years later, Connor returned to recruit missionaries for this project, and Wright responded.

Milton saw this field as a strategic point in the crusade to advance the gos-pel on the advancing American frontier, and particularly his commitments to preventing the extension of slavery and secret societies, as well as the addictive quest for gold that seemed to be sweeping through the frontier. In his mind, these were prominent markers in the onslaught of infidelity that threatened the formation of a Christian society. Traveling by steamer from the port of New York via the isthmus of Panama, he contracted a life-threatening case of typhoid before reaching his destination. With his physical constitution being severely weakened, his ministry duties in Oregon had to be restricted. Nevertheless, he found a suitable venue for ministry as principal and head teacher of Sublimity College, a new frontier United Brethren school in Oregon, where he presided as a strict disciplinarian. He also contributed from his own income to provide for additional missionaries in the growing Oregon project.[8] After recovering from his illness, he resumed the activities of an itinerant preacher, but interrupted his travels to return to Indiana to wed a former student at Hartsville, Susan Koerner. Due to her weakened health, he then chose to remain in the ministry of his home district, the White River Conference. Here he quickly rose to leadership as pre-siding elder and then professor in the new theological program at Hartsville Col-lege.

In his tenure as the sole appointed theologian in the denomination, Wright distinguished himself by developing what Elliott has called a Baconian view of truth, reflecting Francis Bacon's universal perception that human knowledge is of one piece, in its religious and scientific expressions. This outlook was based in an inductive philosophical approach which valued empirical data over rational theory that tends toward the speculative and the metaphysical. Truth that is sci-entific is based on observation and a "common sense" analysis of the observed facts of nature. [9] On this ground, all truth deemed scientific could be harmonized on the basis of the grid provided by orthodox Christian doctrine, as reflecting revelatory truth in Scripture. In brief, there is, to Wright, no qualitative differ-ence between truth in religion and in science, since this definition of the scien-tific method provides the only acceptable paradigm for making truth claims.

This methodology could work for Wright to oppose Darwin's theory of biological evolution, on the one hand, or to defend the prerogatives of women's right to expression, whether in the ministry of the church or in popular suffrage (as the right to vote in civil elections). It was an Anglo-American "common sense" paradigm of truth, well suited for a practical, frontier ethos, though it generally became discredited through the rise of new epistemological options in twentieth century philosophy.[10] Wright's thinking was formed by his in-depth reading of leading nineteenth-century scientific thinkers, including the natural scientist Alexander von Humboldt (1769-1859), with his emphasis on observation and classification. Wright hoped that his sons, Wilbur and Orville, might exemplify the fusion of this disciplined pursuit of science with genuine religious piety. [11] Darwinism was for Milton Wright the epitome of the dangerous liberal spirit because its methodology is predicated on a relativistic and non-theistic foundation. He also had little sympathy for clergy who accommodated this fashionable thought, which he put in the same category as their repulsive attraction for worldly fashions of apparel. All were expressions of the carnal human nature.

At the 1869 General Conference, Wright was elected editor of the denomination's periodical, *The Religious Telescope*, which to him became a venue for advancing his campaign against membership by United Brethren in secret societies. He had come to regard this issue as the next great obstacle to be overcome in advancing the Kingdom of God in America, after the defeat of slavery in the Civil War. Like the defenders of slavery, he thought this practice drained its participants of strength and commitment to the cause of Christ, in this instance by prescribing a regimen based upon a deistic and all-inclusive or latitudinarian view of religious truth. [12] He would resign this office in 1877 when elected bishop.

Wright's Vision for a Universal Pentecost

In advancing his commitments, Wright was appealing, at least implicitly, to the vision of a renewed Pentecost which had first launched the United Brethren in Christ at the Otterbein-Boehm barn meeting on Pentecost, 1767. In a published account, he acknowledged that he had in his possession one of the few extant letters from Otterbein—a letter concerning the millennium, in which the latter declared his postmillennial belief in a coming "more glorious age of the church on earth". [13] Wright indicated his agreement "that the millennium will consist of a happy general spiritual reign of Christ on earth previous to his second personal coming." [14] This will be the age of Christ's kingdom on earth, for which Christians pray "Thy will be done" in the Lord's Prayer. It is an age where "all willing to be saved in harmony with the gospel plan" will receive that salvation, and where "justice and righteousness" will be enacted in every land. And, it will be inaugurated by a final, "universal baptism in the Holy Spirit," as a "universal Pentecost" that will "complete the world's salvation and usher in the millennium." [15]

In his later years, Wright's conviction that this millennial goal was imminent receded in intensity, as he witnessed what he regarded as intractable opposition not only within the larger American society but also within his own United Brethren in Christ to his program for advancing the ideal of a Christian America. This sober reassessment of the prospects for the future germinated during his combative years as bishop of his denomination. This shift was only

somewhat ameliorated by the delight he took in his daughter's hopeful advocacy
for woman's suffrage, and his sons' successful breakthrough in one of the greatest challenges that had held back the human race, the mastery of humanly controlled aeronautical flight.

Ironically, it was during his fitful tenure as bishop among the United Brethren in Christ that he discovered, and perhaps himself helped to foment, the parti-
sanship and disunity that, to early United Brethren, was the mark of fallen human nature. That ecclesial body which was raised up to bear witness to the
coming unity of a renewed Pentecost became in itself a testimony to the persistent human fratricidal strife that had precipitated its rise in the eighteenth century. How we assign responsibility to Bishop Wright in this development is a
matter to be adjudicated by careful historical research. It is sufficient here to
recount the basic elements in the dispute which bedeviled his episcopal career.

Our inquiry has shown that Wright did not come to his position as a funda-
mentalist but as one sharing the postmillennial outlook prominent in nineteenth
century American evangelical Protestantism. As a churchman, he was committed to guarding the confessional tradition of his denomination against the challenges to Christian orthodoxy, whether from the side of Darwinian science or
"deistic" secret societies. To his view, both represented challenges to imple-
menting the kingdom of God in America, based on biblical theism.

Wright had found an ally in this crusade in the person of Jonathan Blanchard, a Wesleyan holiness leader who also served as president of a newly founded
revivalist school in Illinois, Wheaton College. Blanchard and Wright agreed in
their perception that secret societies, like slavery in the antebellum era, were
each condoned by clergy to attract and retain affluent members in the church,
whose love of wealth threatened devotion and obedience to Christ alone.[16]
Blanchard formed a new organization to advance this agenda, called the National Christian Association (1867), which had strong United Brethren participa-
tion. Wright became its vice president in 1876, the year before he was elected a
United Brethren bishop, with assignment to the West Mississippi District.[17] His
election to the episcopacy of his church occurred with the help of his anti-
secrecy supporters. He was initially assigned to serve in the Iowa area of the
denomination.

His opponents succeeded in defeating his re-election to the quadrennial office of bishop in 1881. That gave Wright opportunity to begin publication of an
anti-secrecy United Brethren newspaper after relocating to a major center of
earlier abolitionist activity, the important Quaker city of Richmond, Indiana.[18]
However, his commitment to his church continued, leading him to distance himself from Blanchard's abortive efforts to form a new anti-secrecy denomination.

As the United Brethren moved toward denominational schism over the anti-
secrecy issue in the 1880s, Wright found himself being outflanked by the "liberal" faction, that linked rescinding of the disciplinary article prohibiting secret
society membership with support for a new church constitution favoring lay

representation and other democratic reforms in church conferences. Wright was a proponent of the latter, especially as it impacted women in ministry, but as leader of the so-called "radical" faction on anti secrecy, his predicament was that defense of the old constitution would prevent him from garnering support from those favoring these reforms in the church.

In 1885, Wright's "liberal" opponents formed a church commission to re-write the denominational confession of faith and constitution so that the anti-secrecy references would be muted. One could now participate in Masonic ac-tivities so long as "Christian character" was not harmed. Ironically, Wright was also re-elected bishop during that quadrennium, although his opponents in the church hierarchy consigned him to episcopal duties in the Pacific area, appar-ently to distance him from the debate. After returning to the Midwest, his con-frontation with his opponents took the extreme form of challenging the decision to replace him as bishop in the White River Conference (Indiana). He ultimately withdrew from his beloved, now "apostate" denomination when a referendum of the general membership, and the official vote of the General Conference, ratified the new constitution in 1889. The expelled minority of radicals then proceeded to reorganize under Wright's leadership as the Church of the United Brethren in Christ (Old Constitution).[19]

In the last sixteen years of his public ministry, Wright waged his ongoing campaign for the coming universal Pentecost that would usher in the millennial reign of Christ in a Christianized society. However, he now did so from the posi-tion of a bishop in the minority branch of the United Brethren, and the continu-ing controversies that swirled around him served mainly to dampen his opti-mism for the imminence of that kingdom. After his final resignation from the episcopacy in 1905, he devoted much energy and attention to the meteoric aero-nautical careers of Wilbur and Orville Wright.[20] His support for their promising project would occupy his attention, signifying his continued commitment to linking orthodox Christian belief with advances in science. This outlook would soon be outflanked in conservative Protestant circles, torn by the fundamental-ist-modernist controversy that came on the heels of the First World War. With his death occurring in 1917, that was one controversy that Milton Wright did not live to engage.

Notes

1. See Paul Goodman, *Towards a Christian Republic: Antimasonry and the Great Transition in New England, 1826-1836* (New York: Oxford, 1988), 21.
2. See J. S. O'Malley, "German-American Contributions to the Ongoing Search for American Evangelicalism with Reference to the Radical United Brethren Secession of 1889," in *Methodist History* (October, 2008); and Daryl M. Elliott, *Bishop Milton Wright and the Quest for a Christian America* (PhD dissertation, Drew University, 1992).

3. H.A. Thompson, *Our Bishops* (Chicago: Elder Publishing Company, 1889), 536.

4. Thompson, *Our Bishops,* 536-537.

5. "Annual Conference Minutes of the White River Conference of the Church of the United Brethren in Christ, 1847-1856," Transcript of originals, Methodist Library, Drew University, Madison: NJ, 82, as cited in Elliott, *Bishop Milton Wright*, 34.

6. See Bruce Behney and Paul Eller, *History of the Evangelical United Brethren Church* (Nashville: Abingdon Press, 1979), 184.

7. On this, see Hans Schneider, *German Radical Pietism* (Metuchen, NJ: Scarecrow, 2007).

8. *The Sixth Annual Report of the Board of Missions of the United Brethren in Christ, and the Proceedings of the Annual Meeting* (Dayton: U.B. Printing Establishment, 1859), 6,18; cited in Elliott, 70.

9. Elliott, *Bishop Milton Wright*, 322-323.

10. Examples of this paradigmatic challenge is the rise of existential and phenomenological thought in thinkers like Karl Barth and Edmund Husserl.

11. Milton Wright, "Alexander von Humboldt," in *The Religious Telescope* (September 22, 1869), 20; as discussed in Elliott, *Bishop Milton Wright*, 325.

12. See discussion in Elliott, *Bishop Milton Wright*, 167-252.

13. Philip William Otterbein, "Letter Concerning the Millennium," in Arthur Core, ed., *Philip William Otterbein; Pastor, Ecumenist* (Dayton: Board of Publication, 1968), 102-103.

14. Milton Wright, "The Millennium's Approach," *Christian Conservator*, (December, 1887), 1,5., cited in Elliott, *Bishop Milton Wright*, 127-128.

15. Wright, "Millennium's Approach," 5; in Elliott, *Bishop Milton Wright*, 129.

16. For an analysis of Blanchard's relation to Wright, see Elliott, *Bishop Milton Wright*, 182-207.

17. United Brethren Bishop David Edwards was its first president. "The National Anti-Secret Society Convention," *Religious Telescope* (13 May, 1868), 254; Elliott, 183.

18. The masthead of this paper, *The Richmond Star*, was "First Pure, then Peaceable." Its successor was *The Christian Conservator*, the official organ of the "radical" United Brethren that would be published at their new headquarters at Huntington, Indiana. See Elliott, *Bishop Milton Wright*, 212.

19. Contention centered upon the question of whether the old constitution had intended the required vote for amending that document to be two-thirds of the total membership or only of those voting, with Wright's party arguing for the former, and hence contending for the illegality of the majority (liberal) position.

20. Wilbur died of typhoid in 1912, cutting short his promising career in aviation. Both brothers were also actively involved in supporting their father in the church struggles.

The United Brethren Publishing House, Dayton, Ohio, 1869. Image courtesy of the Center for the Evangelical United Brethren Heritage, United Theological Seminary, Dayton, Ohio.

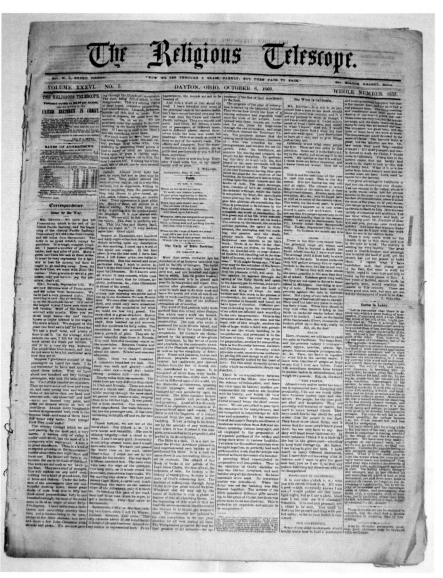

The Religious Telescope as it appeared in October of 1869. Image courtesy of the Center for the Evangelical United Brethren Heritage, United Theological Seminary, Dayton, Ohio.

Prologue

July 7, 1869   Editorial Salutatory

DEAR READERS OF THE TELESCOPE:—It has fallen to my lot, very unexpect-
edly, to assume the duties of the editorship of the principal periodical of our
denomination. I enter upon those duties with a deep sense of the responsibility
of an editor's position, and not without sincere diffidence respecting my capability of satisfying the just demands of the Church for piety, ability, literary taste,
knowledge of church affairs, etc.—qualifications so essential to that position.
While I rejoice in the fact that the RELGIOUS TELESCOPE has not, for many
years, been without an able managing editor, making its columns instructive to
our people and an honor to our denomination, this very fact increases my diffidence, as it does the capability required of the successors of such editors. The
prospect, however, of having the assistance of my worthy predecessor, who has
managed the editorial department of our paper through a period of great success,
and who has made a record of which himself and the Church may be justly
proud, is not a little comforting. I hope I shall have the prayers and moral support of the very many dear brethren throughout the Church, who are alike interested in the success of our Church periodicals, and the prosperity of our denomination. I hope that, as hitherto, many valuable correspondents will
contribute able articles to enrich the columns of the Church paper. Of the reasons which induced my election, my sense of the proprieties to which those used
as candidates are amenable, would forbid my speaking, and even preclude all
desire to say a word. Every minister and every layman in the Church has a right
to expect of one in my position magnanimity, equanimity, and discretion. The
whole Church will expect me to discharge the duties of my office with all the
ability, grace, industry, and impartiality of which I am capable. Unaccustomed
to the editorship, there will be much to learn that experience alone can teach,
and much that practice alone can acquire; hence I shall expect to have the kind
forbearance, for a time, at least, of all our dear brethren in the Lord.

I shall hope to contribute something toward the diffusion of sanctified knowledge, toward the promotion of real Christianity, and toward the encouragement of the cause of missions, education, and the Sabbath school. I hope to be alive to the interests of our itinerants, and to those of their people; for their interests are the same. I shall seek to not be local in my attachments, nor in my views. I shall seek to not be partial on account of personal friendships, nor prejudiced against any with whom I may differ in sentiment at any time in my editorial career. I shall seek to avoid hobbies, and yet endeavor to make our Church paper expressive on every important question which should properly be entertained by a religious journal. I should desire to have the RELIGIOUS TELESCOPE not a sectarian sheet, yet a *United Brethren* paper. I hope to be able to recognize in any denomination, or any organization, or any public man, whatsoever is commendable, however much I may dislike some things pertaining to that organization, or regret some things attaching to that person. The sentiments which I shall express from time to time in our editorial columns, will be the honest convictions of my mind, and I hope to speak the truth in love, remembering that I shall answer for those sentiments, and the spirit in which they are expressed, to *Him* before whom we must all soon appear in the judgment. But I know that words to be effective must have some edge.

That I shall be able to satisfy my own desire in those things, or meet the expectation of my friends, I sincerely doubt. I can only try. This is all I can do; but in it I will persevere, and in the strength of grace, in humble reliance on God, yielding to no discouragement, I will, with prayer unceasing, diligence unflagging, and vigilance not slumbering, labor to have the support of my brethren, the approval of a good conscience, and the favor of God. Time unfolds the future before us; it is ours to labor and to wait.   MILTON WRIGHT

September 8, 1869   Our New Volume

We begin with this number of our paper the THIRTY-SIXTH VOLUME OF THE RELIGIOUS TELESCOPE. More than a generation since, our paper was first issued and was then a semi-monthly folio of medium size. From the first, it has taken a high stand on the moral questions which have arisen for the solution of the age. Though for a time unpopular in consequence of its boldness and zeal in support of these measures, it has lived through trial and obloquy to see most of history, we trust that our church organ will still, through evil report or good report, stand in the front ranks on every question of moral reform. On Slavery, Temperance, Secret Societies, and other moral questions, the TELESCOPE has made a record which it is to be hoped will never be reversed or tarnished.

We are very largely dependent upon the free-will offerings of the talented writers of the Church for the attractiveness and efficiency of our church paper. We hope they will feel this, and let their contributions respond to our invitation to furnish our columns with their chosen thoughts in carefully-written articles abounding with gems thinly clad with graceful, but soul-stirring words. It is our desire to make the TELESCOPE not so much our own exponent of thought, as the exponent of the thoughts and feelings of the wise and pious throughout the Church. This is our ideal of what a church organ should be. We would that our beloved brethren could realize our desire, and the importance of making our weekly periodical the repository of the choicest gems which they gather in their studies, in their meditations, in their labors, and in their communion with God. Some articles, even from good writers, for various reasons, may not find a place in our columns; others may be delayed for a time. It is impossible, in the columns of our paper or otherwise, to explain those reasons in each instance; but our contributors may rest assured that we often share their disappointment very keenly, without a word of reproach from them. We love to please them, and even delight to publish other communications from them.

It is highly desirable that the circulation of the TELESCOPE should be greatly enlarged. While the membership of the Church has been greatly increased, the circulation of our chief periodical has not kept pace with our advance in numbers and means. It is to the ministers and members of the Church that we must mainly look for such an advance as shall place our paper as nearly as possible in the house of every member of our Church, and extend its circulation and influence beyond our membership. Will you not for the sake of the Church, and for Christ's sake, do what you can?

Again bespeaking, as in our last week's issue, the prayers of our beloved brethren and sisters in Zion, we address ourselves anew to the task before us, assuring our readers that we will endeavor, with a single eye, a good conscience, and an honest heart, to labor to make the RELIGIOUS TELESCOPE a continued and increasing success.

Religious Telescope composing room, circa 1893. *Image courtesy of the Center for the Evangelical United Brethren Heritage, United Theological Seminary, Dayton, Ohio.*

Chapter 1

Theology

September 8, 1869   The Prince of Peace

Christ, of old, by the spirit of prophecy, was denominated "The Prince of Peace." This will lead us to inquire, "Wherein is the title appropriate to him?"

If we refer to temporal warfare, he may be called the Prince of Peace. He ever, by his example and precepts, condemned violence. The weapons which he used, and which alone he authorized his disciples to employ, were spiritual. The principles which he taught are those which underlie the peace of the world, and which, if universally received in faith and practice, would usher in the millennium for all nations. Wherever his doctrine has been published and to any considerable extent has been received, it has ameliorated the condition of the nations, modified the rules of carnal warfare, and lessened its prevalence, even though the true votaries of this religion have been very few and have never directly controlled for an age any great nation. Christ, in his providential government, has made the wrath of man to praise him, turning the affairs of nations to the promotion of his own glory. He has not, however, willed man's wickedness, nor delighted in his wrath, but only accomplished the best results in the application of his own overruling power. Could we properly consider the conflicting condition of the nations without the gospel, and then mark the change wrought by even a few embracing its truths, and those progressing so little in its purity, we should not be astonished at the title divinely given to Christ, "The Prince of Peace."

There is another view we may take of Him of the increase of whose peace there is no end. Truth is clear and peaceful; error is a tangled conflicting maze. It has not a set of dogmas universally acknowledged by its subjects; but there is no limit to the number and diversity of errors which swarm in this world of ours. Error wars with error, and is often most intolerant. It can never cease its strife while it exists. By increasing ignorance, error is only limited in its arena. The universal prevalence of truth alone can produce universal peace in the universe of thought and intelligence. In the past, thought has contended with thought, and errors have struggled with heated zeal, and sometimes truth has been thereby evoked. Errors in premise—incorrect first principles,—necessarily involve conflict; and conflict is the only road to truth; but truth itself, received and adopted, has no conflicts in itself, and the greater its prevalence, the more of peace;—and in its final, eternal field, peace prevails forever under the fostering reign of its Prince.

But, finally, we notice that peace which we have with God "through Jesus Christ our Lord." In Christ all the attributes of God harmonize. In him mercy and justice meet together—righteousness and peace embrace each other. He was set forth as a propitiation that God might be just and the justifier of him that believeth in Jesus; and now the glory of God is "seen in the face of Jesus Christ." Not only do the attributes of God harmonize in the Prince of Peace, but it is through the cross of Christ that the enmity is slain, and the sinner is subdued by the power of divine love. Justice may threaten, duty may call, heaven may invite; it is alone a crucified Redeemer which slays the enmity of the carnal soul through the workings of his divine power.

And with the prevalence of his kingdom shall peace be established. It is the harmony of heaven. It is the unison of the song of the redeemed, in which a believing Abel, a sanctified Enoch, a righteous Noah, a peaceful Melchisedec, a faithful Abraham, a persecuted Joseph, a meek Moses, a holy Samuel, a sweet-singing David,—and the holy prophets and apostles, and martyrs, and confessors,—the redeemed of the Lord from every part of the earth shall join in singing: "Thou hast redeemed us out of every nation," and the angels, delighting to look into these things, shall sing: "Just and true are all thy ways, thou King of Saints." All in heaven is one holy concord of harmony in thought, and affection, and worship,—one everlasting song of peace. Christ, all in all there reigns the eternal "Prince of Peace."

February 2, 1870   God Hiding His Face

Perhaps the general experience of Christians is that at times God's presence and favor do not seem manifested as at others. There are certainly causes producing this; but they may not always be well understood by us. We can well understand why willful sin should cause God to hide his face from us, but not so well why, when we are earnestly, industriously, and conscientiously endeavoring to do his will, a cloud should seem to intervene, our light and comfort flee apace, and we be left wondering as well as mourning. Perhaps our devotions languish, our hopes sink, our zeal flags, our communion with God seems interdicted, and we have hardly enough spirituality left to adequately wonder, or mourn our loss. Many reasons can be suggested for this experience; but are we not apt to feel that they are not correct? We may say that faith is wanting; but we may be conscious of no unusual declension in this grace till the cloud was upon us, and of course then our faith was not in lively exercise. We may say that there was too much self-confidence or vanity, too much yielding to the carnal nature, or too much shrinking before the frowns or yielding to the caresses of the world. While all this is true, we may be conscious that there was no more but even less of this than when our skies were clearer and our joys were fuller. We may endeavor to explain it by all those methods which are in many cases true and applicable, but, after all, from a long experience, be compelled to reject all of those ordinarily-given explanations. While this is true of the darker shades of Christian experience, is it not also true of the sunnier hours of Christian life? Are there not times when the religious sentiments and emotions of the soul seem all awake and alive? Joy flows like a stream from a full fountain. Communion with God seems like a spontaneous flowing out toward Deity, and an inward flowing of spirituality to the soul—an appropriate meeting and sweet commingling of a Divine Spirit with a soul rendered holy by a sacred and heavenly renewal. While enjoying this communion, which seems to embrace all that heart could wish, are we able to explain satisfactorily why such is the state of our religious experience and enjoyments? None of the reasons ordinarily assigned will fully answer our inquiries.

We are led to inquire whether it may not be the good pleasure of the Father to give us special seasons of refreshing from his presence? Whether there are not times, too, when he allows our souls to be subject to especial trials? Was it not so with the Master, when on earth he was being tempted in all points like as we are? Was the conflict, after his baptism and after the divine recognition, when he encountered the adversary in the wilderness, a matter of no trial? Was the sorrow which he expressed as he walked with Peter, James, and John toward Gethsemane nothing? Were his "strong cryings and tears," of which Paul speaks, without an adequate cause? And yet he did no sin.

Again; we are subject to chastisements. Are these to be continuous?—unintermittent? or shall we believe that the chidings of reproof and the rod of correction are administered in the seasons which are of God's own choosing? Are there no seasons of respite and days of grace, when the weight of the rod is not laid on us, and when the chidings of reproof are not chilling our souls? The severer strokes of our Father's chastisement surely are not falling continually and mingling all the time with the most endearing caresses and sweetest comforts which our souls receive from him.

Further; have not the circumstances which surround us and the state of our physical system much to do with our souls? While a high degree of grace enables us to measurably triumph over these, and oftentimes to rise above them in ecstatic, joyful victory, it requires no mean degree of grace to enable us so to do; and when this is wanting, or the soul is found off its guard, or is attacked at some peculiarly vulnerable point, it may find itself measurably cast down, and, perhaps, like an army attacked at an unexpected hour of the night, somewhat bewildered; yet the hopeful exclamation following the temporary inquiry of the soul, "Why hast Thou forgotten me?" is soon heard, "I shall yet praise Him for the help of his countenance." The well-trained soul turns to God with the assurance that though "weeping may endure for a night, joy cometh in the morning."

April 20, 1870   The Resurrection

When some in the apostle's day heard of the resurrection of the dead, they mocked. It is just so still. Jesus and the resurrection were then prominent themes; and a good share of mocking must have been done by the wise Greeks. Had the apostles been skilled in modern conservatism, they might have avoided the opprobrium which they seemed to court. As it was then, so it is still quite natural with the earthly mind to call in question the doctrine of the resurrection. Some still think the creation of the body a slight exercise of Divine power compared with the resurrection from the dead. Why the latter greater than the former?

That there is to be a resurrection is too plainly taught in the Scriptures to require much argument. Christ's body was buried and came afterward out of the tomb. It was a fleshly body. He "was made flesh." And if there is no resurrection from the dead, then is not Christ arisen, as Paul forcibly argues. If Christ is not risen, then our hopes are vain, and the whole Christian system falls to the ground. If Christ has arisen from the dead, then he is the first fruits of them that slept, and is the surety that they shall rise also. Why should the first body be discarded forever rather than the soul? Have not both become corrupt, and do not both need renovating? Is not the change which Christ accomplishes marvelous in both? The change accomplished in the soul of the profane Bunyan and that of the slave-trading John Newton was marvelous on earth, and would be more marvelous still, could we part the veil and see them around the throne; especially if we could see them with immortal vision. But is their identity destroyed by the change? What if our mortal bodies put on immortality? What if our natural bodies be changed to spiritual ones? Is the change more marvelous than that of the soul? And if the one does not lose its identity, why must the other? But the Scriptures teach that these vile bodies shall be changed and fashioned like unto His glorious body; that they that are *in their graves* shall come forth; that they which sleep in the dust shall awake. Why are the dead spoken of as *raised up, as raised from the dead*, if they are not the same which have sunk to the grave?

But is there no comfort in the doctrine of the resurrection? Although it might be enough to us that God wills it, that he wills it because he sees best, yet there are other considerations which present themselves to the contemplative soul, endearing the doctrine to us. The man sold into bondage gladly hails his children with whom he parted twenty years since in their infancy, and whom he now greets as men and women. He would have given the wealth of the world rather than not see them once more before he closed his eyes in death. Will it avail for the philosopher, to tell him that not one particle of their infant bodies remain for his view? There is an identity which he will hail. He recognizes those as the eyes that once sent the light of a child's love through the chambers of his soul, and those as the lips that once sent the thrill of filial affection to stir all the tenderness of a parent's heart. Yes; those same lips, though now compressed with thought and guarded by discretion, he recognizes as those that once sent ringing through his whole being the magnetic glee of a childish mirth and joy, as the free flow of juvenile thought and laughter parted those lips asunder. So, will it be nothing to us to see again the eyes that poured the sweetness of holy love into our souls; to see the lips that instructed, comforted, and blessed us; to see the hands that cherished and ministered to us? Why is the shadow of the artist so dear to us, and the soul's sacred picture of the departed dearer still? Why is the holy soul filled with longing to see the departed again? Why are the heart's finest and tenderest emotions stirred with the hope of greeting them in the morning of the resurrection?

It would seem that those who see no comfort and gladness in the doctrine of the resurrection have either strangely miscomprehended it, or have but little considered its beneficent features.

October 26, 1870   Secularizing Religion

There is a strong tendency in our times to secularize religion. If we reflect that many in seeking it take into account how it will affect their temporal, worldly interest to obey Christ, we need not deem it strange that such, if mistaken in the attainment of religion, or if afterward backsliding from it, should again resort to such considerations. One method of secularization, is to see how much of the love of the world will assimilate with the Holy Spirit. By degrees it may be introduced into a converted soul, and the Spirit of God may be so gradually withdrawn that a will disposed or resolved not to recognize its absence may fail to acknowledge the loss. With much reflection the conclusion may be reached by the help of the adversary, that the emotions and experience of the early days of conversion were the excesses of the weakness of a new-born soul, and that a settled purpose and good habits are about all that is necessary to constitute the very first order of Christian character.

Some try what degree of passion, mirth, or even dishonesty, they can indulge and yet retain the jewel of the soul. Of course the dishonesty indulged is such as the world calls respectable, and, hence, not to be discarded by the accommodating conscience. This method is often a complete success, and to find the dead bodies of Christian professions lying around somewhat loosely is not an uncommon sight.

Whatever is customary and well reputed among respectable people is, by many, received as consistent with Christianity; and any who do not see things in this light are regarded as singular, weak, or bigoted. There is enough that is thus of good repute among respectable worldly people to secularize any one's religion. Many whose consciences are a little too tender to appropriate such things directly, save the good opinion of the world and their own self-respect (?) by indorsing such things and seeming to appreciate their excellence. Such an indorsement really in the sight of God involves all the responsibility and in the sight of men gains all the honors without any of the profits, if these things afford any profit even of a carnal nature. Thus do those liberal souls indorse for the devil, for which they are repaid with the smiles of his most respectable children. Thus these secularized religionists guaranty [*sic*] peace with Satan and yield him undisputed sway over the world, including the secularized portion of the church. They can say, "Though opposed to slavery, we hate abolitionism; though abhorring the liquor traffic, we can not favor interfering with the freedom of commerce; though loving the Bible and the Christian Sabbath, we can not favor the retention of the one in our schools or the enforced observance of the other on our streets and highways, or even among our children; we hate gambling, horse-racing fairs, but we must patronize them. We have qualms of conscience about church-fairs and festivals, but *the Lord needs the money!* We do not approve of secret societies, but we must secure their friendship and patronage, and lay our hearts near theirs, though they are treasured with the machinations of darkness, sealed with strong oaths, or equally strong 'obligations.' We love simplicity of worship, but we must have an eye to the preferences of the world when we pray, and to the taste of the fashionable when our quartette caterwauls so that pandemonium suspends its discord to catch the 'melody' which we should lose caste not to esteem as second only to the chanting of angels." Thus religion is secularized, or rather the church is secularized at the expense of religion. And this is often done in the name of "enlightened liberality." That is "enlightened liberality" indeed which magnanimously cedes away, not our own but the Lord's, giving with mincing affectation of kindness the purloined treasures to the much obliged adversary of God and man! Well might Satan contemplate a treaty of peace, and conversion itself, if he could have them on terms which would give his silver-slippered majesty the throne, with the Lord second only to himself in honor and dominion. He offered Jesus the same in the temptation in the Wilderness of Judea, if he would only fall down and worship him. His benignity has, in these days, more successfully approached many of the professed followers of Christ. They are agile in shunning the cross, rather than patient in bearing it. Indeed, they have not much more of the cross in their creed than they have of Christ in their souls. They have for fathers in their sect those of whom Paul wrote, saying that a certain class shunned suffering "persecution for the cross of Christ."

The true followers of Christ are not conformed to the word but transformed by the renewing of their minds. They marvel not that the world hates them, and think it not strange concerning the fiery trials through which they pass. They count themselves but pilgrims and sojourners here. They are only careful that they may win Christ and be a peculiar people zealous of good works, keeping themselves unspotted from the world. They are not ignorant of the devices of Satan. They do not expect his conversion; neither are they purposing a truce with him, nor contemplating a treaty of amity and co-operation. They have enlisted for the war. They regard the maxims of the soldiers of the cross in the first century as suited to the present. They rally around the cross of Christ. They seek not the new-phazed [sic] but the old kind of religion. In Christ they win the battle; and with him they shall be crowned victors at last. The seal of the living God is upon them.

November 9, 1870   Why Excluded from Heaven?

The inquiry may and no doubt often does arise, Why are sinners excluded from heaven? Especially does this inquiry press upon the thoughts of those listening to solemn warnings who have never yet learned the exceeding sinfulness of sin. But are sinners excluded from heaven? or do they shut themselves out? It is more their own work than the decree of God which shuts heaven's door against them. First their sins excluded them from the kingdom of heaven. Then when grace is offered, through Christ, their own rejection of its offers prevents their pardon, their admission into the family of God, and their inheritance with the saints in light.

They are excluded because they love falsehood in preference to truth, sin in preference to holiness, the world in preference to God. They choose disobedience, though fraught with self-evident ruin; they reject grace, though laden with the richest blessings and though its claims are pressed by the most importunate pleadings of goodness and love. Sinners wade through years of blessings without being moved with gratitude, and reap astonishing harvests of goodness without being won by divine love. In vain do all the efforts of divine grace seek to remove the hardness or overcome the impenitence of the sin-hardened and rebellious heart. It is as cruel to itself as to God. How terrible the depravity which rejects all grace, withholds all sacred affection, and courts condemnation, wrath, and everlasting ruin, preferring those to the claims of right, purity, and goodness. How terrible the enmity, how persistent the rebellion, how desperate the defiance, and how fool-hardy and inexcusable the risk. How little is there to palliate the guilt, and how absolutely impossible it is for men or angels to find any plea to offer in justification of the unyielding rejection of Christ on the sinner's part. Is not Christ with his requirements, his economy, and his gifts, perfect? With every reason in favor of acceptance, with no just reason for refusing, how irrational is the rejection of God and his grace. Indeed, it seems a terrible insanity; but even the plea of insanity can bring no relief; for the sinner has a conscience which forbids seeking justification in the plea of unaccountability. That conscience, though torpid now, may yet awake before death shall rend the veil that intervenes between the soul and eternity. If its wakings here make a hell on earth, would its quickenings in a future state find a paradise in heaven? If all the means employed—love, mercy, and grace—have been spent in vain, how shall the soul, unless robbed of all volition, be reclaimed? It must be excluded from the saint's everlasting abode.

It could find no genial home there. Then why should it enter? Must pollution tarnish the habitation of God? If not, sin must be shut out. Must discord and rebellion be intruded into the family above and the peace of heaven be sacrificed to the unyielding adherents of Satan? Is there any righteousness, benevolence, or mercy in mixing hell and heaven? Surely the incorrigible sinner must be excluded from heaven for truth's sake, for righteousness' sake, for goodness sake. There can be no admission to heaven only through repentance and faith. Regeneration is essential to an heir of God.

March 22, 1871   Trust in the Lord

Multitudes have perished, perished eternally, but not one of them trusting in the Lord. Not one soul staying itself in humble reliance on God, has ever been cast away. All manner of lessons will man learn besides, but how slow he is to receive that, the earliest and most taught in the sacred volume, reliance on Jehovah. This trust is the concord and harmony of the inhabitants of the celestial world. The want of it on earth is the chief source of disquietude, discord, and disaster to Christ's militant host. His soldiers are too often weak in their own strength; too rarely strong in implicit reliance on his promises. Their defeats are but exemplifications of truths which he has made known, and are to his glory, as showing the truth of his warnings, though exhibitions of the verity of his gracious promises would, doubtless, be more acceptable to him, as well as more happifying to his people.

Many can say, "If he will give me a sign, I will trust in him;" and yet, sign after sign given would be met with calls for their being supplemented by more, and those more wonderful. It would seem to be easy to trust the Lord when his hand of blessings is almost visible, and when his hand of protection canopies our heads, almost as a visible shield. Faith in the Lord may seem quite natural when his dispensations are to the furtherance of our most cherished personal wishes. But when God's providences gather like dark clouds; when our hopes are blasted and our fondly cherished desires are set at naught; when our loftiest aspirations are humbled in the dust; when the cherished ideal of our own life-struggle and its consequent victories float like a wreck on Time's restless wave, how hard it is to summon faith for such an hour. It then seems like a palpable contradiction of facts before the eye of the carnal soul. It seems not only to insist upon an incredible thing, but also an impossible one. Yet such faith is in accordance with truth. It is the most precious requirement and gift of Jehovah; and it is the safety and happiness and salvation of a soul lashed by the trials and persecutions of earth. Happy is he that can say of the Lord, like Job: "Though he slay me, yet will I trust in him." The strength of such a one is in the Lord; hence it may be truly said to be like the strength of a unicorn. This trust in God, which is sufficient for the most soul-confounding trial, carries with it salvation and eternal glory. May it be yours, dear reader.

April 19, 1871   Christ Crucified

The world has ever hated the doctrine of the cross. Christ crucified has ever been a stumbling-block to the Jews, and foolishness to the Greeks. Yet there is salvation in no other. Christ crucified reveals the wisdom of God and the power of God to save. An atonement only can deliver from the guilt of sin, and its Author only can rescue from its power and bring its captives into the relation of prisoners of hope. Christ crucified is precious to the sin-sick, despairing sinner, as he lifts his eyes to the cross as to the star of hope. Christ, to the saint ever precious, is doubly so in affliction and in a dying hour. He is inexpressibly precious in the assembly of praise in heaven.

The world are not disposed to reject Christ in some respects. That is, they are willing to admire the Christ of their own anointing. As a teacher they confess him wise. They can not deny the excellence of his teaching. The confession of the awe-stricken ones, who had been sent to arrest Jesus, is the confession of every candid, well-informed infidel; Christ spoke as never man spake. Christ will do for them as a teacher of pure, sublime sentiments; but as an atoning Savior, he is to them at once the object of horror and ridicule. Their loathing is intense; their satire is sharpened with the venom of depravity and rebellion. The gall of hell is in it. Christ as a teacher is tolerable, but as a crucified Redeemer he is to them most insufferable.

The man of this world can endure Christ as a martyr. He may even be excited to admiration for him; but let not the shade of the cross fall near! He may admire his noble spirit of self-sacrifice, but can he endure him as a sacrifice for sin? Anything suits him better than that which he most needs, a Redeemer.

The world can even bear Christ as a prophet. A degree of inspiration, without offense, may be attributed to him. He may be called the antetype of the sacrifices of a long and illustrious dispensation; he may be recognized as at the right hand of the Father, as the reigning power in heaven. Almost anything may be admitted except the glory of the cross. Its luster is, in the eye of the earthly soul, the essence of hatefulness. There is something marvelous in this enmity. It has moved alike the scepter of kings and the impotence of the helpless pauper. It has called forth the satire of the sage and excited the spleen of the boor. Why is this enmity so implacable that neither reason nor witnesses to the blessedness of the doctrine of the cross can disarm it?

The prevailing feature in the fall of our first parents was their desire to be what God did not admit their claim to be. Man's ambition must now be scaffolded on his self-conceit. The very lesson of the cross concerning man's desert is the sting of shame to his vanity and self-appreciation. He had almost (or quite) as lief vault into into [sic] perdition as to receive salvation on the humiliating terms of an atonement such as Christ has made. It not only testifies to his sinfulness, but magnifies the guilt of his sins by an infinite atonement. Humiliation and contrition for sin is absolutely essential to harmony with the doctrine of the cross. To go to heaven as pardoned rebels, as reprieved culprits, is more than the carnal mind can bear. It can bear the cross only when it is kept on the background. Even then it is an unworshipful Mordecai, whose execution alone can appease the wrath of a self-exalting Haman. Christ crucified is a monument of reproach to a guilty conscience.

But, after all, the doctrine of the cross it is that wins the soul of him who feels his need of a Savior. When the candid truth is felt and acknowledged by the soul, as respects its sinful condition, the need of an advocate with a plea no less efficacious than that of a ransom through the blood of the atonement is felt with great force. A friend is loudly called for, and no friend is so lovely as He with the ransom price. His love, his magnanimity, his loveliness, looms up before the admiring soul, while gratitude wells up from the fountain of affection. The soul in praise, as it contemplates its Deliverer, feasts on the loveliness and glory of Him who trod the wine-press alone, and comes with dyed garments on the mission to seek and to save.

Christ crucified is tenderness to the heart, hope to the soul, life to every good work, and the inspiration of true worship among men. It gives the pulpit interest and power. It imparts union to the followers of Christ. It is their watchword, their battle-song, their theme of praise. The effectiveness of this doctrine is seen in its transforming power in the soul. It melts opposition. It wins by its heavenly magnanimity. It gives a triumph over death which is marvelous to those who have not felt its wondrous power. It is light in the dark valley. It sways the souls of the redeemed, and moves the acclamation of angels. It is the highest glory of the heaven of heavens. Man may despise it, but God honors it on earth and in heaven.

January 24, 1872   The Soul After Death

Some maintain that the soul after death has no conscious existence till the resurrection of the body. Much has been said and written on the subject of the intermediate state, and little remains unsaid; but we propose to present a few thoughts pertaining to the subject.

The doctrine that the saint of God passes at death into a state of unconscious existence, from which he is to be aroused only by the sounding of Gabriel's trumpet, is gloomy and forbidding. It has no inspiration to the dying Christian, nor consolation for his bereft friends. It contradicts the ecstatic, joyful anticipations of myriads of dying saints, who have soared from earth triumphant as conquerors to their thrones. It sets at naught that wondrous power which religion manifests in the presence of death. It treats as a delusion the unearthly joys of a dying Stephen, Paul, Polycarp, and the whole army of martyrs, who triumphed amid showers of stones, beside the executioner's block, before the glare of wild beasts, or in the midst of encircling flames. Stephen while dying could say, by inspiration, "Lord Jesus, receive my spirit." Paul could say in prospect of death, "I am willing" "to be absent from the body and to be present with the Lord;" "I have a desire to depart and be with Christ, which is far better." Martyrs could kiss the stake and sing joyfully amid the flames. They could say, "Welcome is the cross of Christ, welcome everlasting life." Does the doctrine of the soul's unconsciousness from death till the resurrection contain any of the elements of such joys and triumphs?

The doctrine of the unconsciousness of the soul from the death of the body till its resurrection, taxes with delusion the dying hopes and joys, as we have said, of the most eminent Christians of all ages. Let us notice this a little more particularly. When in 1546 that eminent servant of God, George Wishart of Scotland, being sentenced to the flames by the papacy, was led, with a rope about his neck and a chain around his body, to the fire, he said, "For the sake of God's word I now suffer not sorrowfully, *but with a glad heart and mind.*" "*I fear not the fire,* and if persecution come to you for the word's sake, I pray you, fear not them that kill the body and have no power to hurt the soul."

When Richard Baxter was on his death-bed, he said, "I have pain, there is no arguing against sense; *but I have peace, I have peace*." He expressed his firm belief that he was approaching his long-desired home, and his joy was the most remarkable when death seemed to him nearest.

Philip Henry on his death-bed uttered these sentences: "God's Israel may find Jordan rough; but there is no remedy, they must pass through it to Canaan." "I am ready to be offered, and the time of my departure is at hand." On the point of expiring, he exclaimed, "O Death, where is thy sting?" and resigned his soul into the hands of his Redeemer.

John Janeway, when he approached death, exclaimed, "Oh, that I could express a thousandth part of that sweetness which I now find in Christ;" "Now I am going to the complete eternal enjoyment of Christ. Would you keep me from my crown? The arms of my blessed Savior are open to receive me;" "Come, Lord Jesus, come quickly;" "I shall shortly be in eternity, singing the song of Moses, and the song of the Lamb."

Samuel Walker, an able and learned minister of England, when near his death, said to a young clergyman at his bedside: "O my young friend, had I strength, I could tell you such news as would rejoice your very soul; I have had such views of heaven; but I am not able to say more."

Risdon Darracott, another eminent minister of God, exclaimed when dying, "He is coming, he is coming! but surely this can not be death! Oh, how astonishingly is the Lord softening my passage; surely God is too good to such a worm! Oh, speed thy chariot wheels; why are they so long in coming! I long to be gone!"

William Grimshaw, an eminent preacher, when dying, said, "Never had I such a visit from God since I knew him." To one who asked him how he did, he answered, "As happy as I can be on earth, and as sure of glory as if I were in it." "I have nothing to do but step out of my bed into heaven. I have my foot on the threshold already."

When David Brainerd, so illustrious and precious in the annals of Christian missions, approached death, looking upon the Bible, he said, "Oh, that dear book! that lovely book! I shall soon see it opened! The mysteries that are in it, and the mysteries of God's providences, will all be unfolded!" One day, when he lay apparently dying, he whispered in broken sentences, "He will come! he will not tarry! I shall soon be in glory! I will soon glorify God with the angels."

The sainted Toplady, when near his death, said, "Oh, how this soul of mine longs to be gone; like a bird imprisoned in a cage, it longs to take its flight. Oh, that I had wings like a dove, then would I flee away to the realms of bliss and be at rest forever! Oh, that some guardian angel might be commissioned, for I long to be absent from this body, and to be present with my Lord forever." Nearer, still to the river, he said, "Oh, what delights! Who can fathom the joys of the third heaven?" "The sky is clear. Come, Lord Jesus; come quickly."

The great Count Zinzendorf, just before dying, said to a friend, "Now, my dear sir, I am going to my Savior; I am ready, I am quite resigned to the will of my Lord."

Robert Hall, when in the last struggle, in reply to the exclamation of his wife, who said, "This can't be dying!" answered, "It is death—it is death— death! but added, in answer to her inquiry about the comfortableness of his mind, "Comfortable—very comfortable," and immediately exclaimed, "Come, Lord Jesus, come—." His voice failing, his daughter added, "quickly," to which he nodded assent with an expression of complacent delight.

Richard Watson, while suffering great pain a few days before his death, exclaimed, "Oh, how much labor and pain it costs to unroof this house; to take down this tabernacle and tent, and to set the spirit free! And when shall my soul leave this tenement of clay! I long to quit this little abode, gain the wide expanse of the skies, rise to nobler joys and see God."

The pious Payson, on his death-bed, speaking of his sufferings and joys, said, "I have suffered twenty times—yes, to speak within bounds—twenty times as much as I could in being burnt at the stake, while my joy in God has been so abounded as to render my sufferings not only tolerable, but welcome." On another occasion he said, "I can find no words to express my happiness. I seem to be swimming in a river of pleasure which is carrying me on to the great fountain." On another occasion, speaking of his meditations the night previous, he said, "I felt that death was disarmed of all its terrors; all he could do would be to touch me, and let my soul loose to go to my Savior."

Wilbur Fisk, the able and pious president of Wesleyan University, Connecticut, when scarcely able to speak, said to his wife, "Think not when you see this poor, feeble body stretched in death, that it is your husband. Oh, no! your husband will have escaped, free and liberated from every clog! He will have new plumed his glad wings, and soared away through the ethereal regions to that celestial city of light and love!"

When David Marks, a Freewill Baptist minister of remarkable talent and piety, neared his final home, he said, "I am weaker—thank God for it! Oh, I am happy, very happy! I am going to my Father, to the society of disembodied spirits, to the sweet labors of eternity. The tomb is not gloomy. The Savior has passed through it. My bloated limbs look beautiful to me, a sign that I am nearer my home."

When P. Kemp, one of the early fathers in the Church of the United Brethren in Christ, was dying, being asked if the love of Christ was present with him, he answered, "Oh, yes! bless the Lord, I shall soon be with him."

The accomplished and pious Guething, when dying, said, "I feel as though my end had come. Hark! hark! Who spoke? Whose voice is this I hear? Light! light! what golden light!"

William Otterbein, as he was expiring, exclaimed, "Jesus, Jesus,—I die, but thou livest, and soon I shall live with thee." Then to his friends he said, "The conflict is over and past. I begin to feel an unspeakable fullness of love and peace divine. Lay my head upon my pillow, and be still."

That doctrine which denies all conscious existence between death and the resurrection has, then, not only a host of clear Scripture proofs to overcome, but also an army of witnesses—of which those mentioned in the foregoing are but specimens—to confound before it can be received by the Christian church. It is also clear that the very nature of Christ and God is opposed to it.

Is it reasonable that Christ should, at death, extinguish that flame of spiritual life kindled by his Spirit, suppress rudely that love which despises death for his sake, suspend that holiness which qualifies to see his face, and cast from his presence for years and ages the *very existence* of the objects of his love, atonement, intercession, and communion? It is as unlike Christ as it is unlike the teachings of his word. Then not only the triumphant power of religion in a dying hour, but also the very nature of Divinity teaches that the soul has a conscious existence immediately after the death of the body.

February 14, 1872   Our Faithful Creator

Innumerable millions of intelligent, accountable beings have been called into existence by the Creator. Contemplating those existences, well may we pause and inquire the object of their creation. Inspiration declares that they were created for the pleasure of God. They are, doubtless, formed for his glory. It would not be in harmony, however, with the revelations of the divine character if we were to suppose that the myriads of creation are called into existence, and endowed as they are, merely that there might be spectators of the power, wisdom, and perfection of the Creator. Creation is the fruit of Divine love. God, nowhere called power or wisdom, is revealed as love. "God is love."

It pervades his whole being; his whole nature is in harmony with it. His creation, his laws, his administration harmonize with it. His power is not stronger, his wisdom more penetrating, nor his holiness more sensitive than is his love. His is perfect love, full-orbed love. Is it not unaccountable that any of his creatures should be estranged from him, or should even hesitate to confide in their faithful Creator? It would be inexplicable if we should not consider the nature of man, the designed manner of his being. He was placed in the world, a creature of choice. Without volition, man's love, gratitude, obedience, and worship toward the Creator would be robbed of everything calculated to elevate man or glorify God. Man as a mere machine, acted upon by irresistible power and moved to the Divine service, loses that position, and, if conscious of it, a large degree of that happiness which attaches to voluntary service. If such, how can he esteem his service as ennobling? or the Creator, whose own act it is in every sense of the word, as less than self-serving, self-praising? To be fit for communion with God in the highest sense, to be qualified for a noble order of being worthy of the purchase of a Redeemer's blood, to be fit to be among the choristers of the skies, man must be a creature of choice. Volition is as inseparable from the dignity of man's immortal being as it is essential to the praise and glory of God.

In considering, then, God's administration in heaven, earth, and toward hell, we must ever keep an eye on the fact that intelligent beings are creatures of choice; and considered in this light, heaven, earth, and hell itself will perfectly harmonize with the all-pervading benevolence, the inexpressible love, attributed to Jehovah and his Son, Jesus Christ our Lord. We may not comprehend it all; for we are too finite in the grasp of our minds as well as too unskillful in our adjustment of the balances of reason to sit as infallibilists in judgment on the doing of Him whose goings forth are from everlasting.

In connection with the foregoing, it might be well to add that there are diversified ideas of benevolence in its application to temporal as well as eternal things. It would have been deemed by extremists entirely consistent with that benevolence which should crown the character of a great nation, to have executed every prominent traitor in the late southern rebellion, to have confiscated the property of every rebel and applied it to the liquidation of the national debt, and to have disfranchised perpetually every one of those who fought against the Union cause. In the estimation of others it comported better with the fraternal regard due to erring citizens, to restore as speedily as possible the great body of participants in the rebellion, to civil and political rights. But not a few of those who strove hard for the success of the rebellion, thought it most accordant with national benevolence to give unrepentant rebels absolute control in the late rebellious states over the persons and liberties of the loyal colored people who had befriended those fleeing from Libby or Andersonville prisons, or who had faced the cannon's mouth fighting under the flag of the Union. God's benevolence may be unappreciated by fallen man, but in the light of immutable truth it will not cease to shine most gloriously.

We are encouraged in the sacred word to commit our souls in well-doing to God as to a faithful Creator. There is something peculiarly comforting in this exhortation of the Apostle Peter. The fact of God being our Creator implies a care and affection for us corresponding with the nature of that relation. His care will evidently be even more tender than that exercised over the flower of the field or the sparrow that falleth not to the ground without his notice. His mercy and pity for us will be very tender. Like as a father pitieth his children will be the sweet sympathy of a faithful Creator toward his children who fear him. And as he has created us, how willing will he be to assist us and lift us up when we attempt that service which seems so like the first steps of an infant. How willing will he be to help us in carrying out the purposes for which he made us, and for which Christ came to redeem us. What ample means will he provide for our salvation if we will but avail ourselves of their use; and how abundant will be the glorious reward which our faithful Creator has provided for us through Jesus Christ, our precious Redeemer.

April 10, 1872   Wrath of the Lamb

There is something terrible beyond expression in the phrase, "the wrath of the Lamb." The very idea of Deity being moved with anger—though of course we do not regard it as passion like that prevalent with sinful men—carries something awful in it. But it becomes still more awful if we associate it with Deity clothed in the likeness of humanity—if we ascribe it to Him who was the very embodiment of all that is gentle, sympathetic, and affectionate. This pity turned to stern severity, this benevolence to wrath, is like the wormwood and the gall. While it carries the idea of the most considerate justice, and even the most exquisite tenderness, it also reveals the awful turpitude of sin which so moves the stern displeasure of the meek and tender-hearted Jesus, and adds awfulness, dignity, and grandeur to that wrath which, towering above mercy and love, pours a flood of vengeance upon the head of the presumptuous and incorrigible sinner.

The very meekness, tenderness, and delicate sympathy, exhibited in the life and teachings of Jesus,—that gentleness that spared the bruised reed, that meekness which bore the indignities of his merciless persecutors, that sympathy that wept at the tomb of Lazarus and on Olivet,—join in hightening [sic] our conception of the awfulness of the wrath of the Lamb. The humiliation of Christ, the sacrifice he made of previous elevation, the sufferings which he endured to redeem a world of enemies, the tenderness as well as the heroism exhibited on the cross, unite in intensifying the awfulness of that divine pleasure and fury expressed in those apparently paradoxical words, "the wrath of the Lamb."

But, while it must be remembered that Christ excels in all that is gentle and meek, we must also remember that he, in superlative sense, hates, loathes, and abhors iniquity. There is, in the perfect holiness of his character, an intense repulsion of all unbelief, hardness of heart, and impenitency in sin. All manner of violations of the pure law of Jehovah, in the sight of the immaculate Son of God appears in its moral turpitude what it really is,—exceedingly sinful; and as virgin delicacy shrinks from impurity and obscenity, so does the pure soul of Jesus hold in loathing and detestation the iniquities and even the tolerated sins common among men. How terrible, then, must be his displeasure when manifested against the incorrigibly impenitent! How awful are those words, "Depart from me, ye cursed." The curse of some poor vagabond might be received with indifference, the imprecations of some brainless youth might be born with composure, but the curses of a dear brother, a loving sister, or a revered parent, would tear the soul with the violence of anguish, would crush the heart as beneath a mountain of lead. How shall any one then be able to endure the wrath of the

Lamb—the curse of Christ? Shall the hand that was nailed to the cross be raised, and the sweet lips which have interceded for the transgressors pronounce the curse! Shall the very love of Christ which passeth knowledge be turned to gall in its denunciation and punishment of the offender against not only the law but the mercy and grace proffered in Christ Jesus! Oh, how doleful the procession of despair which shall then crowd into the gates of perdition! With that curse stamped upon their very being, and sealed with the signet of the Judge of all, how awful their final state, where forever they are wholly given over to the power of sin and to the dominion of the wicked one!

The displeasure of Christ against sin is not of caprice. It is a deep-seated, nay, an eternal principle. It is as old and as firm as the throne of Jehovah. It is as spontaneous as the radiation of the glory of God; and it shall at last prove more terrible than the fire, and thunderings, and earthquake which did clothe and shake and vocalize Mount Sinai at the giving of the law. When the great day of his wrath shall come who shall be able to stand!

In view, then, of the awfulness of that wrath, which is, as it were, the very essence of abused love, mercy, and grace, how should the sinner tremble; how speedily fly for refuge to the now interceding Savior; and how carefully ought the servants of God to work out their salvation with fear and trembling. To this end how earnestly ought all to seek that divine grace which works within the followers of Christ to will and to do of his own good pleasure. There is no necessity that any one should incur the eternal displeasure of the Son of God—the wrath of the Lamb. It is in the power of every one, through grace, to find acceptance in Christ Jesus.

June 19, 1872   Spiritual Life and Death

The Christian lives; the man of the world "is dead while he lives." The Christian is alive to the existence of God, to his infinite power, to his all-pervading presence, to his awful majesty, to his precious love, to his stern justice, to his amazing condescension, and to all the marvelous perfections of his divine character. He is alive to his own sinfulness, to his entire dependence on God, to the obligations he is under to his Maker, his Redeemer, and to his fellow-men. He is alive to the great salvation of which he has been made a partaker, to the inheritance to which he has become an heir through Christ, and to the fearful responsibilities which rest upon him in the church and in the world. He is alive to the prosperity and glory of the church, to the woes and joys of the people of God, and to the sweet communion of saints. He is also alive to the condition of perishing sinners, to the awful degradation of a world lying in wickedness, and to the sentence of condemnation resting upon the impenitent sinner. We may say he is alive to God, to heaven, to earth, to hell,—alive to himself, to his fellow-beings,—alive to all that is good and to all that is evil,—alive to the past, to the present, and to the future. He that is dead to these things is a poor specimen of the grace of Christ, who gave himself for us that we might have life. He that liveth is dead to that which is evil, in that he loves it not and takes no pleasure in it; but he is alive to all its hatefulness and ruinous power.

The man of the world is alive to the pleasures of sin, but dead to its loathsome character, to its deceitful workings and charms, to its awful guilt, to its heritage of woe. He is insensible to the existence and character of God, to his presence, to his creating and upholding power, to his law, to his grace, to his warnings, to his impending judgments, to the terrible inflictions of that wrath which hangs over the impenitent. He sees not his own true character in the sight of Deity; he does not realize his own attitude toward God and the divine law; he calls good evil and evil good, and even glories in his own shame. He is insensible to the beauty of holiness, to the glory of Zion, and to the excellence of saints. The joys of God's people are mysterious; their sorrows seem to him fictitious; their aims appear to him to be visionary. He hastens to destruction with his fellows, oblivious of the awful judgment and final doom which are theirs as well as his. Truly the man of the world is dead while he lives.

The worldling is alive to sin, but not to its true nature; to the world, but not to the real side of it. He is alive to himself, but not to himself as he is. He is alive to pleasure, but to that only which is as fleeting as it is false. He is like one that dreams. He is a walking somnambulist. He is alive to nothing in its true relation to God and to eternity. He sees but one world, and is not duly sensible of the over-ruling influences which govern it. His ideas of a future life, if he has any, are like those of a feeble dreamer. To him the present assumes undue proportion to the future.

The judgment of the man of this world concerning the things of time, without reference to God and eternity, may be good; but when he tries to think upon the future he is liable to the greatest errors, especially in weighing the present in the scale opposite to the things to come. If he is of a philosophic cast of mind; if he possesses fine reason and discernment; if he is not carried away by passion, he may reason with considerable accuracy about the things to come as compared with the things which he now sees; but unless quickened by grace, he does not realize the truth of his own better theories. His better judgment and the real feelings of his soul are at variance with each other. Were it not for the quickenings of God's grace, which visit all without partiality, there could be no escape from the delusions of the devil, who binds with power of spiritual death all those who, despite divine grace, yield to his delusive dominion.

It is to be feared that the Christian does not always sufficiently realize the difference between spiritual life and death; that yielding to carnal influences he is often so benumbed that he may almost be said to be dead while he has a name to live. If so, he dishonors God and but poorly represents that spiritual life which he professes to have. But the man of this world generally has very little realization of his true condition. He is so dead as to not realize his dead condition. When we talk to him of his state, our solicitude and tears and entreaties seem to him a delusion, and he is more inclined to laugh at what seems to him a delusion, or pity what he deems our fanaticism, than to heed the counsel given.

The scriptural idea of spiritual death means more than many realize, and the scriptural estimate of spiritual life is far more just and real than many seem to suppose. It is high time that carnal professors should weigh this subject and seek for greater abundance of life, that they may the better glorify God and do more to awaken others from the slumbers of spiritual death.

February 19, 1873   Man's Frailty

Frailty is the common lot of humanity. Man is frail in body, mind and spirit. Born weak and helpless, assailed by the rudeness of the elements and the ignorance and recklessness of so-called nurture, it is almost a miracle that he lives through the tender years of childhood. He breathes poison in the atmosphere, eats dyspepsia in his food, and runs the gauntlets of innumerable accidents, which stand ready to wound, maim, or push him to the tomb. It were no wonder if he should be blind or deaf, decrepit or maimed. It would not be strange if he would be dyspeptic, consumptive, or dropsical [sic]. It were rather strange if a myriad of chords should remain in tune, if innumerable cells should perpetually perform their functions, and if external and internal conditions should, through long years, stand so adjusted as to report no painful intelligence to stir up a heedless mind to the discharge of its duties as a guardian of its less valuable but very essential partner, the body.

It turns out just as might be expected. The world is a grand hospital,–much more extended and multitudinous than truly grand. The wonder is that so many are regarded as convalescent. Few can said to be well.

With so much painstaking to exclude the pure food of the lungs and retain the excrescences of the breathing and perspiratory [sic] functions of the physical system, it would be a signal though happy failure if human beings should not treasure up wrath to be dispensed in corporeal or capital punishments in the name of violated law. The capital form of punishment lays the fabric waste, while the diminutive penalties retain it in a state of melancholy preservation. Sighing in the vale of affliction and mortality, the psalmist exclaimed, "Lord, make me to know mine end, and the measure of my days, what it is: that I may know how frail I am." Death and corruption shall swallow a world of pride and vanity; and it is but one step to the charnel-house. There all caste is lost in kindred charnel-dust, however varied be the urn on which caste sits and smiles in mockery upon all human glory.

But if man's body is frail, what shall we say of the mind? It inherits not only the frailty of the physical system, and, through its imperfect organs, reaps a harvest of mental imperfections, but it has a spiritual realm of discordance, darkness, and death to deal with. Its ignorance is so profound as to leave the universe of thought almost untouched, and when touched scarce else than disordered in a ratio corresponding with the degree of interference.

The mind, though so profound in its ignorance, is often equally profoundly opinionated. Yet its opinions are often based on whims or molded by the dictum of others. Its creed, in nine cases out of ten, is borrowed, and often miserable patchwork at that. It builds on history, much of which is mere fabrication, or distorted truth, which is but the more a lie. It builds on science, which is often but successive crops of speculation, current under the head of this misnomer. It shapes its mental structures, often, after the fashion of legends, dreams, or fancies,—perhaps fascinating fiction. Milton, with the pencil of his imagination, has sketched out the heaven and hell—with all the intervening regions—of a multitude of candidates for both worlds, and with the brush of his genius gilded the one and darkened the other. But his paradise and his hell may be, and are, far less the reality than those before which the sons of holy inspiration shrink, abashed, at but the slight unveiling of them. His Adam and his Eve, his angels and his devils, his paradise and his hell, though ever so far superior to the products of a multitude of vile or foolish dreamers, may be widely unlike the primitive pair as witnessed by the shouting sons of God at the planting of the top-stone of creation, or unlike the angels seen by Jacob in his dream or the shepherds in their vision, or unlike the devil scanned by Michael in his disputation over the body of earth's greatest law-giver, or unlike the paradise beheld by the apostle in his ecstatic elevation, or the hell in which the rich man in torment lifted his beseeching eyes. Man, though possessing endowments that are self-surprising as well as self-confounding, will, if he lean to his own understanding instead of that of God's word and God's Spirit, find himself drifting on the tide of thought, or, more often, its vagaries, without chart or compass, with little better ideas of the true bearings than those of the inebriate searching skyward for his lost footing.

But above all, how frail is man in his spirit. Fire may flash from the granite bowlder [sic] before the smiting of a rod of steel, but the hammer of truth may echo, in its vain resounding, through the chamber of man's moral being without its smitings [sic] of the stony heart yielding one spark of love or gratitude to man's Maker and Redeemer,—unless a power such as brooded over chaos move with a force almost surpassing creation itself; and then but a spark is produced, perhaps never to be fanned to a flame. "Haters of God" is the inspired appellation of that fallen spirit which, in its multitudinous representatives, may be called unconverted man. "Hateful and hating one another" underlies every motto of fraternity which is the bond of union with the carnally-minded. Wicked men are frail,—more than frail. Their frailty is unto death and destruction. It fathoms, at last, the depths of perdition.

The variances and stifes [*sic*], the piques and alienations which beset societies of believers, are not very creditable to human nature, which overrules a better power within, that will not arbitrarily reign. The peevishness, the caprice, the selfishness of some whom we dare not call else than Christian, tell a sad tale of the frailty of the spirit of man. His slowness to do good, to press after holiness, and his readiness to tire and faint in the divine service, all unite in testimony to his frailty of spirit.

Truly man is frail. But God is without infirmity. His love, his mercy, and his grace are all in which we can hope and trust. We can find safe anchorage nowhere else than in the goodness and mercy of Omnipotence as revealed in Christ the Mediator. In him frailty is swallowed up in strength. Our weakness, realized by faith, gives us access to divine might. Mortality is at last swallowed up in immortality. And, finally, glory and infinite strength embrace the child of frailty and the culprit of offended law. Then shall human frailty enter the songs of everlasting praise only as a theme in ascriptions of gratitude and everlasting honor given to him who loved us and washed us in his blood and transferred us from frailty below to power and glory among the sons of light around his throne on high.

May 7, 1873   Not Our Own

It is not easy for man to accept some obvious truths. Some of these are so averse to his carnal nature that it requires much grace to reconcile him to them. Among these is the total non-ownership of himself or anything called his own. Not that the Creator has not committed many things to him as his. But all these are given him to be used in harmony with the divine will, which is in accordance with wisdom, righteousness, and man's best interest. To require less would be neither holy nor benevolent. Perfect conformity to this law would make earth a paradise, would raise man to almost angelic happiness. Yet non-conformity is almost the universal fact, and from it come nearly all the woes of humanity. Perfect obedience to this law, founded in the very nature of the relations of God and man, would, in the church, effect a happy revolution, and, by its influence, change the moral condition of the world. But it is a lamentable fact that many in the church manifest an almost total non-comprehension of this truth. By their practice they show that they regard themselves and all their possessions as their own in fee simple. It is a presumptuous and most pernicious untruth.

The doctrine of man and all that is his belonging wholly to God, is rejected by the world, because it does not realize the relation of the Creator and Redeemer to the objects created. An additional reason for its rejection is the enmity of the carnal mind against God and all that is holy. The church, in a great measure, relinquishes or compromises this doctrine because of the power of current practice or respectable example averse to it. No wonder if the people reject what the minister holds in contempt. Nor is it strange if the minister questions his own better judgment when the almost universal practice of Christians condemns his views as fanatical. If a few Christians would insist upon a close practical application of the doctrine of man's non-ownership of himself and his endowments and possessions, not only would the world, but the church, also, regard them as demented or fanatical. The fact is that the world is not only demented upon the subject of salvation, but the church is miserably beclouded with reference to its duty to its great Head. A multitude of Christians are living much as if they were not the servants and stewards of God.

This doctrine of man's ownership of himself, and all that is called his, being wholly subordinate to the divine right of Christ to man and all claimed as his, is most reasonable. All is from Him by whom we are created. We were plunged in bankruptcy and despair, but the Redeemer paid our ransom. We and ours are the purchase of his agony and blood. By purchase we are his. By gratitude we are bound to lay all at his feet. Our all-wise and infinitely-compassionate Redeemer is certainly entitled to direct our all. To deny this right or be indifferent to it is unbelief, rebellion, ingratitude, and presumption. When we see how far short professors of religion come to the measure of duty in this regard we wonder not that the righteous are scarcely saved. We are almost constrained to limit the power of grace by saying: "Who, then, can be saved?"

If the true doctrine of God's complete right to us, with our all, had proper possession of the minds and hearts of Christians, the church would be abundantly supplied with ministers, and these would be fully sustained by those to whom they minister. Missionaries would flow out to heathen lands spontaneously, and means for their support would scarcely need to be asked for, so gladly would contributions be made. Millions of money, in Christians' hands, now spent for selfish, vain, or useless purposes, would be poured out for benevolent and evangelizing objects. Christians would have power with God, power with each other, power in the world. The excellence of Christianity would become incontrovertible. Heathendom would soon be permeated with the light and influence of our holy religion, and false religions would fall, like Dagon, before the ark of the Lord. Infidelity would lose its plea and be ashamed. It would be silenced, if not convinced. The church would become a grand workshop for the Lord. The fruit of Christian labor would become the glory of every land. Alas! this doctrine is very little regarded by many who take the name of Christ.

The result of the full conviction and practice of the doctrine of Christ's complete ownership in the purchase of his blood, is the contempt of a vain world, the affected pity of worldly-wise Christians, with slighting, reproach, and other forms of persecution. By superior endowments or peculiarly favorable circumstances, some such may challenge the respect of the world or of a worldly church; but detraction in some form will inevitably attend them. Yet as shining lights are they in the church, and their labors will tell in eternity. There they shall shine as the stars forever.

November 5, 1873   Questioning God's Love

It is very natural in fallen man to doubt the love of his heavenly Parent. It is against light, against reason; it is to his own injury; yet he persists in it. Even converted persons fail to realize the fullness of God's love. No wonder that the apostle prayed so earnestly that his brethren should be enabled to comprehend the breadth and length, the depth and hight [sic] of the love of Christ that passeth knowledge.

The evidence of God's love is so full that it may seem marvelous that any should doubt it. His works, providences, and word declare it. The very nature of Deity renders it self-evident. No one can consult his own reason and consciousness and deny the greatness of this love. Yet the contradiction of sinners against themselves is universal. Some better sentiments have a place in every thoughtful mind; some higher theory has a hold on every philosophic soul; yet life is lived and actions are performed universally by sinners on entirely a different assumption. God's counsel is regarded as averse to man's interests, and man is engaged in fruitless efforts to over-reach the Almighty—under the supposition that, slumbering or impotent, he will permit it. This tribute to a morpheic God is astounding. Yet it is far from being hypostatical. It is a ruinous reality. It may be added that it exercises a very deleterious influence even in the very borders of the church of God.

If it be inquired as to why this questioning of God's love is so prevalent, it may be answered that Satan infused it into our first parents in Eden. It has been a part of fallen human nature ever since; nor has Satan failed in its diligent culture. It is the sheet-anchor of his success with the impenitent, and he could do little in the church without it.

Jacob questioned God's merciful providence when called to go down into Egypt, though it had been so plainly manifested at Peniel, in Haran, and at Gilead. Moses doubted it, though the burning bush was blazing before his eyes. Israel doubted it at the yet uncrossed sea, though Egypt had been plagued for their sakes, while they were exempt from providential chastisement. David's beautiful humility and trust while retreating before the rebel forces of Absalom was not more marked than were the overwhelming of that prodigy of faith, Elijah, retreating from the wrath of the idolatrous queen, Jezebel.

This heart of disbelief in God's love is displayed by the sinner in leaning on an arm of flesh in preference to the arm of Omnipotence, in rejecting the counsel, overtures, and mandates of God, in trusting in his own righteousness instead of Christ crucified, and in putting confidence in the flesh instead of the Spirit.

The whole life of the sinner says to Christ: "I believe thee not; I need thee not; I abhor thee; I fight against thee under the black flag—slay or be slain." The results are a life devoid of peace. Carnal pleasure is alloyed with bitterness, fear, and the stripes of chastisement. Death is gloomy, miserable, or even awful; and eternity is wherein to bewail everlasting defeat. When the Christian questions the love of him who gave his life for him, who has called him, regenerated by his grace, adopted him into the heavenly family, and sealed him by the testimony of his Spirit as to his acceptance with God, it is no wonder that he has fears, doubts, and disasters; that he is barren of Christian graces; that his strength is turned to weakness; that his hope is lost in gloom. His promises and assurances demand a better return for his love and goodness. The spirit of a child toward a heavenly Parent requires better things.

It is wicked and disastrous not to trust in our God and our Redeemer. It is wicked in the sinner, but it seems more out of place still in the child of grace. It is inward blasphemy against Gethsemane, Calvary, and the mediatorial throne. It is reckless defiance of the judgment-seat of Christ. If Christians all would cease to question a Savior's love, trust in him implicitly, and obey him fully, how gloriously would the light of Zion shine. How happy would God's people be; how victorious; and what marvelous power they would exert in the world.

February 4, 1874   The Savior's Ascension

The birth, teachings, miracles, sufferings, and reign of Jesus Christ are often discoursed upon, but rarely his ascension. Yet its interest is attractive, and the event itself glorious. It was the ascension of a once suffering but now triumphant conqueror to his everlasting throne.

After the resurrection of Jesus he showed himself to the disciples twelve times. First alone to Mary Magdalene at the sepulcher; then to the other women; next to Peter; fourth, to the two disciples on their way to Emmaus; then to the apostles, all, except Thomas; then to them again when Thomas was present; afterward in Galilee, at the sea of Tiberius; next to the disciples on the mountain in Galilee; and then to more than five hundred brethren at once; after this to the Apostle James; next to all the apostles as they were assembled together; and last of all, at the time of his ascension.

It is due we should say that he, after his ascension, revealed himself to Stephen, Paul, and John; but we mention twelve times that he showed himself to his disciples, in abundant proof of his resurrection from the dead, previous to the heavens receiving him out of their sight.

Forty days after his resurrection, having led all the eleven apostles out from Jerusalem onto Mount Olivet, to a spot about a mile from Jerusalem, near Bethany, the home of his dear friends Martha, Mary, and Lazarus; while he was conversing with the disciples, and they were looking upon, he began to ascend, and rising in their view, higher and higher, a cloud at last received him out of their sight.

Let us for a few moments consider the circumstances connected with the ascension. Companion-like, yet shepherd-like, he led them out, conversing as they went, as a bosom friend yet with all the dignity of the great Teacher, the Son of God. He, in answer to their question, silenced their query about the restoration of Israel's temporal power. He talked to them of the Holy Spirit, which they were promised after a short tarrying in prayer at Jerusalem, and which they did receive, ten days after this, with the sound of a rushing mighty wind, accompanied with cloven tongues of fire. He told them of the witness they should bear of him and his truth in the capital of Judea, and in the land, and to the uttermost parts of the earth. He was now completing his personal mission on earth,—his last until he should come with all his holy angels in power and great glory, at the time of the general resurrection and the glorification of his saints, when they are caught up together "in the clouds, to meet the Lord in the air, and so shall" "ever be with the Lord." He had been born in the depths of poverty in Bethlehem, had been an infant refugee in Egypt, a rural youth in the village of Nazareth, esteemed a carpenter's son, perhaps a carpenter himself. He had appeared as a teacher, (heralded by the rudely-clad, earnest-voiced John the Baptist,) speaking, himself, as man never spake. He had fed thousands, healed multitudes, giving agility to the lame and impotent, hearing to the deaf, sight to the blind; and he had even raised the dead. He had cast out demons, and had stilled the tempestuous waves of the sea. He had wrestled in Gethsemane, endured scourging as a criminal, received the reproaches of rulers and the execrations of the multitude. He had been nailed to the cross, and had expired amid the revilings of enemies, in agonies beyond human knowledge, upon the sight of which the rocks were rent, the sun hid his face, and the earth trembled as if in astonishment, and of the inhabitants of the tombs many arose and showed themselves in the city of his enemies. Laid in Joseph's new tomb, he had the third day arisen from the dead, appeared to the disciples twelve times, and now while conversing with the apostles, he ascends up while they are looking upon him, till a cloud receives him out of their sight.

Ah, whither is he gone, the Master? Wondering, gazing, perhaps longing for his return, swallowed up with thoughts produced by the scene, they scarcely at first noticed the appearing of two men in white apparel, who come less to rebuke than to instruct and comfort them. Why gaze in astonishment, perhaps in grief? He shall come again: come in like manner as they have seen him go into heaven. Every eye shall see him; even they also which pierced him. He shall come in the clouds of heaven in power and great glory. "The heavens shall pass away with a great noise, and the elements shall melt with fervent heat; the earth also and the works that are therein shall be burned up." For he shall come with all his holy angels. "The Lord himself shall descend from heaven with a shout, with the voice of the archangel, and with the trump of God." "He shall come," not only taking vengeance on his enemies, but "to be glorified in his saints, and to be admired in all them that believe." But meanwhile he has a great work to do. He is to sit at the right hand of God as an intercessor, as a great and merciful high-priest. He is to make "intercession for the saints according to the will of God." He is, too, to sit as a king, and his dominion is to extend from "sea to sea, and from the rivers to the ends of the earth." The heathen shall be given unto him "for an inheritance and the uttermost parts of the earth for a possession." Indeed, "the kingdoms of this world shall become the kingdom" of Christ. "He must reign till he hath put all enemies under his feet." At last he shall be revealed without sin unto salvation. He shall appear to the joy of his apostles,—and "all those who love his appearing"—whose bodies "shall be fashioned like unto his glorious body," who shall see as they are seen and known as they are known, who "shall be like him," and shall "be kings and priests unto God and the Lamb forever."

March 4, 1874   Justification and Regeneration

Superficial Bible students often fail to discriminate between regeneration and justification. That both go together is clearly taught in the Scriptures. But the one is done in the soul of the believer by the cleansing, renewing power of the Holy Spirit; the other is done in heaven by the will of God, in accordance with his prerogative, through the atoning merits of Jesus Christ. The one is the creat-ing of the soul anew in Christ, making it a partaker of the divine nature; the other is freeing it from all the guilt of past sins. The one is of regenerating grace; the other of pardoning mercy. Of every regenerated person it may be said, in part or in whole, that his soul is cleansed of indwelling sinfulness; of the other, that *all* his sins are pardoned. Both are obtained through faith; neither could have been righteously conferred but for the purchase by the atoning merits of the Savior; yet the text, "The blood of Jesus Christ his Son cleanseth us from all sin," and similar ones, applies only to justification, the pardon of sins being in reality a part of the scriptural doctrine of sanctification; for the soul's cleansing from guilt is essentially an element of its sanctification.

When a soul is pardoned, it is *wholly* pardoned. Otherwise it can not be jus-tified, but it is under condemnation, and, hence, an heir of perdition. The one justified by faith has peace with God. He is in that described by David, whom Paul quotes as saying: "Blessed are they whose inequities are forgiven, and whose sins are covered. Blessed is the man unto whom the Lord *will not impute sin*." He may not be all that he could desire, nor all that Christ desires of him, in spiritual attainments; but he does not willfully cherish sin. He loves righteous-ness, and mourns his conscious shortcomings before God. He labors and prays for complete victory over sin. He is longing and striving for increased spiritual attainments. But in the free grace of God's pardoning love, he is complete—not in the knowledge of all its marvelous richness, but in the reception of pardon and justification. While he stands, by faith, in this grace, "the Lord will not impute sin" unto him. He is *fully* justified; he is thoroughly regenerated; he is sanctified,—that is, he is cleansed (in part, at least,) from indwelling sinfulness and from sinful habits; he is cleansed from guilt, this cleansing being found in God's pardoning grace; and he has the rich internal fruits of the Spirit in his soul, which will also be manifest to others in his life. Sanctification not only involves the cleansing of the soul from indwelling sin and all guilt, but also a new creation, or, in other words, the furnishing of the soul with spiritual graces to occupy the newly-cleansed dwelling. It is the cleansing of the soul-palace, and then the furnishing of it with the Lord's spiritual furniture. This is what the apostle terms "the *washing* of regeneration and the *renewing* of the Holy Ghost." This is being born of *water* and of the *Spirit*—that is, *cleansing* and *renewing*. These go together; but the one is a driving out, and the other a furnishing process. It is the taking away of unholiness and the establishment of holiness in its stead. If the new furniture of the soul is not ample, other pieces (graces) should be added; and if such as are now there are not well cleansed and well polished, this ought to be attended to promptly and efficiently.

Regeneration is always a *decided* work. This one, recently a child of Satan, has become a child of God. He may not be a perfect child, but he is *altogether* a child of God. He has not a double paternity. God and Satan are not co-parents of any child of grace. All such are fully the children of God; yet they are not all wholly sanctified.

It would seem scarcely necessary to say that quite a translation and transformation must take place in every soul in its passage from the life on earth to that in heaven. It certainly ought not to be supposed that the converted soul will, with all the errors and weaknesses inseparable from this life, be removed to heaven without these being taken away. Undecidedly we shall there see as we are seen and know as we are known, and our souls shall no longer be adapted to the nursery below, but to all the intelligence and perfection essential to fit us for membership in the family of God "with the spirits of just men *made perfect.*"

There is a great deal of foolish talk about regeneration in death, and about the regeneration of children, etc. We may not look too confidently into these things, nor dogmatize where all is mystery. It is doubtful whether we will learn more than God has revealed, and whether we will more than become wise unto salvation. Yet it is evident that if the heavenly state is what the Bible represents it to be, the best Christian will undergo quite a transformation in passing from his imperfect state here into that of angelic perfection. Some reach a high state of humble spiritual elevation in this life; yet their shortcomings and imperfections are known to their most discerning Christian associates. Truly they dwell in clay and exhibit traces of the carnal. But all these faults shall be left outside of the heavenly city. "When that which is perfect is come, then that which is in part shall be done away." For this the Lord shall have eternal praise.

March 25, 1874   Acquaintance with God

A man may have been well-versed in the Scriptures and yet be unacquainted with God. He may have poured over the account of creation, the fall of man, the deluge, the call of Abraham, the lives of the patriarchs, the deliverance of Israel from Egyptian bondage, the giving of the law, the conquest of Canaan, the history of the judges and kings of Israel, the sublime words of the poets and prophets. He may have pondered the remarkable teachings and career of John the Baptist, and of Christ and the apostles. He may have committed to memory large portions of the gospels and the epistles, and yet know not God nor his Christ. This lack of knowledge may be illustrated by the case of one who passes through the grounds and palace of some illustrious and opulent man, viewing with a degree of admiration that arrangement, these productions, and the taste and skill of those combinations, but who never yet saw the face of the possessor of all this, nor ever heard his voice. He is a stranger to the one whose grounds or whose palace he explores. The very presence of that lord might be embarrassing. But should all this change, and were the visitor to become intimately acquainted with the person whose glory he has viewed only in his possessions or in such orders as he has left for his domestics, or such notices as he gives to strangers,— what a change. What a change, especially if he become an intimate friend of the possessor of all this beautiful, sweet home, and a joint owner with him of it all, through the affection of its legal possessor. How differently now would be tread those walks. What a change when he sits in that parlor. What a sense of home, of affection, of joy, would thrill through all his experience in that mansion and in those grounds. And would not the dearest of all be the countenance, the loving voice, and the tender caresses of that friend? The palace and the grounds would seem as nothing without the noble, magnanimous possessor of it all—the partner with the recipient of all those favors.

So some go through God's works and peruse his word, but never become acquainted with him. They may not even learn his true character. They may be really averse to the elements composing it, and denounce and abhor those very characteristics in another that are reflections of the attributes that shine so brilliantly in Deity as revealed in Christ. Alas! there is often a sad lack of acquaintance with God.

This lack of acquaintance with Christ is not alone seen in the unconverted; but it is found, alas, with so many who have visited the mercy-seat. Some lingered not long enough to hear his voice, saying, "My peace I give unto you."

They fancied the touch of the mercy-seat enough. They did not wait for the falling of its baptismal dews.

There are others who came away from a warm reception by the blessed Redeemer. But their visits to the place where the special manifestations of the divine presence are given have been too few and too formal. They know little more of Christ than in the day of their first introduction to him. They have not carried his remembrance in all their walks, nor pressed his image continually to their hearts. They do not talk with him. They do not sing to him the song of love, to which a refrain by the Spirit is returned sweeter than that of all human love, or than any finite love; and though not heard by the ear of flesh, it is the essence of joy unspeakable and full of glory.

Without acquaintance with God's word, the knowledge of God must be imperfect and difficult. Indeed, hearing is by the word. But we must learn that word in living, thrilling connection with its Author, if we would have light in our minds, warmth in our hearts, and joy in our souls. Without prayer we can learn little of the great Giver whose hand is opened to the petitions of his saints. But we must come to him in the prayer of faith, of real communion. Oh, how guilty ought the formal worshiper to feel in the absence of that communion which Christ invites, in the secret devotion and in the place where two or three assemble in his name.

If we would have this acquaintance with Christ we must be very careful not to depend on public worship alone for that acquaintance. But if we love to converse with him by the way, we will love to meet him in his banqueting-house, where the wine of his cheer fills every soul, where eye speaks to eye, and joy flows from heart to heart.

October 7, 1874   The Great Love

The apostle says that we love God because he first loved us. But how great is this love toward us? It must correspond with his other attributes. We think of his power; it is infinite. We talk of his wisdom; it, too, is without limit. How great, then, must be his love; for "God is love." His love, then, as exercised toward us, must be greater than we have ever realized. Its hight [sic]—who can reach it? Its length—who can measure it? Its breadth—who can comprehend it? The great employment of learning to know the love of Christ—when shall it be completed? "God so loved the world." How inexpressibly much is wrapped up in that little word "so;" and the provisions this love has made are for whosoever—"whosoever believeth in him." Yes; we may thank God for a whosoever salvation.

But this love must be greater than that required of us. If ours were with all our hearts it would but come up to the measure of our duty to him. Such love would exceed the strongest and the most tender known on earth. But God's love to us must exceed all this. Then how can the mind grasp or the heart realize the greatness of God's love toward us?

Again: this love, as it is manifest in the soul of the believer, in whose heart it is shed abroad by the Holy Ghost, is beyond all expression. For the love of God is manifested toward us, as well as produced in us, by the Holy Spirit. And how ardent the love it inspires when admitted in its fullness. The one who receives it counts not his life dear, but is willing to suffer all things if he may only win and please Christ. This love is full of ecstatic pleasure, as when it shone in the face of George Wishart as he went to the stake kindled by papal malignity; as it was with the sainted Payson as he wrote back from "the land of Beulah;" as it was with John Fletcher when he triumphed day after day with increasing joy as death drew nearer. Yes, how wonderful that love which so charmed that noble army of martyrs that they would not accept deliverance. Truly it passeth knowledge. This side of immortality we shall not know all its sweetness, nor appreciate all its richness. Even in heaven who shall comprehend that which pervades an attribute that is in itself infinite! How that love shines in the sight of angels; and how does it find its corresponding flame in the bosoms of the redeemed, whose everlasting songs attest their hallowed joys!

But if God so loved us how ought we to rejoice in him; how ought we to praise him! Truly, as with the psalmist, it is not wonderful if our "glory rejoiceth."

But praise in the heart or on the lips is not all of it. No; our love should be displayed in lives devoted to his service. To visit Christ as suffering in the person of his destitute and bereaved ones, and to keep one's self unspotted from the world, are more than sacrificial gifts upon the altar—more than whole burnt-offerings. Through toil, through reproach, through sufferings, and through the trying ordeal of death, let us bear the sincere profession of our love to him who has loved us with so great a love.

September 29, 1875   God's Law Benevolent

Many evidently regard the law of God as the enemy of man. This is a great mistake. As it has been truly said, "God's commandments are his chiefest benedictions" They are his greatest blessings. Though the above aphorism is without doubt designed to apply chiefly to the commands to labor in the vineyard of our Lord, it is worthy of a far more extended application. The apostle declares the law to be "good" as well as "just and holy." Indeed, it may be doubted whether the goodness of God shines more brightly anywhere—except in the gift of his Son and in the final home of his saints—than in the great moral law contained in the ten commandments, and in the precepts of the prophets and those of Christ and his apostles. The commandment "is exceeding broad." There are "wondrous things contained in" the law of God. Indeed, "the law of the Lord is perfect, converting the soul." If "the law is our school-master to bring us to Christ," it is surely worthy of regard as our benefactor. All this is true, though incorrigible violators of the law find it to be their death. Indeed, few of God's blessings may not be turned into curses.

The foundation of the law contained in the decalogue is in this, "Thou shalt love the Lord thy God with all thy heart," and this other, "Thou shalt love thy neighbor as thyself." Upon these two commandments hang the law and the prophets. And a blessed world we should have if these commandments were kept in their fullness. Our sin cursed earth would be turned into a paradise.

If any man would love the Lord with all his heart from his earliest years, that indwelling love and the divine communion which it would bring would afford unspeakable happiness. His peace and joy would be unceasing, and beyond all expression. The union and communion of the soul with Deity would far surpass the sweetest conjugal felicity known on earth. And as the will of God concerning each and all is perfect in benevolence,—entirely in harmony with the highest good of man,—it follows that the obedience resulting from so great affection toward the Lord would tend to the most complete good of himself and all mankind. As the glory of God and his good pleasure are in entire accord with the good of the human race,—and indeed with that of all the holy throughout the universe,—it follows that this love toward God tends to the pleasure of the Father of all, and to the showing forth of his glory on earth—and indeed in heaven. Truly the commandment to love the Lord with all the heart—thus teaching, prompting, and enjoining a blessed duty—is one of the chief benedictions of the Lord.

The command to love our neighbor as ourselves is, on its very face, so blessed that it seems unnecessary to show that it is one of our Lord's greatest benedictions. Love toward our neighbor is sweet and peaceful, and is promotive of all that is favorable to individual and social happiness. It tends to gracious and profitable words, to works of usefulness and benevolence, and in every way conserves the highest good of the community, and tends toward the general good of the world. With the full and universal prevalence of obedience to this commandment the spirit of envy would not sparkle in the eye, slander whisper on the tongue, nor violence and malevolence appear in the actions of men and women. War would no longer startle cities with alarm and spread devastation and untold horrors over mountain and plain. Jails and penitentiaries and courts would lose their vocations. Even hospitals and almshouses would scarcely be needed under the universal prevalence of the law of love in its fullness, so great would be the readiness of the community to relieve suffering. Besides this, the universal and complete observance of this law would greatly limit the prevalence of disease and misfortune, and would tend toward the reduction of extreme indigence.

What has been said of the benevolent results of conformity to the great law of love applies with similar justice and force to every one of the ten commandments. The command to have no other God than Jehovah is a very benevolent injunction against polytheism, which ever tends to confused ideas of Deity, and also to a very low order of theology. Polytheism, as heathen mythology demonstrates, brings up, in theory, a terrible conflict of deities, and these of a very corrupt and degraded order. All this, in soul and life, as also in the history of society and of nations, brings forth vice, superstition, and the unhappiness and the misery resultant from these.

The command against the worship of idols is an injunction against degradation and consequent vice and misery, as well as spiritual destitution and disaster resultant therefrom [sic]. Idolatry is the shame of its votaries and the degradation of the nation given to it.

The commandment against profanity is one against a most foolish and wicked vice which carries alienation from God and searedness [sic] of heart with all its desolation.

The command to keep the Sabbath day holy appears benevolent in that it conserves the physical, mental, and moral health of those who observe it in its fullest degree, and that every individual or nation that disregards it is corrupted and degraded, as a consequence. This commandment is clearly and abundantly benevolent.

What has been said of these commandments is equally true in degree of every commandment of the decalogue. Each is for a man's own good, for that of his fellow-beings, and for the good pleasure and glory of God.

What is true of the commandments of the decalogue is also true of every precept of God's word, every precept of Christ and of his apostles. They are full of goodness to the individual observing them, and to all others. They are as benevolent as they are wise and righteous.

It might also be shown that even the penalties attached to the violation of God's law are benevolent instead of malevolent—for too many are inclined to think the latter. But this we must not discuss in this article.

The conclusion of this whole matter is that the custom of many—even of some Christian ministers—of looking on the frowning side of the law is unwholesome as it is also erroneous. The terrors of the law should be preached often and freely. In truth, they are too apt to be suppressed in this age. But, in all ages, the goodness of the law—which emanates from our God, who is not only holy, but *is love*,—is too little realized by the sinner; it is not enough proclaimed by the ministry, and it is too little valued as a doctrine in the creed of the church of Christ. Will it not be well for all to consider this doctrine, hold to it, and give it due prominence in their minds and hearts? Then each Christian could exclaim with the psalmist: "Oh, how love I thy law."

February 16, 1876   The Ever-Abiding Spirit

An Indiana correspondent has recently heard some strange preaching,—such as we heard years ago,—which has prompted him to ask us a few questions. One of them is: *Did the Holy Ghost leave the world when the last apostle died?* In answer, we will say that Holy Ghost and Holy Spirit are one in their meaning, and that this Spirit has ever dwelt and reigned in the hearts of God's children on earth, as well as in heaven. Yet certain marvelous manifestations and gifts of the Holy Spirit were not given in the apostolic days till after the ascension of our Lord; hence, *in this sense,* there was a time in which it could be properly said that "the Holy Ghost was not yet given."

The Holy Spirit, as is clearly taught in the Old Testament Scriptures, dwelt in the hearts of God's children in the ages prior to the coming of the Messiah. The Lord promised Israel that after his judgments for their iniquities should have been fulfilled he would cleanse them from all their idols. He says: "A new heart also will I give you, and a new spirit will I put within you: and I will take away the stony heart out of your flesh, and I will give you a heart of flesh. And I will put my Spirit within you, and cause you to walk in my statutes, and ye shall keep my judgments and do them." This giving of "a new heart," a "new spirit;" this making of the hard heart tender, is all represented as being the effect of the Lord's putting his "Spirit *within*" the people of Israel. The prophet is next brought to see the valley "full of bones," and "very dry." The Lord caused breath to enter into these crisp bones, which had been so greatly shaken, and they soon sprung into life. "Thus saith the Lord God: Come from the four winds, O breath, and breathe upon these slain, that they might live;" and soon the dead skeletons "stood up upon their feet, an excellent great army." How this great revival, like that in the days of Joshua,—and not wholly unlike that of Pentecost,—was accomplished, appears in that the Lord says: I "shall put my Spirit in you, and ye shall live, and I shall place you in your own land." (Ezek. xxxvi. 26, 27; xxxvii. 2, 5, 6, 9, 11, 14.)

The direct agency of the Spirit of the Lord in cleansing and preparing the heart during the old dispensation is clearly taught in the following scripture: "The Lord thy God will circumcise thine heart, and the heart of thy seed, to love the Lord thy God with all thine heart, and with all thy soul, that thou mayest live." This is in entire harmony with the prophetic promise given to Israel upon their return from captivity in Babylon: "I will give them one heart, and one way, that they may fear me forever, for the good of them, and of their children after them." Again he says: "I will put my fear in their hearts." A similar promise concerning the gathering together of Israel is found in the book of the prophet Ezekiel: "I will give them one heart, and I will put a new spirit within you; and I will take away the stony heart out of their flesh, and will give them a heart of flesh." (Deut. xxx. 6; Jer. xxxii. 39; Ezek. xi.19.)

All this is in perfect harmony with David's prayer when interceding for renewal, after his sin concerning Uriah. He says "Create in me a clean heart, O God, and renew a right spirit within me;" and he indicates most clearly the agency by which this is to be accomplished by saying: "Take not thy Holy Spirit from me;" and again: "Uphold me by thy free Spirit." (Psalms li.10, 11, 12.) The doctrine was so well taught that Christ's reproving question to Nicodemus, "Art thou a master of Israel and knowest not these things?" was most just.

The New Testament doctrine of the agency of the Spirit in quickening the soul and cleansing the heart is very clearly expressed. We are taught that we must "be born of the Spirit;" that if such we have "the love of God shed abroad in our hearts by the Holy Ghost;" that the converted gentiles are sanctified by the Holy Ghost;" that the Corinthian disciples were "washed" and "sanctified" "by the Spirit of our God;" that Paul prayed unto the Father that the Ephesian brethren might be "strengthened with might by his Spirit in the inner men;" that salvation is through the "renewing of the Holy Ghost;" that the election of believers is "through sanctification of the Spirit." (John iii. 5, 6; Rom. v. 5, xv. 16; I Cor. vi. 11; Eph. iii. 16; Titus iii. 5; I Peter i. 2.) Nor should we wonder at this, for the new dispensation is most emphatically called "the ministration of the Spirit;" and it is contrasted as such with the less fervent spirituality of the old dispensation, which, on account of its burden being the law, is called "the ministration of death." (II Cor. iii. 7, 8.) Was it to be expected, then, that the spirituality of the new dispensation should after 'the death of the last apostle" be entirely wanting? Of course not; though some "having not the Spirit" may so affirm. (Jude 19.) Though there be some who "have not so much as heard whether there be any Holy Ghost" (Acts xix. 11), yet the apostle speaks of "the Holy Ghost, whom God hath given to them that obey him." (Acts v. 32.) Those "having not the Spirit," then, are the disobedient.

The Scriptures clearly teach that the Holy Spirit *dwells* in all God's children, *witnessing* their acceptance with him, giving an *earnest* (foretaste) of their eternal inheritance, and *sealing* them unto the day of redemption. Paul says: "Ye are not in the flesh but in the Spirit, if so be that the Spirit of God dwell in you. Now if any man have [*sic*] not the Spirit of Christ he is none of his." (Rom. viii. 9.) Poor man is he who even tries to teach others the way, himself "having not the Spirit" of Christ. Paul again says: "And because ye are sons, God hath sent forth the Spirit of his Son into your hearts, crying, Abba, Father," (Gal. iv. 6,— also I John iii. 24, iv. 13, Rom. viii. 16); and he says to the Ephesian brethren: "After that ye believed, ye were sealed with that Holy Spirit of promise, which is the earnest of our inheritance." So those "having not the Spirit" are not *sealed* of God, nor have they an *earnest* (foretaste) of the spiritual inheritance on high. (See also II Cor. i. 22; Eph. i. 13, 14; iv. 30.) The Spirit also assists the believer in his prayers. (Rom. viii. 26; Jude, 20.)

Christ, while on earth, taught very clearly that the Holy Spirit would be given freely of the Father to *all* who ask him for it. He says: "If ye then, being evil, know how to give good gifts unto your children, how much more shall your heavenly Father give the Holy Spirit to them that ask him." This was true before Pentecost; it is yet true. All that ask of the Father will receive the Holy Spirit, bestowed most freely and willingly; and such as receive it may *abound in hope through the power of the Holy Ghost.* (Rom. xv. 13.) And Christ's promises to be with his ministers "through all days" and to be in the midst wherever two or three disciples are gathered together in his name are in clear proof that the Holy Spirit is ever-abiding.

The mode of interpretation by which the New-Testament Scriptures are represented as being "all the Spirit that there is now in the world" is too puerile to demand much reply in this connection. It is like that of the papists, who maintain that Christ's words, "This is my body," "this is my blood," teach that the consecrated bread and wine of the eucharist are the actual body and blood of our Lord. When the language of Jesus, "The words I speak unto you are Spirit," are quoted to prove that there is no Holy Spirit only in the records of the inspired volume, and when the language of Paul, "The gospel is the power of God," is quoted to prove that there is no spiritual power for the conversion of souls except that contained in the literal Scriptures, it reminds us not only of papistic puerility, but also of that attributed by the poet to the fledgling of Eton College, who told his uncle that he could prove that a jack-pie is a pigeon; because "a jack-pie is a John-pie, and a John-pie is a pie-john (pigeon)." The student's reward of a chestnut horse, which on the invitation of his uncle he came out one fine morning, in boots and spurs, with eager expectation, to ride, is just such a one as those puerile expounders of God's word merit. The uncle shook a horse-chestnut from a tree and bade his nephew saddle and ride it; for according to "Eton logic" "a horse-chestnut is a chestnut horse.' The whole logic of those who try to argue away the proofs of the true nature and operation of the Holy Spirit in the gospel dispensation is after the jack-pie, horse-chestnut order.

April 19, 1876   Religious Emotion

Some greatly fear the emotional in religion. They are constrained to speak and write against it. We see little occasion for so doing. There is far greater excess in indifference and inanity in religion than of emotion. The congregations of some who speak and write against the emotional are fearfully intemperate in indifference and inanity, if the pastors are not themselves afflicted with the same. Rarely is there too much religious emotion. There is nearly always too little, and it is the curse of the church.

Men may have the wrong kind of feeling or emotion. They may have those but little affecting the heart or the intellect. These may be based on natural feelings mostly or entirely. Men may, as is often done in fashionable society in other

things, simulate emotion. These are either spurious emotions or feelings, or of a
low species. We may as well condemn the true bill because of the counterfeit, or
the best species because of inferior resemblances. Counterfeits indicate that
there are true bills; and monkeys derive much of their attraction from resem-
blance to mankind.

Some may institute contrasts between emotions and abiding feelings to the
discredit of the former. Very well; deep feelings rarely exist without breaking
out into manifestation by emotions, just as the deep currents or tides are not in-
imical to the billows which swell and dash upon the surface and lash the shores.
The glory of old ocean is greatly enhanced by its waves and billows; so the
glory of God is more clearly manifested in the expression of the feelings and
emotions of the soul in the depths of which the tides of divine love and joy are
constantly moving.

Intellectuality is a good thing; upright and comely conduct is good; but the
heart is the main thing. It is the gold of the coin; it is the aroma of the herb.
There is too much tendency to formality in every one of us. Too generally cold
hearts lie back of formal worship and formal lives; and too often they *lie* in more
than one sense of the word—when they talk of faith and hope and experience.

There is too little feeling, too little emotion, in nearly everything connected
with religion. Mr. Ever-so-much-pious talks of God and heaven with an expression too much like that of a dullard yawning in his expatiation on the glories of a
doll, or of an auctioneer bristling with simulated admiration of his wares. The
parson warns of the dangers of damnation too much like foolish parents tell their
children of fabled evils. The church needs emotions; yes, those too big to find
rest and concealment. We need a little more gospel sincerity. The realities of the
great salvation, the ineffable glories of the blessed Redeemer, man's deep sinfulness, and the struggles of the great conflict with sin call for more active, intense feeling, deeper and more manifest emotion. True revivals always bring
intense emotion, and they never tend in opposition to true religion, to fervent
piety, or to holiness in life. The reality of divine things needs above all to be
realized by Christians, to be powerfully expressed, and to be infused into a
sleeping world by the aid of God's grace. We do not wish too much of the emotional—oh, no; but, alas! We are almost sure to fall very far short enough of it.

May 3, 1876   Divine Guidance

The nature and extent of divine guidance is one of the difficult questions for the
solution of Christians generally. The psalmist says, "Thou shalt guide me with
thy counsel, and afterward receive me to glory." Jesus told his disciples that his
Spirit, the Comforter, should guide them into all truth. These scriptures certainly
give us good grounds to predicate our hope of divine guidance. But in what

shape we should expect this guidance is not so easy for many to determine. Some conclude that it is to be wholly by the Scriptures. In this they are no farther advanced than the psalmist, who said, "Thy word is a lamp unto my feet, and a light unto my path." Truly such the revealed word is; but is there nothing else of divine guidance to be expected by Christians? Paul earnestly desired that the Lord would give to the Ephesians "the spirit of wisdom and revelation in the knowledge" of Christ, "the eyes" of their "understanding being enlightened." This certainly implies more than mere acquaintance with the words of scripture. The apostle also prayed unceasingly for the Colossians that they "might be filled with the knowledge of his (Christ's) will in all wisdom and spiritual understanding." This certainly implies an internal work of God's Spirit enlightening the eyes and giving spiritual discernment. The apostle also thanks God for "the grace" given to the Corinthians by which they were "enriched" "in all utterance and in all knowledge." Indeed the familiar words of James teach us that God gives wisdom "liberally" in answer to the prayer of unwavering faith. We are certainly, then, entitled to believe that spiritual guidance is to be expected through the direct agency of the Holy Ghost.

But some fly to the opposite extreme from those who understand this divine guidance to consist alone in the words of revelation, as found in the Holy Scriptures, and they expect, at their own pleasure, to be gifted with inspiration. Much that does not at all indicate heavenly wisdom—some of it nonsense, and other proved to be false—has been palmed off as dictated from on high. Should we expect inspiration in the highest sense of that word? It was thrust upon the prophets, instead of their summoning it at pleasure. The apostles were called, being divinely appointed. Perhaps it is but rational for us to conclude that we can not draft revelation into service at our pleasure. Nothing written, as if divinely inspired, which dates this side of the apostolic age deserves the name of divine revelation, the book of Mormon and the writings of the learned and accomplished visionary Swedenborg being included in this remark.

Well-meaning men, whose ideas of revelation are of the modern prophetic type, are liable to mistake human fancies for revelation from God. It is in the very nature of thought to be, sometimes at least, quite spontaneous. The same is true of language in a remarkable sense. Men are liable, then, to mistake fancies and words, merely human in their origin if not sometimes instigated by the wicked one, as being by the inspiration of God. We once knew a man of fair gifts and sincere purpose to arise in a meeting, after the first prayer for penitents at the altar had been offered, and speak before a large audience in substance as follows: "The Lord told me to-day to come here to-night and perform a duty. I told him I wouldn't do it. But after going into my house and sitting down and reflecting I concluded that if I did not I should suffer for it. So I have come here, and if you will bear with me, and the Lord will help me, I will endeavor to perform that duty." And, walking to a man sitting in the front part of the congregation, who had been under conviction for some time and afterward professed conversion, the "inspired" man laid his hand upon the thigh of the penitent, and, kneeling, said: "The Lord told me to lay my hand upon this man and pray for him. He has been my enemy and has crushed my heart; and now I see spotted demons around him ready to drag his soul down to hell." With a few words slightly resembling prayer, he concluded the performance, to which he sincerely believed the Lord had called him. It is not easy to describe the feelings of the whole house. Some pitied the penitent so outraged at such a time and under such circumstances. Many were indignant. All were astonished and shocked. It was a severe damper on the evening's services. This was done, not by one devoid of intelligence, or of evil life. It was done by a professed minister of the gospel, a member of another denomination than that under whose government the meeting was being conducted. We give this case (for we have known many professed revelations just as captious and unseemly) to show that men may mistake the suggestions of their own minds, or perhaps those based on quite a human feeling of their hearts, for the revelation of God. It is due that we should add that in a prudent way this conduct was reproved, afterward, and a repetition of its like deprecated; but although we never heard of any one besides crediting this supposed revelation as from God, the sincere perpetrator of the sacred farce and outrage may to this day believe that the Lord told him to do so. While Christians should not take the extreme of discarding real spiritual guidance, they should avoid the presumption which attributes their own fancies, and spontaniety [sic] of thought or word, to the inspiration of the Holy Ghost.

May 10, 1876   Holiness

It may be that many have very inadequate conceptions of holiness. That which is holy is pure; but not all that is pure is holy. Lilies are pure; the snow is pure; but neither is holy. Why? Because unendowed with God's Holy Spirit, which alone is holy—the very essence of holiness. We mention this because so many are liable to overlook the great component element of holiness. With man it is the Holy Spirit dwelling in him as a pervading, prevailing, ruling power. Yet it is true that holiness implies freedom from guilt, cleanness as distinguished from the pollutions of sin. This cleansing from the guilt and defilement of past transgressions is *all* that is meant by the scriptures which represent the blood of Christ as cleansing "from all sin."

The true idea of man's original state, and of his depravity subsequent to the fall, is often lost sight of. The Edenic nature was upright; as the scripture says: "God hath made man upright." "In the image of God created he him;" that is, in his moral image. This was manifested by Adam's inspiration, which enabled him to name all the beasts and fowls and to utter those beautiful and authoritative words when the Lord brought Eve to him. But as soon as he had fallen, what a change. So at enmity with God was his carnal mind that he shunned him, seeking to hide from his sight. He began at once to excuse sin, attributing it to woman, and ungratefully reminding the Lord that he had given him this tempting companion, and apparently seeking by prevarication to deceive his Maker. His sense of guilt is shown in the fig leaf dress and in his attempt to hide from the divine presence.

How did the generations following illustrate the terrible depths to which man's nature, from its original uprightness—in the image of God—had fallen. The murder of the second-born by the first-born, the ambition and violence of the renowned giants,—the earth being filled with violence,—the general corruption that prevailed, so that every imagination of the thoughts of men's hearts was only evil continually, show an awfully fallen state; and the history not only of the ancients, but also of modern times corroborates in an awful manner the antediluvian lesson on depravity. Even the history of God's ancient people and of his church in modern times is quite in harmony with this appalling testimony.

None have a keener sense of the tenacity of human depravity than those who are eminent for the piety, and intelligence in sacred things. The best of men often think the most lowly of themselves; as the wisest most feel their ignorance. This arises from their having more self-knowledge and a finer sense of right and wrong than have others of less judgment and conscience. It matters not that there are spurious imitators of these; their piety is none the less genuine.

The question arises, Can men be holy? "Without holiness no man can see the Lord." Can he be free from sin? From its guilt he must be freed or he can not be justified in the sight of God. There is no condemnation to them who are in Christ Jesus. Can a man in this life be made free from the reigning power of sin? He can; for Paul says to his brethren, "Sin shall not have dominion over you; for ye are not under the law, but under grace." Man can be so free from sin as to not sin flagrantly nor willfully. "He that is born of God can not sin." This doubtless means that such as truly possess a regenerate nature—"the divine nature"—will abhor sin, and, acting from a higher principle than that of the carnal mind, will obey God. Yet such may err; they may feel that they have come short of the full measure of duty; they may be conscious of their need of praying: "Forgive our sins," as the Savior taught to pray. What! do they sin? Not in the sense of flagrant or willful sin. They can say of their shortcomings, "To will is present, but how to perform I find not." "It is no more I that do it, but sin that dwelleth in me." It takes an effort to abide in grace. The Apostle Jude exhorts that "praying in the Holy Ghost," we should "keep" ourselves "in the love of God." We should, as Peter says, "resist the devil;" we should not be "ignorant of his devices." We must pass through self-crucifixion.

We can be free from selfishness, anger, malice, and lust. We can have continual faith, love to God and to man, spirit of prayer, consecration, and victory. Many of the differences existing on the subject of freedom from sin consist mainly in difference in the understanding of terms. We ought to be and must be free from sin in the same sense so earnestly contended for by the Apostle Paul in the sixth chapter of the epistle to the Romans.

There are strong incentives to earnest effort to have dominion over sin, and to be filled with holiness. It is the will of God. Ample provisions are made in the atonement, by the Holy Spirit, and by providences and trials; for we, too, have some Philistines left to try us. Besides, holiness brings deliverance, happiness here, glory to God, and finally insures everlasting happiness. Why should not all seek it, long after it, struggle for it, lay hold of it by self-crucifixion, self-consecration, and faith in Christ. It is ours through the Holy Ghost.

August 16, 1876   The Gospel for the Poor

One of the chief points in the message of Jesus to John the Baptist in prison was, "The poor have the gospel preached to them." According to the prophet, as quoted by our Savior himself, Jesus was anointed of "the Spirit of the Lord" "to preach the gospel to the poor." The Apostle James says, "Hearken, my beloved brethren." Why this special call for attention? Because he is going to announce a truth so liable to be overlooked or forgotten. It is this: "Hath not God chosen the poor of this world rich in faith, and heirs of the kingdom which he hath promised to them that love him?" Paul taught that of the called there were "not many wise after the flesh, not many mighty, not many noble." It is the poor rather than noblemen and nabobs who are "rich toward God."

It was a happy time when the poor had the gospel preached to them. If Jesus were on earth he would see to it that the gospel should still be preached to the poor.

In our day the rich have the "gospel" preached to them, in some places at least. They have fine churches, luxurious pews, splendid organs. Then they have ministers of their own choice—and shall not the men of heavy purses have heavy votes in choosing a pastor? So they have such a minister as suits them. He has learning, talent, and accomplishments. He is a giant in logic, an adept in rhetoric, and a silver lute in eloquence. In politeness he shines in the best society. Socially he is the ornament and favorite "everywhere." Then he is so well trained that his preaching is of the most docile kind. When he preaches the law—which he does occasionally, for he is very orthodox—he makes the voice quite lute-like. The fire and thunder and earthquake of Sinai he makes as sweet and gentle as an infant's lullaby. His discourses are prismatic, tearless, and unawakening. Who can say that, in our day, the rich have not the gospel preached to them?

It is true the poor can come also to those fine churches; for they are rarely filled to overflowing. They can come if they would contrast their own clothing with the jewels and purple and fine linen of the chief pew-holders. They can come if they would bask in the shade of self-asserting aristocracy. They can find a church-home there if they can be at home in services dictated by wealth and fashion and supported by the same. They can sit there if everything is not so in contrast with their dress, their manners, their habits, as to make them feel uncomfortable. But one thing is certain: The great body of the poor are not reached by the fashionable churches of our cities. And it is noticeable that when a pastor comes to a city to organize a mission-church, he is too apt to do so with aspirations for competition in style, methods, and other respects with the churches which are now but half filled, and which seem to be accomplishing but little for that class to which Christ was specially sent, and which he reported had the gospel preached to them in his day.

We know that it is easy to overstate the situation of popular churches. We must not imagine that all city churches are void of regard for the poor, and that they are never attended by any of that class. But there is a field in nearly every city for one to succeed who goes there and makes it it [*sic*] his prime object to reach the poor by methods and services adapted to their tastes and modes of life. And if he shall succeed in preaching the gospel indeed to the poor, and if it is made to them the power of God unto salvation, there will be enough of the more pious men of wealth, or of liberal means, who will be drawn toward him in his labors; and he will not be long without means to carry on his work, nor without influential members to aid him in his mission of preaching the gospel to the poor.

October 11, 1876   The Indwelling Spirit

One of the common devices of the adversary of souls is to minimize the essential elements of Christian faith and doctrine. Accordingly, false teachers among the Jews of old said, "Thou shalt love thy neighbor and hate thine enemy.["] These would reduce the divine command to love to objects only which all may easily love, and give free scope to the carnal inclination to hate those who render themselves obnoxious. Faith many would have to mean little or nothing more than historic credence, and charity little else than the distribution of means which had been assured by the payment of advance fees. So it is of the Holy Spirit. Some would believe, and have others believe, that the Spirit is deposited in the written word, and that such as read it or hear it read and expounded, and retain it in the memory, are filled with the Holy Spirit. "They do greatly err" not understanding "the Scriptures, neither the power of God." Nehemiah tells us that the Levites of his day, in their solemn confession, acknowledged that the Lord had given to their fathers his "good spirit to instruct them;" and Jesus said this Spirit should "teach" the disciples "all things," bring to their remembrance his teachings, and guide them into all truth. This is "the anointing" which the apostle says shall teach the followers of Christ. So he prayed that to them might be "given, by the Spirit, wisdom."

The Spirit upheld David. It quickens; it comforts; it reproves; it sheds abroad in the heart the love of God, helps our infirmities, renews, and sanctifies us. Without it none can say from the heart that Jesus is Lord; with it, none can deny him.

The Holy Spirit is the great agency in the enlightenment, the conviction, the renewal, the transformation, and the growth of the soul. How strange it is that some speak so slightly of this Spirit. Is it that they do not understand the agency employed in their conversion and sanctification, or have they never known the power of God? Surely such can enjoy little of God's grace, if they are not wholly destitute of it. It is to be feared that many such know not God. When we remember the words of Jesus, that much more willing is our heavenly Father "to give the Holy Spirit to them who ask him" than we can be to give good things to our children, how strange it is that any devout person should be destitute of it, and not so much as know "whether there be any Holy Ghost."

Many are destitute of the indwelling Spirit; and why? Jesus tells them that the Father is most willing to give. The question then arises, Have they desired it? They should have sought his help to know its value and loveliness. To such as desire it, truly appreciating how valuable and precious it is, it will be given in answer to fervent, persevering prayer; and such will pray. In the hearts of such the degree of its presence and power can be increased by sacredly cherishing it, and by faithful obedience to it. Its increase must be sought with strong desire, diligence, and importunate prayer. How many are there who spend days and nights seeking the Holy Spirit, pleading for it, cherishing it? Alas, how few! But what better could they do? Many are worse employed. In all things religious, how many try to get along with the form without the soul? How often it is that even teachers show a sad lack of skill in things relating to the soul's welfare.

Want of the Spirit is what ails so many family Bibles, which grow musty or dusty for want of use. It is this which haunts so many secret and family altars. It depletes or demoralizes so many prayer-meetings, chills or misfills so many pulpits, and makes so many unworshipping choirs. It ruins so many protracted meetings, and cuts short or mars so many revivals. It is most ruinous in its consequences wherever it prevails in the church.

Pastors should pray like Paul, that their brethren might be filled with the Holy Spirit. From every pulpit, from every family altar, and from every heart entreaty should be made to God for the Holy Ghost.

It is scarcely necessary to say that we should distinguish between the real presence of the Holy Spirit and that fanaticism which imagines its presence without its reality. We may discriminate between the hypocritical and the real. We need not be deceived by others; we should not be deceived by our own selves.

We need the Holy Spirit above all things for the labors which lie before us the coming months, which ought to be months of revival, sessions of edification to the church, occasions for establishing more firmly the faith of individuals and of the churches. If we have, as we ought, the Spirit of the Lord, he will raise up instruments to accomplish his work; and the barren fields shall bloom, and the desert places shall sing for joy. The church needs, above all things, the baptism of the Holy Ghost. This will give her people the higher life without any need of theories about it, and in the absence of well-meant controversies concerning its methods and composition. It is the Holy Ghost, dear reader, that you, yes, *you*, need, and need it now, *just* now; and before you lay aside this paper your heart's resolve should be to seek a full baptism from on high—seek it henceforth and perseveringly.

October 25, 1876   What we Live for

What do we live for? is a hard question for many. They do not exactly know. Some fancy it is to eat and drink; others for show; and some seem to think it is merely to run a career. With very many, self-interest is at the bottom of all their calculations. All seem to center around themselves. That which is near is magnified; all at a distance is diminished. The loss of their own property shadows, in their minds, the loss of communities, the ruin of states, and the woes of continents. The present, too, outweighs, as many think, the future; this world, the world to come. To such, God, Christ, the soul, their fellow-men, are held as of little account. What huge children such are. They act as if demented.

There is really one great interest for all creation and for its Author. It all centers in God. It affects, too, all creatures. True, it is, that the divine interest is in the individual—in each and all of them. In our case our real interest is doubled by sharing the good with others. There are various departments of interest. Our interest is largely in humanity, and this as relates to them on earth. It relates to them, however, as probationers for eternity. What a world for labor we do live in. What interests we have to live for—ours, our fellow-beings, God's glory. Who is there that has no aspirations for a useful, noble life?

In order for us to live as we ought, and for what we ought, we must know God, know our relation to him, to our fellow-beings, and be brought into harmony with those relations. How are we to know him, understand his will, and comprehend our relations to him and to mankind, but by his revealed word, by meditation, and by spiritual illumination? We must, then, be Bible students, give our minds to the consideration of sacred things, and seek spiritual assistance. By self-abasement, by resignation to the divine Will, by study to know the same, by heeding it, and by the Holy Spirit, conferred in answer to fervent prayer, it is, that we are to learn to know ourselves, our relation to God and to our fellow-men, and our duty to God and to man.

We should live for God's glory. Benevolence and goodness appear to be the moving cause of creation. For his pleasure, (and he is love,) all things are, and were created. A debt inestimable is placed upon us to seek God's glory. This is in entire harmony with our own well-being and that of our fellows. To glorify God we must be correct in our faith. We must not only believe in a God, but in Jehovah and his Son Jesus Christ; not only believe in the true God, but also believe what he says—believe him. Unbelief is not from want of evidence but from a wicked heart; there is "an evil heart of unbelief." Some seem to regard unbelief as a mere weakness; the Scriptures uniformly treat it as a heinous, damning sin. Belief opens our minds and hearts for instruction and correction, for knowledge, and to duty. By it we know our relations to our God and to our fellow-beings. All is in darkness without it. Unbelief casts discredit on God's revealed word, his worship, Bible ethics,—it destroys all the authority of ethics—licenses sin, prevents the love of God—for who can love a may-be God,—and confuses what God would harmonize. Harmony, like that of the physical creation, ought to exist in the moral world. Eclecticism in religion relies on man's fallible and shifting, varying judgment, instead of the revelations of the Infinite. It is the weakest of all systems of religion in its faith, and a perfect nullity in its authority. It is a mere sentimental theory. Its votaries are ever ready to cast off any of its tenets, ever ready for a change. It is a patch-work of all religions, true and false; its beliefs are mere caprices. By *true* faith we are prepared to live for God's glory. It must be *pure, strong, live* faith.

But in glorifying God the heart is essential. There can be no real family without love; no real state without patriotism; so heart is the real essence of all true purpose and all real moral prosperity in society. A great heart is a power, as has been demonstrated by philanthropists, evangelists, reformers, patriots, and parents. There is no genuine glory to God without it. All the ascriptions of saints and angels, all the homage of heaven, would be cold as icebergs without it, and as repulsive as putrefaction. It is holy affection that gives excellence to all the services of the sanctuary here or those on high.

Those of true faith and pure hearts are well prepared to glorify God. Their lives must be cheerful yet sober, buoyant yet consistent, unascetic yet pure, given to active pursuits yet devout, mindful of others yet consecrated to God, unostentatious yet exhibiting fruit. Their private worship must be sincere, constant, and voluntary; their public worship orderly, harmonious, and with unction. Their lives should be adorned with peace, intelligence, judiciousness, prudence and diligence, and success in business, public spirit, philanthropy, Christian love, and with domestic affection and faithfulness.

What do many live for? Who knows, though some of these are church members, and think themselves Christians? The world would have them shine. Satan gloats over their foolish or aimless lives. But the true church mourns, the

Savior mourns, the Holy Spirit grieves. We ought to ask ourselves the question, What are we living for? How many can say they are living for holiness, for usefulness, for Christ, and for heaven?

March 14, 1877   Spirituality of the Church

There are many interests of the church of Christ. Chief among these is its spirituality. If it have all else besides and want this, it is nothing. If it have this, though poor, though despised, though scattered, it is the jewel of Christ; it is clothed with the power of God. He is its shield, its glory in time, and its exceeding great reward.

What do we mean by spirituality? We mean the indwelling, cleansing, illuminating, strengthening power of the Holy Spirit. We mean no imitation, no counterfeit of it. There may be that which is called spirituality. It may be the hypocrisy of the deceived or deceiving. It may have a show and a boast, but little or no reality. It may consist in ranting, or in swaggering profession. Real spirituality is spirituality discerned.

There was a church in the apostles' day which said: "I am rich, and increased with goods, and have need of nothing." It knew not that it was "wretched and miserable and poor and blind and naked." It needed repentance instead of boasting. So it is now with those who indulge in works of darkness, or sympathize with them, and yet boast of spirituality or other prosperity.

A sect in our Savior's day had numbers and wealth and learning and reputation and power, and thought its members better than others; but Jesus said: "Except your righteousness shall exceed that of the scribes and Pharisees, ye shall in no case enter unto the kingdom of heaven." It is those who are born of God that know what spirituality is, and who realize that all not born of God lie in wickedness. While men indulge in, approve, or tolerate darkness they have no right to claim *that* light enjoyed by those born of God; for such "know that he that is born of God sinneth not." So far as possible the child of God keeps himself "unspotted from the world." He bears the reproaches of those who think it strange that he runs not with them to the same excess of riot, in revelings and banquetings.

But how shall spirituality be attained, preserved, and increased? Sects, or bodies, or organizations having it not have need of a radical reformation. Nothing short of this will do. Death and perdition are at the door. By awakening, by repentance, and by humbling themselves under the mighty power of God, alone, can spirituality be attained by such.

But properly we have to do with such as are not devoid of spirituality, even if somewhat deficient in it. To such we address ourselves. How shall our spirituality be preserved? Not by indulging sin, not by indulging maxims and practices, but by forsaking and avoiding everything condemned by the letter or spirit of the divine precepts. This must be done in our every-day life, in our associations, and in all our co-operative affiliations and doings. By sin we forsake God and drive away his Holy Spirit.

But we must seek after spirituality. More willing than earthly parents to give good things to their children is God "to give the Holy Spirit to them that ask him." All spirituality not the gift of the Holy Spirit is carnal instead of true spirituality. There may be man-made spirituality, but it is deceptive and baneful. Its source is the carnal mind, of which Satan is parent. To our heavenly Father we must look for spirituality. Ezra says: "The hand of our God is upon all them for good that seek him; but his power and wrath is against all them that forsake him." If we seek the Lord he will not take his Holy Spirit from us, but pour out his Spirit upon us.

Not only must we ask for spirituality, but our works must proceed from it. God's Spirit is not dead, but fruit-bearing. The Master is glorified in the much good fruit of his disciples. Words of benevolence and usefulness must proceed from the truly spiritual soul. It must, it will, worship God and seek to promote his cause. It will consecrate a man's time, labors, and means to objects dear to Christ.

He who mediates not much in the Lord's garden is not likely to have his soul make him "like unto the chariots of Aminadab." It is he that meditates much on holy things who can say: "My heart was hot within me; while I was musing the fire burned." The flippant tongue or arrogant speech indicates that too many are deficient in sacred meditation. What a lamentable dearth there is in the church of Christ of those precious, well matured sentiments and purposes which can be had only by holy meditation and persevering communion with God. In this bustling age, too many fancy that without much sacred meditation and communion they can, by activity in Christian works alone, warm their hearts and progress in spirituality. It is a sad mistake.

There is too much disposition to try to reach heaven and induce others to do so without either they or we attaining to any high degree of spirituality. This diluting of the saving power of God is corrupting and weakening the church militant. The lowering of the standard by which the average Christian is to be measured tends to give us an army of pigmies [sic]. The lowering of the standard of loyalty to Christ results in filling the ranks with half hearted or alien soldiers. Better one that can chase a thousand than ten thousand who can be put to flight by two. We need an increase of spirituality. It is not so much that technical holiness about which some make so much ado, as it is that holiness—that spirituality—which has no graduating standard this side of the gates of eternal glory. There are degrees conferred by institutions of learning called "bachelor of science," "bachelor of arts," "master of arts," etc., but most of the field of learning is beyond these. So in spirituality, sanctification, holiness. Too many fancy themselves graduates, and it is proclaimed that they have taken the degree or degrees; but most of the realm lies beyond the degree to which they have attained. A little less display of holiness parchment and a little more address to the work yet to be attained would in some cases be very refreshing.

We must cast aside everything averse to spirituality. We must preach, pray, and labor for it. We must have it in our souls, genuine and constant. We must live it in our lives. It is not so much numbers, wealth, or reputation that the church wants as it is spirituality—the genuine life of God in the soul.

The Wright family home at 7 Hawthorne Street, Dayton, Ohio. Photograph by Orville Wright, 1900. Image courtesy of Special Collections and Archives, Wright State University, Dayton, Ohio.

Chapter 2

Piety and Morality

September 29, 1869   Sinfulness and Danger of Ambition

There is scarcely a sin more universal or more baneful than ambition. It expelled our first parents from Eden, and cast down the angels which kept not their first estate. It is found not alone in congress, in parliament, or in minor legislative bodies, but it enters every collection and organization of society. It manifests itself in the neighborhood, in the church, and even sometimes in the family circle. While it seeks glory from others, it worships self. It seeks to have its own self-awards ratified by the concurrence of the opinions of others. It is founded in inordinate self-love. Men of talent often possess it; yet it is a contemptible weakness. It is most ridiculous in seeking after the homage of others. It claims merit, while it could only justly claim demerit; hence it is a falsehood. It most presumptuously invites, and even seems to dare, high heaven to an exposure of its pretenses, and to an unveiling of its hideousness. It seeks that homage which belongs to God alone, and craves the gratification of a sinful propensity; hence it seeks the worship of a sin. It often ignores and sacrifices natural affection, however dear the objects of such affection may seem.

As this was the sin of Adam and Eve, it is no wonder that in their children it has no affinity to true religion. Its existence in the heart is most destructive to real piety.

Its undertakings are of no small magnitude. It would not only rule empires and compel the homage of millions, but it would even dethrone the King of heaven, if such it could do. Failure often, and, in truth, most generally, attends

63

its projects. Disappointments beset its pathway, and the mockeries of fortune goad it to fury. Its attempted flights generally end in flounderings in the dust.

Its possessor, even if successful, is far from being happy. He has not the elements of happiness within him. The inward state is such that no principle of happiness can take root in the cheerless climate of such a soul. He experiences such a state of continual disquietude as those who array themselves against the government of Jehovah should expect. Anxiety loads the poor victim down with fancied or anticipated burdens.

Ambition has spread devastation in this world of ours, far and near, by land and sea. It has brought violence, famine, and distress. It has destroyed magnificent cities, and desolated populous and productive lands. It carries the venom of hate to poison its fangs. It feasts on falsehood and riots in violence. Its devices are most subtle; its schemes are most reckless. It strains every nerve and avails itself of every advantage to make its means of execution commensurate with its plans.

It early sought the overthrow of primitive Christianity. It spread the sable curtains of error and oppression over the dark ages. It still infests the church with dissensions, and robs many a congregation of peace and prosperity. It has caused many of those who did run well for a season to make shipwreck of faith. It has cast many a brilliant watchman from the walls of Zion.

It is not only hard to eradicate from the gifted soul, but it often puts on the guise of virtue so skillfully as to deceive its possessor. While he fancies that his motives to action are chiefly Christian energy and zeal, his real motive is self-glory.

If there is anything that the church should carefully guard against encouraging, it is this godless ambition. It is as guileful as the serpent in Eden; and it has bitten its thousands, and is still carrying havoc in the ranks of those otherwise promising in the church. Individuals should look to it that it does not steal, unsuspected, into their souls and ruin their eternal prospects. If we could get the attention of every gifted, especially of every aspiring, Christian, we would say, Beware of an ungodly ambition. Struggle and pray to be delivered from it. If it is not put under your feet, it will destroy your peace, desolate your soul, and end in your eternal destruction. Especially would we entreat the minister of Christ to guard well against it. The example of our Lord, who, though equal with God, made himself of no reputation for your sake, demands that you should for his flock set such an example as he has given for you, that the weak in faith may follow you as you follow Christ.

October 6, 1869   Novel Reading

It is clear that far more than half the literature circulated in our day is fictitious. Even of that class not rated as such, there is a large portion which mainly aims at catering to a perverted taste. These assertions will not be controverted. Yet the sale of such literature goes on, and the energies of many minds are absorbed with or perverted by it. There is no doubt that to many minds fictitious reading is very attractive; and it may even be claimed that it has its advantages. It may be said that many writers of fiction are distinguished for fine taste. While this may be true, it may be added that many writers who repudiate fiction are no less distinguished for good taste. This is surely an age which furnishes solid reading in abundance, composed by the best of authors. It may be said, also, in defense of fiction, that such writings are well calculated to cultivate the imagination. While this may be, to some extent, true, it is also true that in works of truth there is abundant material to furnish the mind with the necessary food for the healthful cultivation of this faculty. It is no great recommendation of falsehood to say that the youths who practice it cultivate the imagination with great success. Yet it is certainly true. We do not, therefore, praise departure from truth in the ordinary walks of life.

We notice among the evils of novel-reading that it mingles fiction with our reading of truth, and is therefore calculated to confuse the memory. The mind is not calculated to retain all that is thrown into the memory, and, consequently, whatever of fiction is introduced must displace a measure of truth. Not only can not the man of prudence afford to read the dreams of some novelist, but he can not afford to read books and periodicals of greatly inferior merit, even if not fictitious. For the finest memory can not afford to be loaded down with that which can not profit.

Fictitious writings present characters which are not real. Though the author may paint well, the composition of characters and events are at the caprice of the author. In this way false theories of character are set up as real, and romance takes the place of truth. In this way a sickly ideal is often placed in the stead of truth and nature. When we remember that a large part of the writers of fiction are quite mercenary in their authorship, and many of them are perverted in their principles, may we not justly deem it dangerous that the youthful mind, so easily captivated by that which is brilliant and pleasing, should be brought under the fascinating power of the novelist?

It can not be denied that novel-reading inflames the passions. Nor can it be denied that it vitiates the taste. It can not be doubted that it is the cause of many irrational, romantic freaks of love. It has been at the bottom of many an elopement, and of many hasty, inconsiderate marriages. Novel-writers themselves, it is said, have been known to exclude such reading as unfit for the perusal of their own daughters. Such reading is an enemy of solid thinking. It not only takes up the time which should be spent in solid reading, but it perverts the taste, till the best of books are regarded without interest. The person addicted to it is likely to be impracticable. He will base his judgment on fictitious premises, so that his conclusions, however skillfully drawn, must be erroneous. He is disgusted with the tame realities of life, and longs for such as romance parades before his now distempered vision. His family is neglected; his life is squandered; and at last, having wasted the vital forces in delusive speculations, he sinks down to death wholly unprepared for a future state.

The Sabbath-school reading of our country at one time became so largely fictitious that the friends of the cause were alarmed; and it is to be hoped that the opposition to the fictitious juvenile literature will still more increase among the earnest Christians of the land. But the evil of fiction is not limited to writings for the youth. In some of our religious, or semi-religious, magazines, and other periodicals edited by divines—sometimes with the title "D.D." appended to their names—fiction is largely published. Who would think without disgust of some of the holy characters described in the sacred history issuing such magazines and periodicals? Such publications are comparatively pure; yet they are most effectual in breaking down the opposition to fiction in general. They propose to use Satan's devices less wickedly than he does! In this way they bait on the good, especially the young, to a toleration of fiction, and cultivate a taste for it, till the line of demarcation between the two classes of fiction is lost. The world-pleasing tendencies of our age give just cause of alarm. Not only does fiction carry its poison, but catching the spirit of catering to a worldly demand, some leading journals, ostensibly religious, furnish little reading matter which is calculated to make the heart better or stir the spirit of devotion, but mostly that which pleases the world. If we should peruse some popular so-called religious periodicals, we should find the evidence clear that what they esteem the jewels in the composition of their pages is that which breathes not a note of the spirit of Calvary or the hope of heaven through the name of Jesus. Some religious journals in our day are not only too much secularized, but, worse still, are to a great extent under the yoke of bondage to a sinful world.

January 26, 1870   Prevalence and Evils of Gambling

Gambling prevails to a fearful extent in our cities, and its corrupting influence even reaches country places. The law does but little for its prevention. This is not at all strange when we remember how many of our lawgivers and administrators of legal proceedings are themselves addicted to the vice. Few love to condemn their own practices from the judgment-seat, or as executive officers of the government. It has quite a softening influence in a law officer's sentiments when he reflects that he would have delighted to do the same thing under similar circumstances and temptation.

In many of our cities, owing to the indifference of the officers of the law, enactments against gambling are almost totally inoperative. Associations formed for the purpose of abating this evil find themselves hedged in and discouraged whenever they attempt the resort to legal measures to facilitate success. These law-officers give proof that the old adage is true: "A fellow feeling makes us wondrous kind." Their love of the gaming-table softens the asperity of their rough natures in such cases, and turns their judgments to softest mercy.

The evils of gambling are not to be seen and realized by any whose experience has not been involved in its demoralizations and calamities unless they be very attentive and careful in their observations. It makes one addicted to it quite contemptuous of ordinary honest gains. It leads the person who yields to its influence into the worst of society, and brings him under the influence of a most unwholesome excitement. Sentiments of honesty become to him a matter of derision, and when he has once become completely absorbed in the practices and fascination of the vice, all the finer sentiments and tender affections of the soul are kept in almost complete abeyance; and he sits in his gambling-hell or walks abroad a heartless monster. Oaths, intoxicating drinks, lewdness, recklessness of expenditure, resort to balls, theaters, and races follow as almost the inevitable result. The person ceases to live under the natural laws of his being. He is soon carried in the whirlpool of an unnatural excitement, and is consumed with a corroding longing for unmerited gains. Not only is he in the company of the thief, the defaulter, and the swindler, but his very practices are calculated to hasten that assimilation which might justly be expected as the natural result of such associations. Does he move in some of the honorable professions? If this vice does not cause him to neglect the interests of his calling, it will at least infuse its corrupting influence into his pursuits, and make his profession, and the consideration which it gives him, a power for evil.

How often does this vice lead men to the most reprehensible resorts for the obtaining of means to play a magnificent part in the game of chance. How many delusions blind him and lead him on. And if he is for a time successful, on what an uncertain pivot do the vibrations of chance sway his citadel of wealth. Quarrels, collisions, and murders are always at the door, if they do not enter the gambling-saloons to slay the victim of that cherished vice or put the brand of Cain upon his brow. It is but due that the citizens of our country should be aroused to the consideration of the evils of gambling, and be awakened to its fearful prevalence. It is time that the churches of America should discard those practices so much more than merely like gambling with which world-accommodating professors and even divines contrive "to raise money for the Lord," not on his, but the devil's plan!

It is due, also, that our citizens should make every effort to have enacted and enforced, laws which will most effectually restrain such vices. In order to do this they must not place in positions of responsibility those who are themselves gamblers, though they may not claim to be professional ones. We commend the following, from the *Christian Statesman*, to the perusal and consideration of our readers:

As long as these evils are tolerated under the very eye of the Government, there must be something of a sting in the reply of the Mormon, John Taylor, to the speech of Vice-president Colfax, delivered at Salt Lake City. Mr. Colfax had said, "Our country is governed by law, and no assumed revelation justifies any one in trampling on the law." His opponent replies. "Let me respectfully ask, Is there not plenty of scope for the action of Government at home? What of your gambling-hells? What of your gold rings, your whisky rings, your railroad rings?" &c. Now, while we would have Mr. Taylor understand that the United States Government is at home in Utah just as much as in New York or Washington, we would also have our Government so conduct itself towards gambling-saloons, and other infamous places, as to give no opportunity to corrupt Mormons to read it a lecture on morality.

April 13, 1870   Pompous Funeral Obsequies

We presume there are none who do not delight to honor the worthy and illustrious dead. They are and should be embalmed in the memory of the living. The method, however, in which they are honored by a vain world fills some sensible people with disgust. It is related that a wealthy citizen of Maine, in his last words to his heirs, said: "Plant me as soon as I am cold, and don't cart me around for a side-show. *Remember Peabody*." Whether this incident be fictitious or not, it shows that there is a sentiment pervading many minds that so much pomp and parade as was exhibited in the funeral obsequies of even that great philanthropist does not accord propriety. Some one said, a few months since, that there were two things receiving, in the newspapers, excessive attention, of which he was heartily sick of seeing and hearing so much—the Peabody funeral and the Winnipeg war.

That the illustrious dead should be buried in solemnity, with simple, unaffected, and devout honors, not wanting even in chaste magnificence, all will admit. But it is due them and the common sense of a Christian nation that the remains of those worthy of honor should be consigned to the earth without long-protracted delay, and that the bodies of those who have seen the end of all worldly show should be allowed a deposit in the earth from which they sprang, without the greatest pomp and vanity being exhibited over their bodies, from which their souls, disgusted with the folly of these things, have taken their flight. Why not let their corruptible and decaying bodies early sink to the grave, the proper hiding-place of mortality. Who not let them in peace await the resurrection morning.

September 7, 1870   Moral Heroism

There is something in heroic sacrifice and endurance which commands universal admiration. Enemies often reverence it, and pay a tribute to its excellence.

Many, however, capable of admiring its possessor do not have the elements of character essential to its practice. There is a capability of moral heroism, perhaps, in every character, but many fail to develop it by cultivating those principles essential to its composition. There is many a one who would covet the fame of a Leonidas, but few would have been willing to throw themselves in the pathway of Xerxes' millions. There are plenty who would admire the martyr crown of Huss and Jerome who would have been much more willing to compromise their faith than partake of the martyrdom of those heroes. Indeed, zeal to garnish the sepulchers of the illustrious dead is not uncommon among those who detest their principles, and who would, if these worthies still lived, deliver them into the hands of those who would dishonor and crucify them. The proslavery rabble of other days, headed by their leaders, at once loaded those who would emancipate their slaves, with imprecations, while they expatiated on the sacredness of the tomb of Washington, who emancipated every one of his slaves. They prated loudly of the patriotic Franklin, while they ignored the fact that he was the chief in an antislavery society.

Among the most grand examples of moral heroism to which the mind can revert is that of some hundreds of Presbyterian ministers in Scotland, who, being required by the government to do that which was averse to their consciences or give up their several charges, at once chose the latter. Time-servers would readily have found means to reconcile conscience with temporal interests.

The Puritan might, with the slight sacrifice of principles which some are ever eager to make, have remained in the land of their nativity and ranked well as friends of the perverted church whose abuses they reproved, but they would not have transmitted to posterity those glorious institutions, civil and religious, which have blessed the world. More, their influence has done much to reform the church from which they came out.

Another instance of moral heroism is seen in the person of Orange Scott, who, rather than bow the knee to slavery, headed a movement, in New England, striking for freedom from the guilt and domination of slavery. Such bitter persecution as followed him and his co-laborers is among the marvels of modern ecclesiastical bigotry and tyranny. Loving a liberal church government, as antislavery men might be expected to do, detesting secret societies, as the antislavery element in this country generally did, these noble men formed their church organization, including these excellent principles in general. The result is known. Scott, overworked, fell with this armor on. The society of which he had been principal moved into the long-protracted conflict, and fought especially for antislavery principles, which are universally prevalent in the scene of their labors now. This society carried, perhaps, too much of bitterness, as a persecuted people are apt to do, and this militated against their best success—in numbers, at least. But their influence was national. The church from which they came out was agitated by the truths which its people were compelled, not always willingly, to hear. The sentiment of the church from which the Wesleyans came out was essentially modified, and much of this was due to the despised people, who were noble in their utterances against the iniquity which the mother church still harbored under her mantle till it was in its death-throes.

The cruel stab which this society has since received in the house of its friends, we shall not dwell upon. It is enough to say that it still lives and still lifts its voice against iniquities popular in the land while those who sought to betray it are bowing the neck supinely under an ecclesiastical power which none denounced more bitterly than they in the past. As the Wesleyans are quite similar to our own denomination, we could not wish to indicate our desire for the disbanding of our own organization by suggesting that of theirs, though it would be a happy thing if we could be blended into one, which is, perhaps, among the improbabilities, though not among the absolute impossibilities.

Among the instances of this moral heroism, we may mention the political antislavery men of our country. The successful contest of John Quincy Adams on the right of petition, the long-continued antislavery warfare of Joshua R. Giddings in the House of Representatives, the agile pleasantries and yet severities of John P. Hale, the noble arguments of S. P. Chase, the polished eloquence of the classic Palfrey, the noble utterances of Horace Mann, the biting sarcasm of G. W. Julian, and that of others who stood up, unpopular, for the right, are among the material out of which is made imperishable history. The antislavery utterances of Garrison, Phillips, Goodell, and Frederick Douglass will live when the mantle of charity will be sought to cover in oblivion many of the utterances of Clay, Calhoun, and Webster.

Moral heroism generally stems the current of popular opposition in its day, but at last triumphs and receives the garnishing of its sepulcher even from such as would have spit upon it in the day of its fierce contest.

January 4, 1871   Religion in the Family

The importance of religion in the family can not be easily overestimated. From the earliest ages inspiration has recognized its value, and recorded examples of it. The history of the ante-diluvian and ante-exodian periods of the world are meager; but it is evident that the families of Noah, Abraham, Isaac, Jacob, Joseph, and Amram were the recipients of careful, pious instruction. Shem, Isaac, Joseph, and Moses are encouraging and illustrious examples of the blessed fruits of religion in the family. Some, at least, of these are among the most brilliant examples of piety and greatness ever known in the history of the world. Most of the bright stars in the moral heavens, in all ages, have been placed there by the prayers and tears and instructions and benedictions of pious, faithful parents.

What lessons of encouragement do these examples afford for devout, though obscure, parents. How much of Samuel's greatness was due to the piety of his mother, the devoted and devout Hannah! How much of the loveliness, religious heroism, and unrivaled magnanimity of the early life of Israel's shepherd-king were due to the instructions, prayers, and examples of the pious Jesse! John the Baptist, inheriting the piety of Zacharias and Elisabeth, was filled with the Holy Ghost from the time of his birth. Timothy's mother, Eunice,—if not also his grandmother, Lois,—in his childhood taught him the Holy Scriptures, which were most efficient in making him wise unto salvation, through faith in Christ Jesus; and that wisdom made him the most eminent among the immediate successors of the apostles. Luther, Watts, Wesley, Henry, and Otterbein are only prominent examples among thousands who owe so much of their greatness to religion in the family. What a host, among the saved on high, give thanks to God and the Lamb for the benefits received in the pious home-circle!

Moses, by inspiration, enjoined upon parents, through all the ages of the Levitical dispensation, to teach, with persevering diligence, Jehovah's law to their children. Joshua set before Israel the choice of divine service, choosing for *himself* and *his house* the service of the Lord. Solomon taught that the child should be trained up in the way in which he should go, with the assurance that in old age he will not depart from it. The Savior taught that little children should be encouraged to come to him; and the apostles instructed parents to bring up their children in the nurture and admonition of the Lord. John commended the elect lady, whose children were filled with that piety which she taught by precept and example. Surely, Christian parents are without duties at all if they are not in duty bound to see to the matter of religion in their families! What blessings rest upon those who heed this duty; and what darkness is gathering for those who heed it not! Alas! for those parents who raise their children without prayer. May God manifest his mercy by awakening them to a proper apprehension of their duty.

The family lies at the foundation of both church and state. To universally disregard its organization and sacredness would be dissolution, ecclesiastical and political. Justly do genuine Christians resist every attempt to impair the obligations of marriage, or the permanence of its sacred bonds. Without families, California was once the arena of retrograding civilization and refinement. With the family, she has since rapidly advanced to a moral and social equality with her sister states. How happy would be the result of a general prevalence of family religion all over our land, and throughout the world. How happy would be the condition if even all the professedly religious parents would, in spirit and in truth, plant themselves on the sublime revolution of Joshua and his household, determined, whatever may be the customs and choice of others, that they will serve the Lord. How many "home-churches" would echo with the praises of Jehovah! How many a paradise there would be on earth! What influence these would exert in the church and in the neighborhoods of our land. How would our municipal organizations, our legislatures, our congress, and the executive officers of our Government be affected by it! How would the nations of the earth be clothed with righteousness, and canopied with peace! How many a youth would be saved from tragic wreck; and how many an old age would be crowned with the grateful benediction of children and children's children! How mightily and holily would the pulpits be filled, and what a power the church would have in the world! What defeats would thwart and defeat the plans and campaigns of the evil one! How rapidly would heaven be peopled, the rejoicing earth be subdued, and songs of holy joy and victory mingle from heaven above and from the earth! Oh for the universal prevalence of religion in the family!

May 17, 1871   Use of the Wealth of Christians

Christ's kingdom is a spiritual one. The great work designed to be effected by it is the regeneration and salvation of the soul. Yet means and instrumentalities are employed to co-operate with the Spirit in this great work. God not only employs princes and captains and sages to work in the accomplishment of his providential designs, but he employs the arts, the sciences, the literature, the inventions, and the wealth of the world to work in the same way. But especially should such of these as are in the hands of his own people be directly employed to accomplish the designs of the gospel. Here we shall especially notice the wealth of the church. Are railroads to be build? Is war to be waged? Are fine buildings to be constructed? Are great designs of material improvement to be accomplished? How does the wealth of rich church-members flow like abundant streams in those directions. But is it for church-building at home or abroad; is it for the support of missionaries in lands afar, or for the support of preaching at home; is it for the circulation of books, tracts, and periodicals, to carry light into the dark places of the earth, or even for home cultivation and enlightenment, how slow and sparing is the hand of liberality, even though that hand be that of those who claim to be the redeemed of the Lord, and who profess, in soul and body, time, talent, and means, to belong to their Creator and Savior. What a wrong is this— what a burning shame! No wonder the world scorns such evidences of the truth of Christian profession. It is not very strange that the children of such parents are worldlings, and have little sympathy for the religion of their parents—are little inclined to worship "the God of their fathers?" The millions of wealth in the hands of church-members if consecrated to Christ would tell wondrous power on the condition of the world. That which is not so consecrated is that of which God is robbed. When God is robbed it is no wonder that reverential piety mourns and deriding impiety triumphs. A radical reformation in this respect is needed with the great multitude of Christian professors.

February 28, 1872   Ingratitude

The ingratitude of human nature crops out in early life. It manifests itself on the part of the child toward its parents. Though indebted to them for parentage, early care, and support; though deriving instruction, respectability, and often competence from them; though causing them many a sleepless night and many a throb of pain; though their aching hearts have borne with the follies and even ingratitude of the child, how soon does the son or daughter throw off all regard for parental instruction—all respect for parental authority and feelings, and, in some cases, discard the father and mother as beneath their children because some of the accomplishments of artificial life are wanting in those parents, who received their tastes and habits from another age, from, perhaps, less foolish and vicious times.

This ingratitude is often shown toward the church of God. Though the church is the pillar and ground of the truth; though without it man should have wandered in heathenish darkness; though its ministrations and influence have kept it from evil and led to the pure and good; though life's sweetest recollections should cling to it, and though it has been instrumental in bringing the soul from darkness to light, from death to life, yet how little do many regard its honor or prosperity. Instead of liberality in gifts and devotedness in labors for its success, the most trivial whim of their own or ever so well deserved affront received from the church, is quite enough to lead them to forsake its fortunes, and cause them to cover it with reproach and scorn. We have known not a few who have been lifted out of the mire by some particular society or branch of the church of Christ which has borne with their weakness and waywardness when they were in their spiritual infancy, who now return all this with neglect or contempt, or even opposition and persecution.

The same ingratitude is shown to one's country. Patriotism is an essential virtue. Moses, David, Nehemiah, Daniel, and Christ have shone brightly as examples of this virtue. Where patriotism is wanting there is so little warp of character left that the woof of life is in a manner hopeless. There is often a disregard on the part of citizens for their country, its laws and institutions, and for those who in the past or present age have built up and preserved those institutions, that is highly dishonorable to human nature. Not a few despise or smite or sting the bosom that cherished them. This ingratitude for country often takes on the collective form, and treats most shamefully those who have rendered the most important service to the country. Not infrequently have patriots been slandered and abused because they have not contrary to convictions consented to float with the popular current. Some are thrown on the background, and slandered and vituperated simply because they have souls too large to bear the fetters of party. Others have been abused shamefully because a partisan spirit has moved their political enemies to discount the very embodiment of competency, honesty, and patriotism.

While hero-worship is strong enough with most of citizens there is a certain selfishness that exuberates in worship at the shrine of some political or literary god; but that gratitude which goes out toward real service and worth is not to be found in the froth of society on its gala days.

This ingratitude to national benefactors is not greater than is manifested in many instances toward those who have been instrumental in building up the church. Not infrequently those who have entered in where others have toiled and sacrificed to build, look with ill-concealed contempt upon those who yet linger to witness the fruit of that which has been planted with sighs and tears. Some, though seeking to conceal the real animus of their detractions, take especial delight in pointing out and magnifying fancied or real errors committed by those who in the past have taken steps or favored measures the folly of which is demonstrated by the lapse of years, just as it will be ere long in their own case, in a greater number of instances, by the advancing march of time. Those who feast on the defects of the fathers in the church are likely to have a posterity of even greater scoffing ability than themselves, who will not fail to do ample justice to the manifold foibles and blunders of *their* forefathers.

But of all ingratitude, that toward God mounts the highest in its daring and sinks the lowest in its pollution. Though man derives his existence from him, though all his mental endowments, as well as spiritual, are from his divine power, though all the faculties of his physical frame are from the divine Hand, though his preservation and continued happiness are all of God's pleasure and power, yet man is in many an instance entirely devoid of gratitude to his Maker and Redeemer. Though all the elements necessary to sustain man's physical system and well being are derived from God; though friends and the beneficent institutions of family, church, and state come from him; though remnants necessary to sustain man's physical system and well being are derived from God; though friends and the beneficent institutions of family, church and state come from Him; though redemption, regeneration, pardon, and all grace are of his mercy; yet man, in a multitude of instances, is totally ungrateful for all these. It is a terrible indictment against human nature as we find it in its unconverted state, but, alas! the indictment, in part, applies to thousands upon thousands, not only of professed Christians, but of those who have actually tasted of the good word of God and the powers of the world to come. This ingratitude is withering many a soul, darkening many a heart, blinding many an eye, desolating many a church, and destroying many a soul. It is dishonoring God and throwing a baneful influence all over the Christian world. It is a crying sin of every age.

May 29, 1872   Laboring for Spiritual Food

Labor is essential alike to earthly and spiritual prosperity. No great success has ever been attained without labor of the head, heart, and hands. It will be perceived that the latter term is here used to include physical exertion in general. He who will not think on the subject of religion—think earnestly and intently—though with ever such feeble powers or with ever so little system—will not obtain much spiritual food, or lay up much heavenly treasure. He will come out like the careless farmer, the unthinking merchant, or the reckless financier. Satan does not trouble himself about unthinking sinners, or unthinking "Christians," either. He is as sure of such prey as the shark is of the gamboling inhabitant of the sea in which he roams. He who does not think honestly and much on the subject of religion neither has nor is likely to have much religion to assist him in his thinking. Men are often choice about the kind of work they would do, or in their manner of performing it. It is just so in the mental work of most of men. If they would think, it must be either not on the subject of religion, or else they would do that kind of thinking on it which would gratify the carnal nature of the soul. Is not the dearth of real Christian thought in the soul of many a believer a proper subject of humiliation, and even alarm? If our own flattering estimates of our religious thought were but justly discounted so we understood their real value, should we not have occasion to very much change their quality as well as quantity? It is to be feared that many would fall out with any one who would make for them an honest invoice of their stock of religious thought. If they would make such an invoice themselves they would be sure to *fall out with themselves*. Then there might be some hope of improvement.

But the heart-work is of most essential value to a man and to mankind. Saying this does not say that it can exist without the exercise of the intellect any more than either can have the present mode of existence without the physical system. But the great test in the sight of God is the affections. He who loves God has life, and he that loves him not abides in death. It is difficult to think of the affections abstract of the intellect, nor is such abstraction necessary. The affections may be said to be the residence of moral principles in the souls of men. For the want of holy affection the soul is condemned in the judgment and consigned to everlasting destruction. It is one of the essential ingredients of saving faith. It alone can truly inspire the most elevated and profitable thoughts. It is the incense of all real worship, and gives all intrinsic value to good deeds.

The question may arise whether the affections are subject to the control of the will. Though it must be admitted that the will is largely controlled by the affections, it is nevertheless true that even if the affections constitute, in part, the will, they are subject to essential modification under its guidance. If, for instance, the soul finds that according to an enlightened judgment and a good conscience its affections toward its fellow-beings or toward God is wanting in degree, it can will and perseveringly carry out such measures as may secure an increase of affection. It can not secure these by mere resolve, by a mere decree of the will, but it can direct the mind and heart to communion with God, to the contemplation of those perfections and gracious acts toward us and our race which are calculated to enlist the affections. Above all, it may direct us to a throne of grace where in answer to prayer we may receive that divine grace which inspires holy affection. With such grace, with proper contemplation of the relation of our fellow-beings to us and to Christ, and with due consideration of man's nature, motives, aspirations, sympathies, and trials, the affections may be essentially increased and quickened toward our fellow-beings. This heart-work by which we are brought into a closer union with God and into deeper sympathy with our fellow-beings is that which may be and must be performed by every one who would have his own soul fed. There is a vast amount of heart-work needed in the church. Some substitute brain-work for it. Brain-work, if rightly directed, is commendable and valuable, but it will not do as a substitute for heart-work. "God pondereth the hearts," and a great increase of heart-work would produce an abundant advance in the holiness and consequent spiritual power of the church of Christ on earth.

But the body is the servant as well as tenement of the soul. It has much work to do for the benefit of the soul. Its organs serve as a medium through which the soul gathers knowledge and directs its benevolent operations. It must do much seeing and hearing for the soul. Some have eyes and see not, ears and hear not. The members of the body, too, must talk, must bear the soul in transition from place to place in its labors, must confer its blessings—its deeds of charity. They must perform a great portion of its service to God and to man. This work of the body is not only beneficial to others, but without it the soul could not so well live and flourish. As the body without exercise evervates and perishes, so the soul in its present mode of existence can not maintain a healthful state without good works. The works which our hands find to do for the cause of Christ are as essential to the perpetual enjoyment of the food on which the soul feeds as is the work of the mind or heart. The followers of Christ, like their Master, find it their meat to do the will of their Father in heaven. Toil for spiritual food includes, as we said in the beginning of this article, labor of the head, heart, and hands.

May 29, 1872   Prayer

Prayer is the medium through which God confers blessings on his children. It is not arbitrarily decreed as such, but it is adapted to the very nature, necessities, and happiness of God's people. It brings the children of God face to face with their Father in the most direct and confidential intercourse. It enables them to imbibe his Spirit; it acquaints them with his character; it draws out their affections toward him; it affords them the sweetest and most profitable seasons of their lives. Man must have a superhuman object of reverence; for such is the composition of his being, and that being corresponds with holy truth; for the

Creator is worthy of reverence from all the beings who constitute his whole family.

Worshipers in order to be prepared for approaching God in prayer, must feel their need of him. Without this they are in their hearts at variance with truth; for their real need is great. Nor can they pray in sincerity unless they realize their need of assistance. If insincere their prayers will be little less than mockery, and must be unacceptable to God as well as irksome to themselves. But those who intensely feel their need, rejoice in the privilege of approaching a throne of grace. They long for approach as any expectant mendicant would for access to the presence of some noted philanthropist.

Christians in order to properly estimate the privilege of prayer must have faith in God; not merely that he can and does answer prayer, but that he is full of love, pity, and willingness to succor his children. It seems most strange that it should be so, but it is evident that many regard God as a great being, above them so high, and so apart from their state of existence, that he regards with indifference their wants, griefs, and sufferings. Reason as well as revelation would say that this is the very reverse of the truth. The very tender regard manifested in all creation for his creatures, as well as the nature of being which all these indicate, teaches us that God is most sensitively alive to our condition and welfare. His is a tenderness far surpassing that of a mother for her child, though he regards the end from the beginning, and consequently regards as the chief thing, not the present moment, but our whole being; not our individual selves alone, but the whole race, and even the universe of created beings. Proper conceptions of the love and beneficence of God can be best attained in contemplating his glory as seen in the face of Jesus Christ. There we see just the order of that Character who makes intercession for the saints *according to the will of God.* Yes, *in perfect harmony with the will of God.*

Some have vague ideas of the willingness of God to do us good, but no proper idea of the necessity of prayer. The history of the saints of other ages, the direct teachings of the prophets, apostles, and Christ, they admit, exhibit the value and efficiency of prayer, but somehow they feel that the divine Being is of such greatness and perfections that he will of his wisdom and benevolence do all the same for us without our asking. It is enough that God has said that he will be entreated; but if blessings, all the same, were conferred without our asking, we would be unprepared to appreciate them, and should lose all the comfort and assimilating grace received at the footstool of sovereign mercy.

Perseverance in prayer is the test of its reality. What people care but little about they soon forget. Mere mention does not indicate earnest desire, nor does it intensify it. Persevering prayer is dwelling at the foot of the throne and imbibing its holy atmosphere. Persevering prayer has not only obtained wonderful answers, but has been made instrumental in wonderfully assimilating the petitioner into the image of Christ. Prodigies of holiness have been the result of such perseverance in intercessions before the gracious throne of God.

Not only must those who pray believe that God cares for us, but they must believe that he verifies his word in accepting and answering their prayers. They must believe that their petitions are granted, and look for the answer in God's own way. If we ask according to God's will, we know he hears us; and if we know that he hears us, we know that our petitions are granted.

The prayer of faith never fails unless we fail to await its answer. God may not grant it in the same form we ask, but he will do the best for us in the case, which is all we can desire; for every real prayer is offered up in the spirit, "Thy will be done." The Giver of all good gifts takes into advisement every case presented before him by true petitioners, and grants just what will best meet it. Prayer that is unwilling that he should do this is unprayerful. God answers every true prayer and if we can now only accept this truth by faith, we shall see its demonstration in eternity, when we shall see as we are seen and know as we are known.

July 17, 1872   Man Must Worship

The normal condition of the human soul is that of a worshipful being. Only for such a state can a creature capable of intelligent and moral qualities be created by a God who is full of goodness, wisdom, and truth. An ungrateful, irreverent, unworshipful intelligent being—if such were its normal condition—would be an impeachment of the wisdom, truth, and holiness of Deity. Such a normal state would argue that the Creator had given to that being moral and intellectual endowments that were necessarily incapable of comprehending the most essential and beneficent moral truths. It would involve its whole being in the acceptance of the most pernicious untruths concerning the relations of the creature to the Creator, and necessitate the rejection of the most happifying truths on the same subject. It would throw that being out upon the ocean of eternal falsehood, and float it off on the waves of everlasting lies. It would prevent all the happiness found in gratitude, love, and adoration to God. Its mental state would be that of antagonism to the truth of God; its moral condition would be directly opposite to that of every moral and intelligent being in the universe that receives and appreciates eternal truth.

For a created being to truly comprehend and appreciate the Creator is to love, adore, and worship him. Can a God of love and truth otherwise than so ordain the normal condition of man? Can such a Creator be indifferent to the affection and happiness of his creatures, who experience the most exquisite joys in the exercise of the affections which necessarily and involuntarily find expression in his worship. The truth of God, his love, his wisdom, and his holiness, all join in declaring man's normal condition to be that of a spiritually worshipful being.

In the conclusion of this article it is not necessary to assert that man in his unconverted state is not in his normal condition. If he worships at all, his devotions are paid to the god of this world. The great object of the gospel is to restore man to the condition of a true worshiper of Jehovah, who can only be acceptably worshiped through our Lord Jesus Christ. God is a Spirit, and they who worship him must worship him in spirit and in truth, and oh, how delightful is such worship! It is pleasant; it is comely.

August 7, 1872   Pleasures of Moral Purity

There is a pleasure in purity to which the impure are total strangers. Just as the swine revels in the very slough that the lambkin would most carefully shun, so does the swinish soul delight in moral pollutions from which the virtuous would shrink with abhorrence and disgust. But, to pursue the illustration farther, the filthy savage would be astonished if any one were to allude to the discomfort of his filth and vermin. He esteems his ease, which involves all the discomfort of physical indolence, as more desirable than any cleanliness which the fastidious white man might recommend. If he could go to the home of industry and cleanliness he would be astonished at the busy toil which pays the price of a boon so highly esteemed by the pale-face. He does not know the pleasures of a cleanly body, of pure raiment, of purity of food and drink. The sight of the ill-shaped or loathsome, the scent of carrion, the presence of the rancid or unclean in his food, does not pain his mind nor revulse his stomach.

The question arises whether the savage finds, in the absence of esthetic culture and the love of physical purity, those pleasures which the cultivated son of civilization finds in a higher order of life? Does he find in ease, sports, and passions *that* comfort which attaches to civilization? It may be doubted whether the savage is cultured sufficiently to enjoy any pleasure exquisitely. As the unlettered rustic is insensible to the beauties of rhetoric, and the uncultured boor to music or the fine arts, so may the savage be to the intense enjoyment of even the pleasures and comforts he has. His drowsy indolence, cheerless countenance, and indifference to dangers, hardships, and sufferings, do not indicate a high capacity in the savage for enjoyment. Who that has partaken of the blessings of civilization would wish to exchange life with the Esquimau [*sic*], the Pequot, or the Hottentot? Few, we trust, have souls so low.

If, then, we are to conclude that the filthy savage in his insensibility to the sanitary and the esthetic has but a low order of happiness, and that very scanty, may we not by parity of reasoning conclude that though the souls of the morally unclean and the religiously unesthetic may be to a great extent callous to the degradation and unhappiness which clothe their being with pollution and unrest, yet this callous state is less desirable than that which would allow them some rational conception of the pollution of sin and abasement of iniquity.

There is an exquisite pleasure in moral purity. Freedom from guilt, pollution, and the dominion of vice is a heritage in which a regenerated soul may truly rejoice. It is the base of all true happiness. It prepares its possessor for the enjoyment of those graces which are as a garden of spices to the quickened soul, or an orchard of the most luscious fruits. Without it there is no satisfying, enduring happiness. Yet to the unclean there is little apprehension of the excellence and pleasure of this moral purity, this spiritual cleanliness and quickening.

In order that we might be pure Christ entered on his beneficent mission. He gave himself for us that he might redeem us from all iniquity. He gave himself for the church that he might *sanctify and cleanse* it. The provisions are abundant for the removal of pollutions of guilt and for deliverance from the continued power and uncleanness of reigning sin. Here the unwashed heathen of the wilderness, or, of the polished school of a wicked civilization, may find that cleansing essential—*absolutely essential*—to moral and religious decency. Here the Christian convert may find that sanctifying power which will furnish daily, continual, and increasing purity in the sight of God. Many fountains of supposed purifying power have been espied by those who are too vain to accept divine instruction. They have proved, however, but torrents of sand or sluices of miry waters. Their cleansing power has been only such as would satisfy those who revel in the slime of respectable moral reptiles, who are really heaven-defying exhibitors of refined sinfulness that God has assured them to be no better than filthy rags in his sight. It is strange that intelligent men should insist in flaunting these in the faces of saints, angels, and Jehovah, though God has declared them to be an abomination in his sight. As the vermin revel in the carcass do these poor, deluded, heaven-insulting sinners revel in the sweets of respectable sin.

It is strange that even Christians are so slow to learn or so soon in forgetting the source of all true moral purity. They are so much inclined to think of self-cleansing or trust in the delusive specifics of the unessential moralist. Oh, that the multitudes that have taken their first lessons in Christianity had fully learned this first lesson, that in the House of David only, in Christ's atoning blood alone, and in his cleansing Spirit, is found genuine cleansing; for there is only One who can give salvation from the pollutions of sin.

For the professor of religion who is without effort or concern with respect to the complete cleansing of his soul we have no comfort. The cherished pollutions of sin—even tolerated ones—are most abominable in the sight of Him who has neither in his own being nor in his holy habitation a single vestige of uncleanness. When these unconcerned, defiled professors shall stand in the judgment their cherished impurities shall cover them with shame and seal their damnation. The breath of the incense-breathing Judge shall drive away as a whirlwind of wrath those pollutions which they have regarded with so much indifference and complacency.

Every sentiment of safety, duty, gratitude, and of moral and spiritual taste, demands that every follower of Christ should make a prompt, earnest, and effectual work of this heaven-sent purifying. Every motive of happiness, true fellowship, moral honesty, and magnanimity demands that immediately and perseveringly he should seek this fullness of moral and spiritual purity. Complete purity is only to be found in Christ; but it has pleased the Father that in him all fullness should dwell. May we all receive of his fullness and grace in answer to grace cherished.

November 6, 1872   Patience under Opposition

An ardent temperament can only with difficulty be disciplined to endure patiently the opposition brought to bear against cherished principles. It takes culture, and especially grace, to accomplish this desirable object. Yet in reality the disposition to fret because of erroneous theories, or evil doings, results rather from a lack of philosophic thought than from any real occasion for impatience. The world is so arranged by Providence that the vary advocacy of error and the efforts of evil-doing, though directly effecting much harm, are, nevertheless, indirectly accomplishing much good. Just as the gales of the ocean, the terrific thunder-storm, the tornado's fury, and the frigid winter's cold, while occasioning discomfort, loss, and disaster to some, yet bring blessings in their paths, so do many things that are very distasteful to large classes of persons produce many beneficial results.

The opposition of Pharaoh to the liberation of oppressed Israel, made the power and glory of Jehovah known, and has been auxiliary to the declaration of his name and the manifestation of his power, justice, and faithfulness, in all subsequent ages.

The enthronement of Saul, recreant though he proved to heaven-appointed duty, was yet instrumental in shedding a peculiar luster on the character of David and educating him for the grand reign which at once so exalted God's people and so illuminated his worship during the time of this king and his successor. Indeed it paved, indirectly, also, the way for the coming of David's divine Successor on the throne, whose glory is from everlasting.

The opposition of Herod, Celsius, Gibbon, and a host of whom these were types, has resulted greatly in the advancement of Christ's kingdom in the earth, and in placing that kingdom and the evidences of Christianity on a clearer and more widely-known basis that would have otherwise appeared. Through all these ages, opposition has stirred defense: hatred to truth and to the embodied Representative of truth has increased the love and zeal of those fully on the Lord's side. In genuine Christians the truth of the scripture has been fulfilled: "Neither death, nor life, nor angels, nor principalities, nor powers, nor things present, nor things to come, nor hight [*sic*], nor depth, nor any other creature, shall be able to separate us from the love of God which is in Christ Jesus our Lord." Truly, in all these things they "are more than conquerors" through him that loved them.

There is a patience which is ever becoming the servants of God in the great moral conflict in which they are engaged in life. Who has had greater conflicts than Noah, Joseph, Moses, David, Jeremiah, Daniel, John the Baptist, and the Apostles John and Paul. Yet who maintained such a sweet, forbearing spirit amid it all? It is true that they advocated the truth with mighty energy and zeal, and rebuked error and sin in language fitly typified by the scathing lightnings of heaven; but, for all this, there was a life-giving emollient of love and divine dignity which carried with it something of the benevolence as well as truth and judgments of heaven. Peerless as Victory himself can the well-endowed servant of high heaven stand amid the raging elements of conflict, or repose, covered with its debris, in hope of a resurrection to which tarnishing defeat is a total stranger. He who handles the weapons of truth in the spirit of our divine Master carries with him a power that may rouse the antagonism of Satan, the hatred of the emissaries of the arch-fiend, and the resentment of better ones influenced by the adversary's deceivings and devices, but he can afford to wait his reward if he has the approval of an intelligent judgment and good conscience; for he is living for eternal Truth, whose calendar takes note of inconceivable periods which are but the moments of eternity. Through all this, after the brief, troublous present, he shall reign in triumphant victory. Seeing this, the troublous present has sunshine to his eye, and tribulation glory for his soul. Why then be impatient? Why chafe amid the petty annoyances of the conflict? The hero should not fret about the dust of battle nor the petty annoyances of the field. His should be a larger heart, a nobler soul. The Christian soldier should, if impatience arises, take example of Him that endureth the contradiction of sinners against themselves—of Him who was buffeted, spit upon, mocked, derided, and nailed to the cross. He should take a look into Gethsemane's garden, stand by the condemned King at Pilate's bar, and hear one note of the Sufferer's "Father, forgive them," and his impatience will have vanished and he will stand himself as full of spiritual sunshine as Chimborazo's cloudless summit is a solar light. Acrimony and fretfulness should be resigned to errorists and evil-doers. Sunshine, hope, and final victory are the rightful heritage of the advocates of truth.

February 26, 1873   Contentment

Paul said that he had learned, whatsoever state he was in, to be content. What a lesson he had mastered. How few ever learn it. Yet it is a most sensible lesson.

Of what use is it for anyone to fret about what he can not hinder? And why not avoid the evil which can be prevented? Does fretting lessen, or does it not aggravate it? Undoubtedly it generally aggravates the evil, and adds not a few sisterly discords which are equally unamiable.

If our toils are beyond our strength why decrease our powers of endurance by expending our strength in fretting about them? Are they disagreeable? Then why add to their repulsiveness the gloom of discontent? It is better to be a philosophic slave like Aesop than a prince with the discontent of Dionysius rolling in luxury and magnificence.

But is there any just reason for discontent? If we are in the path of sin there is. It is right that we should be discontented with the service of the wicked one. The more radical our discontent the better it will be for us. We need not be discontent with the lashings of an awakened conscience nor the chastenings of a merciful Providence, which are on our side goading us from the service and eternal penalty of sin.

Discontent is not appropriate to Christian life. It does not increase our love and gratitude to God. It does not render our communion with Christ or his church more sweet. It does not give increased unity in the concentration of our faculties in effort to do good. It does not give luster to the habiliments of saints nor angels, as contemplated by the servant of God on earth. It does not gild heaven with increased glories. It has more of the querulous than of song, and more of rebellion than of prayer. It has more of sourness than of the sweet milk of human kindness or of charity. It is a swinish intruder in the Lord's garden of the soul; and it closes more opening buds, mars more flowers, and destroys more fruit than most of satanic agencies. Its grand ancestor is well known as Satan, but nearly all the vices have some claim to its paternity. If it were profitable, its pangs might be endured in hope. If it had some virtue, its vices might be palliated. But it carries so much foolishness, so much hatefulness, so much misery, and so much rebellion against Providence, that it is hard to know why it is so much harbored, unless it is because foolishness is bound up in the human heart.

Paul learned, in the hardest condition, to be content. It had to be learned. It is time every Christian were engaged on that lesson. It is wisdom and righteousness to learn and practice it. The thorough mastery of that lesson by every follower of Christ on earth would add twofold, if not tenfold, to the sum of Christian happiness in the church militant. Let us learn, in whatever state we are, to be content.

March 5, 1873   Sanctification—Holiness

There is nothing more clearly taught in the Scriptures than that every converted person is also sanctified. But it does not follow that this sanctification in each ease is necessarily entire or perfect. Converts may gradually increase in sanctifying grace. Or they may by faith and prayer receive sudden accessions of sanctifying power which may seem almost as wonderful as their first conversion. It would be well, however, for each saint, in such case, to regard this flood of spirituality as but one of a series of installments of grace which he needs to advance him toward that compete fullness which lies before the saint, be he prophet or apostle.

That consecration and that sanctification which give a child of God the complete and continuous triumph of faith over unbelief, and of spirituality over carnality; which make the will and glory of God the full and unhesitating motive of the mind and heart, every day and every hour; subduing the world, the flesh, and the devil with full promptitude and victorious power, may in a very legitimate sense be called *perfect consecration* and *entire sanctification.* But there may be vastly much to be done in the great common lying between such a state and that of the saints around the eternal throne; and fresh supplies of grace as daily bread, and great enlargement and perfecting of the spiritual man, are needed, needed, *needed still,* till out attainments in grace have ripened into a completeness on earth that almost entitles them to be called the first letters of the alphabet of the inconceivable erudition of holiness in glory above.

To the attainment of this finite completeness of entire consecration and perfect holiness, to which we have alluded above, we think every convert ought to press forward with full hope of its attainment in the church militant, and having attained it, to press on with increased ardor toward the infinite. We do not conceal our belief that increased holiness will make the saint more sensitive to all the imperfections which may attach to his own soul and life. So there is no danger of his becoming, by advanced attainments, self-righteous. His humility and self-abasement will increase the more with increased clearness of spiritual sight, and deepen immeasurably as he nears the ineffable throne of Infinite Holiness. The self-righteousness of the Pharisee and the holiness of the genuine saint are as unlike as hell and heaven. The one, if not sheer hypocrisy, has pride founded on spiritual blindness; the other is humble because of divine light shining on limited attainments and showing how immeasurably far they fall short of the perfection of angelic holiness.

The above is but a simple statement of some truths on the subject of holiness, on which there has been full as much controversy as sacred exemplification by the contestants. We believe the essential principles in the foregoing statement are fully sustained both by the word of God and Christian experience. We do not argue the subject, however, further than a simple statement, combined with the scriptural knowledge, the observation, and the experience of our readers, will constitute it an argument.

The perplexity on this subject manifested by an esteemed layman—in a note on our table—has induced the writing of the above; and though what was at first designed for a brief note has grown to greater proportions, we shall not regret its length if it shall prove of any value to any of our beloved readers who may be perplexed on the subject, or subjects, referred to in this article.

April 16, 1873   Lotteries

Whatever the professed object of lotteries may be, they are demoralizing in their tendency. Many a one is inclined to hope that he will prove the lucky ticket-holder in a drawing. Human nature is prone to false hope, or even superstition, about what is generally called luck. Men do not usually take into consideration the fact that if all relating to the lottery-drawing should be fair many chances are against one's self. Besides, the real value of prizes to be drawn may be a very large per cent less than the aggregate purchase price of the tickets sold. If there were a prize of uniform value for every ticket sold, it would not, perhaps, be one half the value paid for the ticket, and in most cases the prizes to be drawn are mainly such as are unsalable,—often mere counterfeits. In the vast majority of cases the ticket-holder is disappointed, and it would be well if his ill luck would cure him of his folly. But in many cases those who invest in lotteries prove more persevering in this delusion than they do in anything else. They hope on, incur new risks, and, though losing much oftener than gaining, they persist in a course that results in the increase of their gambling propensities. They grow worse and worse. Many imbibe the vices usually attendant on such habits, and are ruined in character as well as stranded financially. The eternal ruin of many is promoted by these lotteries, and yet, the churches have sometimes stooped to the employment of them for the purpose of raising money for God's cause! But, hush! Tell it not in Gath!

But the day has come, in Ohio, when churches, benevolent societies, and every one else, are to have some protection against this immorality. The legislature of this state passed a law, last week, providing for the imprisonment of any one who may aid or abet a lottery. So the days of pious gambling without the persecutions of the civil law, are ended in this state! We trust that the good people of this Christian commonwealth are not so chronic in their habits of lottery speculation as to necessitate the imprisonment of any of our church-going people of steady habits, and, we might add, we would regard similar hope concerning all our citizens as very desirable. But it must not be inferred from anything said in this article that the really pious portion of the Christian church ever has sanctioned and patronized lotteries, though the profits of those swindles may have been sometimes ostensibly for the financial profit of the church or some benevolent object. True Christians could not so debase themselves, though some have not been as out-spoken as they should have been against those frauds.

Every friend of good morals ought to heartily thank our legislature for the passage of the Little lottery bill. It is not so small, if Mr. Little was its author. Its passage does honor to his large heart.

When we consider that this lottery business exercises quite an influence in promoting idleness and shiftless habits, that it perverts taste on the subject of the true mode of obtaining financial success, that if it does not bankrupt it prevents many from having any capital to lose, we are compelled to admit that this law is a wise provision for the promotion of the material as well as moral interests of the state.

We do hope that the good citizens of Ohio will see that the law is rigidly enforced. This is especially due from the moral and religious people of the land. It will promote morality; it will favor religious purity; it will reduce the variety of vicious vocations; it will save not a few from gambling habits and financial worthlessness. Let the law be so thoroughly enforced that each sister state may see the advantage of a similar law, and all soon join in the effort to restrain the evil of gambling.

April 30, 1873   Freemasonry and the Decalogue

Freemasonry is a vast system of modern times. It is the soul as it is the mother of secret societies in general. Many are virtually withdrawn members of the order, though their fealty and influence are still claimed by the lodge. Perpetual allegiance is one of the feigned conditions of its yoke. Nearly all systems have adherents both good and bad, in the usual sense of those terms. Freemasonry is not an exception. We owe no unkindness to members of this or other secret orders. We abhor the system the more because it maintains a deleterious ascendancy over many who are otherwise amiable. We owe the same hatred to slavery,—to sin in general,—and for the same reasons. If we say anything hard of Freemasonry it is because truth and duty require it. To trifle with a gigantic evil (claiming to have sealed the lips of its subjects so effectually with oaths and penalties as to have prevented, through the fabled years of its existence, the divulging of its secrets) is treason against truth and the God of truth.

It is of the sinfulness of Freemasonry that we now treat. We showed in our editorials of January 22d and February 5th that the revelations of the system are substantially correct. We now inquire whether Freemasonry violates the commandments of God. It does. It involves fearful infractions of the tables of the law. Sinai loudly proclaims its guilt.

The first commandment of the decalogue says: "Thou shalt have no other gods before me;" or, as Christ quotes: "Thou shalt worship the Lord thy God, and him only shalt thou serve." Who gave the decalogue? He is the author of the flood, the deliverer of Israel, the God of David and Elijah and Daniel, "the God and Father of our Lord Jesus Christ." It is not the god of the Mohammedan or deist. It is Jehovah, who can be worshipped only in the name of Jesus Christ. Jesus says: "No man cometh unto the Father but by me." All worship not in the name of Christ is that of other gods, and is in positive violation of the first commandment of the decalogue. Such is the worship of at least the first seven degrees of Freemasonry, and that of Odd-fellowship. Jesus Christ can not be *legally* introduced into the worship of the lodge. Those who indorse the lodge are responsible for its christless worship. Worship in Christ's name introduced where *lodge-legality* repudiates it, is like the experimental exorcism of devils by the sons of Sceva, who attempted in the name of Jesus whom Paul preached. Then we conclude that the lodge-worship of the "grand architect" and "grand master" is a palpable violation of the decalogue and of the precepts of Christ and his apostles.

The use of images in connection with the ceremonies and worship of the lodge is in violation of the second commandment, forbidding image-worship. The worship of the lodge is not heaven-appointed but man-invented, quite heathenish, and as ritualistic as either pagan or papal Rome.

The third commandment says: "Thou shalt not take the name of the Lord thy God in vain." That the oaths and imprecations of the lodge are in violation of this command is too clear to require an argument. What shall we say of the moral discernment of any well-informed person who would call this in question? The profanity of the lodge is not relieved by the fact that these obligations are administered by no heaven-sanctioned authority. This applies to the obligations of other secret orders in which men, if not sworn otherwise, are sworn by themselves, in violation of the precepts of Christ, which forbid swearing by one's self.

No Christian will need any argument to prove that the Sabbath parades of the lodge are in flagrant violation of the commandment, "Remember the Sabbath day, to keep it holy." Masonic obligations to obey summons that may violate even week-day morality are no better. Protestant Christianity was shocked, recently, in the city of Dayton, by the Sabbath parade of the German Catholic societies. How about the Sabbath parades of the lodge?

The commandment, "Thou shalt not kill," is, in spirit, violated not only by men taking oaths implying the obligation to inflict the most barbarous penalties on others in case they violate lodge obligations, but also in the suicidal assumption of submission to horrid mutilations if they become, themselves, violators of those profane oaths.

The eighth commandment, "Thou shalt not steal," includes the prohibition of all dishonesty, especially that perpetuated in a stealthy manner. It includes all conspiracies by which fellow-beings are over-reached. Frauds by deception violate both the command not to steal and that forbidding false witness. If two, ten, or a thousand persons combine in order to take advantage of others, it is in violation of the eighth commandment. That Freemasonry is a combination to secure financial advantages and preferences over the uninitiated, to secure special protection and favors averse to the impartiality and efficiency of civil and military law, to secure position and preference over others of equal merit, can not be called in question. These are among the well-known claims and boasts of Freemasons. If its wily, stealthy intrigues are not in violation of the command, "Thou shalt not steal," it would be well to cease denouncing the Erie ring and the Credit Mobilier speculation. The methods practiced by secret orders are clear violations of the eighth commandment.

The ninth commandment says, "Thou shalt not bear false witness." The oaths to conceal, imposed by the lodge, involve a multitude of falsehoods; some full of art, some half-truths, and others crowned with effrontery. Its history is fictitious, and its claim to patron saints is in impious disregard of truth. Some one has said of the institution, "It is a lie all over." Truly a tissue of falsehood runs through the whole system. The foregoing is to a greater or less extent true of secret societies in general.

That it is a violation of the tenth commandment, "Thou shalt not covet," appears in the fact that the whole system has in view the securing for its members of advantages over the uninitiated. It abandons that fair principle of dependence on merit and open competition in the struggle of life. It forms its clan for clannish purposes.

We have not pointed out the violation of the commandment, "Honor thy father and thy mother," and "Thou shalt no commit adultery." These are violated by the system, but not so directly in their primary sense as the other commandments. We do not wish to over-press indictments. But any relation, contravening in any degree the heaven-appointed relations of family, violates in a vital sense that commandment which includes honor to parents, love to children, and the sacredness of all that pertains to the family.

Not only do certain degrees of the order *impliedly* excuse unchastity toward females not relatives of fellow-members, but the system involves "duties" and secrets inconsistent with that sacred relation which makes husband and wife one flesh.

The decalogue clearly condemns Freemasonry. The same is true in a greater or less degree of other secret orders. When men say the exclusion of these orders from the church is of human, not divine authority, it must be either in ignorance or in guilt.

It is the duty of the church to require its members to refrain from violating Jehovah's sacred law. It is not a question as to whether some may not have been inveigled into the order through deception, and remained there through want of decision of character or through lack of moral heroism. It is the duty of the church to raise her voice against violations of that law which Christ magnified by his death, and to interpose her authority forbidding such sin.

June 18, 1873   The Spiritual Warfare

There is a contest between good and evil, between right and wrong. When we consider how long it has lasted, and look forward to the prospect of its being continued for ages yet to come, the thought seems discouraging. Must the warfare never cease? Shall we ever endure the din, and the weariness of the battle? Loving peace, and coveting rest and quiet, it is most natural for the Christian soldier to long for that freedom from conflict to which the spirit within inclines him.

Truly, warfare is not pleasant. Yet a good cause may impel the lover of peace to fly to the battle field. The American Revolution was a very unpleasant struggle, yet our patriotic fore-fathers endured all that was disagreeable and hazardous, for its prosecution. So it is with the Christian soldier. A hateful, ruinous power ought to be resisted. The tyranny of its chief is most unendurable. The salvation of one's self and of his fellows demands a struggle. It is a choice between heroic warfare, with assurance of solid fruits in victory, on one hand, and ease, desolation, and death, on the other. Hence the warfare must come; and, though it cost ever so much sacrifice of ease, friendship, and earth's possessions, it must go on.

It is war under the black flag, too. The conflict knows no quarter. It is either victory or death. We must slay or be slain.

It may be natural in the carnal soul to have conflicts. Truly, the way of peace is unknown to the sinful nature. But one sort of a conflict—an uncompromising warfare of good against evil—is not of other than heavenly origin.

No wonder that David—perhaps not wholly meaning carnal warfare—blessed God who had taught his hands to war and his fingers to fight. There are some who think it the very hight [sic] of perfection in a Christian, to possess a frame that will forbid contending for anything. The most timid bird will fight for her young; the most gentle mother will fight heroically for her beloved child. So will the most gentle Christian contend with all his soul's energies against the destructive ravages of sin. He will expend all his energies in the support of the cause of salvation, and maintain, with unyielding vigor, the honor of his Redeemer. Not that he does not love peace. He does love it dearly. But the peace he seeks must not be in the poisonous breath of sin, the loathsome outrage of Satan. There is, for the Christian, no peace in unrighteousness and no cessation of hostilities till sin is finally overthrown.

The conflict may not be, of itself, pleasant, but he looks to God to prepare his heart for the war. He finds in the spirit of his chief Captain that inspiration which gives the courage and impelling power necessary to real warfare against a wily and determined foe. He may well bless God for teaching his hands to war and his fingers to fight. When all is over, and he sees how terrible the loss consequent on a failure to war in behalf of Christ's cause would have been, and reaps the everlasting reward of his service, he will never regret the sacrifices of the warfare.

Our warfare is short. We give place when life's service is over to others who succeed us, and we are placed on the list of crowned veterans. We may be in the very meridian of the great battle, but victory after victory has been gained by the soldiers of Immanuel. Though the cheerless winter of war has lasted long and may still last for ages, yet the sunshine of spring will come, and the garlands of everlasting peace shall crown the brow of every soldier of Christ, and not one in all the universe of God's people shall any more know raging conflict. Then the anthem of peace shall celebrate the complete and eternal triumph of the Prince of Righteousness.

June 25, 1873   Our Motives

Men may be too busy or careless to scan their motives well. Perhaps they are more inclined to recognize the outward quality of actions than the motives from which they spring. Especially is this true when their own actions would appear best if considered without reference to motives.

God regards motives very closely. No act springing from those which are unholy can be approved of him. Yet no motive can justify an evil act. It can only be excused on the ground of unavoidable ignorance.

But sins of ignorance deserve close scrutiny. Some of them are willful, and merit chastisement as such. Much ignorance comes from shutting the eyes, or in some way obstructing the vision. Such merits the avenging wrath of God. In the final day it will receive it. There may be motive in ignorance. Sham and hypocrisy may lie at the bottom of it.

Men may perform "benevolent" acts and yet be serving themselves rather than God or their fellow-beings. They may simulate friendships, at the bottom of which lies little else that selfishness. A man may be a reformer in order to attain fame or position. He may humble himself in appearance to exalt himself in reality. Some may even preach Christ of envy or strife. One may weep for souls, that he may be praised or rewarded for his success. He may be very zealous for principle, as he fancies, while it is the power of prejudice or pride of sentiment that furnishes most of the inspiration.

It is from consideration of the deceit which may be associated with motives, that this article is penned. It is to be feared that many who are honest and conscientious in their own estimation are strangers to their real motives. If the heart is so deceitful and desperately wicked as inspiration teaches, is there not danger that even the child of grace may not always be entirely free from its guileful habits? A penetrating though candid scrutiny of the lives of professors of religion in general will reveal the fact that their motives, though primarily to glorify

God, are often mixed with much that is the result of former habits of mind and heart, or of present carnality. Do we not often recognize in the professor of religion a desire for preferment or promotion? Is it not observed in many cases that his own personal interest influences his judgment in a given case? Does not his own ease or convenience often influence his judgment and action? In how many instances do we recognize, without any departure from charity, these facts with reference to the evident motives of others? But do we always read so candidly our own hearts?

In view of what we have said, does it not become us all to be exceedingly circumspect with regard to our motives? It is dangerous for us to be ignorant of the principles within. Though we may shut our eyes against the internal workings of our own minds and hearts, there is one who knows all about them, and who may call them into judgment. If some of our motives were revealed to us clearly, we might feel condemned. If they were revealed to others, as they may be in the judgment, there would be great occasion for us to be ashamed. It is to be feared that many who are least sensible of defect in motive are so on account of their callousness of conscience. But this can not last forever. The secrets of their hearts will be at last revealed.

They who best know themselves, who most correct their inward, hidden principles, who most repent of all that is wrong in the sanctuary of the soul, who most claim God's strength to regulate their consciences, and are most careful to have all adjusted before they appear at the judgment-seat,—these are the ones whose last hours will be most peaceful, and whose joys will be the richest at the appearance of our Lord Jesus Christ. If our motives indeed be pure, they will lead us to the most enlightened course of action. But if they be evil, they will lead us into increasing darkness, and they may bring us to a terrible reckoning in the day of judgment.

February 18, 1874   Prof. Blanchard's Lectures

Professor Charles A. Blanchard, of Wheaton College, in accordance with previous announcement, delivered, in Summit-street Church, in this city, last Friday, Saturday, and Sunday evenings, a series of lectures on the subject of secret societies. He not only met the expectations of the members of the Philothean Literary Society, under whose auspices he lectured, and the true friends of the antisecrecy cause generally, but exceeded all they had anticipated. His mental culture, his language, his manner of speaking, and his style of argument are all very fine. The personal appearance of the speaker, the manner in which he presents himself before an audience, and in which he introduces his subject, are all prepossessing. His candor, the logical style in which he pursues his subject, his evident sincerity, his thorough mastery of his subject, combined with the win-

ning and impressive manner in which he delivers a lecture, render his efforts
delightful to the decided friends of the antisecrecy cause, and are calculated to
win and convince others open to conviction on the subject, as also to sorely dis-
comfit those who are adherents of the lodge. It is really uncomfortable for
lodgemen [*sic*] to have the folly, the pernicious tendency, and the wickedness of
their orders at once so ably and decently exposed. The very youth of the
speaker—not over twenty-six years of age—is rather in his favor than otherwise.
But his appearance and gifts are nevertheless those of mature manhood. He is a
man which any good cause might well be proud to claim as an advocate, and
which its enemies can hate only because he antagonizes the principles with
which they are infatuated. In few men are the component elements of a reformer
so well combined and so nicely adjusted.

As we hope in a few weeks or months at most to present our readers with
portions of these lectures in a much fuller and more complete form, we shall
little else than mention the subject of each lecture, and indicate a few points that
were made by the lecturer.

The first lecture was against secret societies in general. This lecture had
never been written out by the speaker, and hence gave full play to the vivacity as
well as the strength of his mind, and to that flexibility of language of which he is
one of the best masters we ever heard. It also involved a charm in the delivery
perhaps excelling any of his other lectures. He showed that secret societies had
existed from the very ancient times; mentioned the fact that they are very numerous in this country—that this age can almost be styled the age of secret societies; remarked that this subject is a very important one; and said that it behooves Christians to examine the subject well, and to approve and support secret
societies if they are good, but to condemn and oppose them if they are bad. He
showed that all of them were alike in their general features, and that to belong to
or favor one was calculated to countenance and support the others. In the course
of his remarks he made many telling hits on the prevailing secret orders, major
and minor.

He showed by strong argument that secret societies tend and tempt to deception and falsehood, and in proportion as their principles are imbibed and carried out will men become crafty, double-dealing, and dishonest. He showed also
most clearly the selfish nature of their benevolence and otherwise exposed their
evil tendencies. We have not room to extend mention of the points in this lecture
which was well-arranged, well-timed, and well delivered.

The second lecture was on the initiation of a Mason. It gave a brief but in-
telligible and striking account of the initiatory ceremonies of several degrees of
Freemasonry, quoted from the oaths of the Entered Apprentice, Fellow Craft,
and Master Mason, and exposed the enslaving and degrading nature of the oaths
and ceremonies of the order. This lecture was of especial interest to most of the
audience.

The third was truly a lecture, yet as truly a religious discourse, and it was pronounced by the people of the Summit-street charge, generally, to be altogether fit for a Sabbath-evening meeting. He showed that Freemasonry is a religion, that it has a system of worship and claims that to observe its teachings will save men. He proved this by quoting largely from their highest authorities, as well as by other proofs with which his audience were more familiar. He contrasted the religion taught by the lodge and that of Christianity, and showed their dissimilarity and antagonism in a strong light. He showed that while they carried the Bible as an advertisement in their parades, they not only exclude Christ's name from their prayers, but their published ritual carefully selects from the Bible such passages as have not the name of Christ, or where it does occur in the ninth degree in a somewhat full quotation from one of the epistles to the Thessalonians, they expunge it! striking it out twice in one quotation. After referring in pathetic terms to what Christ has done for us, he uttered his strong conviction that the Church ought not to receive men belonging to such a "church" to the Christian church. What would be the thought of missionaries in heathen lands who would receive into the Christian church the adherents of false worships—of heathen churches? What shall we say of that church in this enlightened country that will take in men still adhering to these heathenish churches, the lodges? He said that one church was enough for any person to belong to, that no Christian church should allow its members to belong to other "churches" with diverse worships and religions. The lecturer closed with a very searching appeal to the audience on the necessity of a deep spirituality, and left a very fine impression, religiously, on the minds of all that portion of his audience not decidedly antagonistic to his antisecrecy views.

March 11, 1874   The Temperance Revival

Great results are sometimes produced by causes which in their first manifestations were quite diminutive. Two children in a day-school in Henry County, Indiana, a few years since, turned the exercises into a prayer-meeting by kneeling down and engaging in prayer, as they, in their Quaker-like faith, felt impelled by the Spirit to do. So the woman's movement against intemperance in southern Ohio towns began in a diminutive way; but it has made Hillsboro and Washington Court-house famous, and will undoubtedly render them historic. That which a few weeks ago appeared insignificant has grown to immense proportions. New York, Philadelphia, Pittsburgh, Washington City, Chicago, St. Louis, and San Francisco, have caught the spirit of the movement that first exhibited itself in a few southern Ohio towns. It is one of the most remarkable revivals in the annals of history, in the rapidity of its growth, as well as in the peculiar subject involved, the methods employed, and the solemnity and courage characterizing it. It is hard to predict the future shape, magnitude, and duration of it. It is carrying all classes of truly wise men and good people in its favor. It is quite likely that Satan's most effectual way of counteracting its power will be by corrupting or misdirecting it. Direct resistance can avail him nothing.

It will be of interest to our readers to have information concerning the history and present stages of the movement. This, gathered from various sources, we now present.

Many of the villages and towns are deeply moved by the tidal wave of temperance revival. But it has also reached the large cities, where a great struggle will doubtless take place. In New York, Dr. Dio Lewis recently delivered one of his characteristic, stirring lectures; and though many of the pastors are said to oppose the movement, on account of wine-bibbing habits personal to themselves or common with the aristocratic people of their congregations, yet the use of the Houston House Variety Theater is said to be offered to the women free of charge. Demonstrations with lively interest have likewise been made in Brooklyn and Jersey City. Philadelphia has not witnessed demonstrations indicating that the more than seven thousand drinking-houses of the "City of Brotherly Love" are to be assaulted by the Deboras [sic] of Israel in the name of the Lord of hosts. Pittsburgh, Cleveland, Cincinnati, Chicago, St. Louis, and San Francisco have also heard the tocsin of war, and are marshaling their hosts for the conflict with the sons of Cincinnati, Chicago, St. Louis, and San Francisco have also heard the tocsin of war, and are marshaling their hosts for the conflict with the sons of Bacchus. In Dayton the assault on the saloons has begun. Some victories have been already achieved in the closing of saloons, and the spirit of the praying league is becoming every day more intense and more general. In Columbus active hostilities commenced even before they did in Dayton. As it has been here since the movement began, the women have not deemed muddy sidewalks too filthy to kneel upon when being refused admittance to the saloons; but the praying women bow at the doors of those dens of legally-protected destroyers of bodies and souls, of home bliss and reputation, of health, of wealth, and of every good thing. Columbus has not a few prominent citizens, including Ex-governor Dennison, who throw their influence in favor of the holy war. In Dayton the business men have agreed to raise $100,000 to sustain the movement. At Washington City the following appeal was made to all the restaurant-keepers:

"We earnestly entreat you, for the sake of your spiritual welfare and for the preservation from ruin of our husbands and sons, that you abandon the immoral and wicked business of selling intoxicating liquors. We will be at your place of business to pray with you next Saturday. Come with us and we will do you good; and may God have mercy on your soul." At Oxford, Ohio, some of the saloonists [sic] have surrendered, and the work still goes on. At Athens most of the saloons have been closed. At Xenia and Springfield the war is being pressed with great earnestness. At Wilmington nearly all the saloons have been closed. At Gallipolis the retail trade in intoxicating drinks is about closed. At Piqua sev-

eral saloons have closed. At Ripley the success is almost complete. At Hillsbor-
ough the most of the saloons have closed, and at Washington Court-house they
have all (fourteen in number) been closed. At Morrow, Greenfield, Waynesville,
New Holland, Sabina, Moscow, McArthur, Lebanon, Circleville, and many
other places the victory is decided, though much yet remains to be done. At Za-
leski, Jamestown, Reeseville, Darbyville, Georgetown, and many other places,
the liquor traffic has been almost entirely suppressed.

At latest accounts, the work is going forward at various places with increasing interest. Indianapolis, Logansport, and Jeffersonville, in Indiana, Madison,
Wisconsin, Leavenworth, Kansas,—indeed, almost everywhere,—the work is
progressing. It is evident that the powers of darkness must suffer great loss. May
God still move in the hearts of the people.

In Dayton, at the time of writing this, (Saturday morning,) the work is active. Yesterday a number of saloons were visited by the praying women. One
saloonist [sic] on Sixth Street surrendered promptly and poured out his liquor in
the street. The women evidently mean success in the strength of God. If they
continue as they have begun,—in faith, humility, and kindness,—they will,
doubtless, have a complete victory. May God strengthen their hearts. The
churches are thoroughly stirred. Many hitherto addicted to occasional or habitual
dram-drinking have come out in favor of total abstinence. The work of the temperance revival is fourfold. It is to suppress liquor-shops, reform drunkards,
drive dram-drinking out of some of the churches, and to convert souls to Christ.
Of course it will also build up believers in their most holy faith.

April 15, 1874   Lack of Vital Godliness

However this age may compare with those which have preceded it, one of its
greatest needs is vital godliness. Indeed, what age has not needed this? Surely
not that of David, Elijah, or Paul. But perhaps the tendency of this age is to the
superficial. It is in most of things, but not in corruption and frivolity. Why, even
the aged are patrons of vain show. Even aged women put on the trappings of the
most recent fashion, and those of high moral and religious standing do not blush
to exhibit themselves in its deformities. Alas! from whom shall reason and common sense proceed? Yet these laugh at the follies of other ages, and flatter themselves as having attained to a higher grade of enlightenment! The follies of pre-
ceding ages—some of them at least—had the apology of sobriety and dignity.
That of this, without much solid claim, must bear the odium of vanity and frivolity. It is a painful truth, but it might as well be expressed; vanity has taken the
place of vital godliness in the hearts of many who are flattered by others as the
leaders of religious society. "Deny thyself," "take up thy cross," are mandates
that have been perverted to mean: "Reason away or sniff at every precept of

Christ that is at war with flesh-pleasing." And it is done by wholesale—and retail, too. It would be better if pastors would warn many whose steps border on Satan's kingdom, if they do not actually tread within his domain.

One of the great causes of decline in the spirituality of the age lies in the want of simplicity in prayer and conference meetings. People, instead of coming to God's house and entering upon his service with souls regardful of him alone, are thinking entirely too much about how they shall perform on the religious stage. They become actors instead of simple worshipers—very mincing, insipid actors at that. The cloak of their skill is entirely too thin to conceal that obsequiousness to the auditors which too often usurps the place of sacred reverence to the great Object of worship.

Another great cause of the lack of vital godliness is the want of God-fearing leaders. Is the pastor not a God-fearing man! Are the class-leaders wanting in sacred reverence and godly awe! Yes; too often these are chosen or prized the more for having but little conscience. People heap to themselves teachers like themselves; and, alas, too many are willing to be thus "heaped." God-fearing pastors and leaders would remove much of the lightness too characteristic of churches exalting themselves, and being exalted by those like them. Fastidious "elegance" and chaffiness too often take the place of the pastor's and leader's tearful exhortation and solemn warning. Oh that God would deliver the church from such teachers. They are Satan's substitutes for prophets filled with the Spirit of God. Some of them are far more apt in questionable gallantry than in warning simpering belles or gay beaux carefully with tears.

Another cause of the want of vital godliness is found in prevailing worldliness. It may be that most persons, truly converted, who tread poverty's vale, would be pious if placed in exalted position, or if abounding in wealth. It may be, but the camel and the needle's eye illustrate most forcibly the precept of Jesus: "How hardly shall they that have riches enter into the kingdom of God!" Worldly people are inclined to throw all this precept away; but worldliness is one of the greatest curses of the church in this age. Alas, it has so blinded many people that they do not see that worldliness prevails in their own hearts and in the church.

Another cause of the lack of vital godliness is the prevalence of a spurious type of religion in the church. The gayly-dressed corpse is not more dead than are those spiritual corpses which some dress up for converts and announce as live souls. Those who begin the Christian life dead, under the care of spiritual undertakers, are likely to become "twice dead."

It is well that Christians have souls; but the soul each one needs is not the soul of expediency, which too often takes the place of guileless trust in God and his counsel. One of the causes of the fearful lack of vital godliness lies in that devotion to expediency which blinds carnal souls to the fact that loyalty to God, the observance of his precepts, and obedience to his commandments, are the highest order of expediency as well as of duty.

May 6, 1874   Internal Communion

This age, at least in this country, is much inclined to be superficial. We live so fast, so excitedly. This is true, at least, of thousands in the more enterprising and more speculating, sections of the country. Even Christians are prompted to live altogether outside of themselves and their homes. One might also fancy them strangers to their own souls. If people wish to get along with outside religion, without any real inward experience, this method is quite to their purpose. But busy and turbulent as was the life of the shepherd king of Israel, he evidently taught and practiced communing with one's own heart. He was not only given to much meditation on the law of God, but he exhorts that others should "commune with their own hearts." There is evidently much in the suggestion. Let us note a few thoughts upon it.

We are so inclined to look after others and after the affairs of others that we may fail to become acquainted with ourselves. And if we fail to keep a reception-room in order for our heavenly Guest, there is a probability that we shall become little acquainted with him. There is no other place besides our own hearts, this side of heaven, where we can hold intimate communion with God. There is no half-way house between our own soul's inner temple and the temple of God on high.

What sort of communion is that when we invite the Lord to come into our souls, while we would be absent if he should come, and perhaps know nothing of his visit? But the wise never make visits on such terms. If they know the situation they stay away. The Lord can not be supposed to visit a soul from which the soul's real self is absent, unless he come to reprove or in some way to assert his sovereign rights.

If indeed the soul has an inner chamber; if indeed one's own heart is susceptible of communion; if Christ truly proposes to have a feast within us and shed his love abroad in our hearts by his Spirit; then we certainly ought to meet God in our hearts—meet him often, or dwell with him there continually.

In this busy world it is quite evident that some—alas! too many,—commune little with their own hearts. Sin may be the cause with some; over-pressure of business or cares with others. Indifference is the cause in still other cases. Such have a very lean experience from whatever cause. The very proposition, "Christ in you the hope of glory," the very requirement to examine ourselves, the very fact that we are temples of God—all teach the duty and necessity of communing with Christ in our hearts and worshiping God within us.

This internal communion implies consciousness of that within, and a realizing sense of Christ's internal presence with all the spiritual impartations which it is his good pleasure to communicate. In conversation with our friends we are not only conscious of our own thoughts, emotions, and permanent feelings, but we are also conscious of those entertained by our visitors. So it is with Christ as a visitor; for he does not come into our hearts as a stranger,—as a mysterious, forbidding stranger—but he is there as our Redeemer, as our Savior, as our dearest Friend.

This communing with Christ in our hearts can only be had by setting apart hours—moments at least—with special reference to it. Even if these be hours of toil we should invite Christ into our hearts, and most unyieldingly and perseveringly devote ourselves to communion with him. To those little accustomed to such communion it may be difficult to obtain this state of uninterrupted devotion to the company of the Master; but perseverance will give the strength of habit, and, besides, that communion will be so sweet and our interest in it will so increase that it will become an indispensable, a continual feast. This communion with Christ in the soul-temple is essential to any intimate acquaintance with him. None but converted persons can enjoy it; but these, without devoting special attention to communion with the Savior, can not be well acquainted with him. On the other hand, they will become strangers to him and to his grace.

They who acquire facility in this communion with Christ in the heart will never be lonely. In a desert or a dungeon they will be in the midst of the sweetest of company. In sorrows and in griefs they will find consolation. They will be strong against the wiles of the adversary. They will be clothed with divine strength for every labor and for every conflict. Their song shall be heard by day and by night. Out of the depths shall be heard the voice of hope and the shout of victory. And finally, when they go home, they will be so much "at home." They will be cheered in a dying hour by the thought that they are going to the palace of that Savior with whom they are so well acquainted, to him whom they have found so kind and condescending, so gracious and so faithful. This communion with Christ would make strong Christians; it would make happy ones; it would give power to the individual, and, if general, to the church; it would clothe the saint and the assembly of the saints with light and fill them with joy. This communion, in a degree, is common to the people of God; but how fitful, how sparing, in so many cases. The whole church needs a great increase of it.

October 7, 1874   Horse-Racing Fairs

Our city was rendered quite lively last week by the Southern Ohio Fair. The attendance was large, that of the great day of the fair being estimated at sixty thousand people. The estimate perhaps admits of a liberal reduction, as is most common in such cases. But the fair was quite a success financially; nor was it wanting in interest to those who attended. The "Exposition Hall" was well furnished; the display of vehicles was good; the show of stock was fine; and the races were, we suppose, all that gentlemen of "the pool" could have reasonably demanded.

We take pleasure in everything that brings legitimate business to our city, that fosters good taste, and promotes progress. We believe fairs, well conducted, to be promotive of the public good, though it has become a question with some as to whether they ever can be so conducted. Yet we will proceed on the supposition that such a thing is possible; nor will we condemn fairs because some evils will inevitably be associated with them; for the same is true of every practicable enterprise. But we can not otherwise than lament the demoralizing influences attendant upon fairs which make horse-racing not only one of their features but their *chief feature*. That this was true of the recent fair in this city appears in the fact that nearly one half of all the premiums offered by its managers were offered on the speed of horses. It further appears from the fact that the great day of the fair, that which called out scores of thousands of people from far and near, was the day on which the exciting races were to be run. The "Goldsmith Maid," which could trot a mile in 2:18, and "Judge Fullerton," which could make the same distance in 2:23, were the glory of the day.

That races are demoralizing in their influence has been proved by hundreds of years of practice in the old world. Their influence in American is too patent to require argument. "Where the carcass is thither will the eagles be gathered together," is quite applicable to those races. They are the joy of the drunken and profane, the occasion of the gathering together of the lewd. Gambling is not only an accompaniment of the races, but the races are themselves the very soul and practice of betting.

It becomes, then, a serious question as to whether it is proper for Christians to patronize such fairs. We doubt, indeed, whether there is much question about it in the minds of conscientious Christians, who attended the recent one at Dayton on the great day of the fair, when horse racing was the chief glory of the occasion. It is doubtful whether they feel any doubts as to the impropriety of their means going toward paying the large sums given to the winners in the races. There were many good Christians there; but it is not likely that the really good and reflecting went away feeling their consciences were at perfect ease about giving countenance and substantial support to horse-racing. Is the Christian church indeed to be brought to indorse horse-racing? This might have been regarded as a startling question thirty years ago. But it is likely to be brought home to the consciences of Christians now. For if the managers of fairs devote half their means to the encouragement of speed in horses, and the greater part of their attention to the same, what is the patronage of fairs but the patronage of horse-racing? If the premium on a horse-race is to be placed at $4,500, and a large sum (reported to be $5,000) is to be paid out of the proceeds of a fair to bring a noted racer on to its grounds whose only utility is the life she inspires in the betting fraternity, what shall we say about patronizing such fairs?

No doubt those who manage fairs have seen Christians in this generation bow before so many things that are antichristian that they expect them still to do so, and that more and more. But we are mistaken if many who have attended the

Southern Ohio Fair have not learned a lesson that will be reduced to practice. It is this: Take careful notice of the programme of a fair, and have strong guaranties that a so-called fair shall not be but another name for a grand horse-race before you give your countenance or patronage in its favor. We suggest the propriety of passing this lesson around, and let it be applied to all the county and state fairs of this country. Christians, like other people, must learn by the experience of themselves or that of others.

October 28, 1874   Backsliding

Against nothing are we more constantly warned in the Scriptures than against backsliding. Backsliding Israel or Christians departing from the faith are alike warned in the Old Testament and in the New of their danger and God's displeasure.

Backsliding may be defined as departing from God. To be away from light involves darkness; to be away from warmth brings coldness; and to be away from the bosom of Life results in death. All these involve unhappiness here, destroy usefulness, and may finally become fixed in eternal death. If salvation means anything every one conscious of being in a backslidden condition ought to be alarmed. He ought to be alarmed because backsliding is displeasing to God and dishonoring to the church. He ought to be alarmed, too, because he is himself involved in terrible danger. And what renders this danger the greater is found in the fact that oftentimes the backslider declines so imperceptibly to himself that he is scarcely aware of his real condition. Large numbers have backslidden, and thus hindered their usefulness in the church and became a burden to Christian society, and often a reproach to the cause of Christ, whereas if they had been faithful they might have abounded in usefulness and might have been happy instead of miserable. Some such may be awakened and finally saved; but, alas, what a failure are there lives! Their record is that of idlers in the vineyard, and false beacons on the shores where wrecked souls are strewn.

One frequent cause of decline is the want of Christian doctrine. Truly, some are well informed in scripture truth, but they have ceased to realize and thus to appropriate it to the benefit of their souls. They have doctrine but they do not use it. There are others who are wanting in a knowledge of the treasures of God's word. They do not read it enough to appreciate or understand it. Those who read little of current news, or little of history, or little of anything else, care little for current news, or history, or whatever else they neglect. Neither are they very well prepared to understand and appreciate any detached paragraph they may read on any of those subjects. So it is the constant and careful reader of God's word that is best able to understand it and value it at its true worth. Bible reading and Bible meditation would save thousands from religious decline and not a few from total backsliding.

But the want of scripture doctrine is likely to involve the reception of much that is very unscriptural, and error is as poison to the soul. Some care very little for doctrine. The reason is that they have very little idea of the value of truth. Indeed, they do not love it. Wherever a people is found indifferent to the distinction between truth and error there will be found but little moral stamina. They may pretend largely and in certain respects do largely, but there is no depth of genuine religious principles there. "If my words abide in you," our Savior says, "ye shall bring forth much fruit." Without careful adherence to God's word backsliding is inevitable. How many ought to brush the dust off their Bibles, to rub their sluggish eye-lids, and open the betrashed avenues of their souls to gospel truth. Yet it is to be feared that many will turn from the perusal of this to neglect, as heretofore, that holy book. But they do so at their soul's eternal peril. The plea of the lack of time will not answer; for abundance of time is squandered which if saved would enable professors of religion to better understand their Master's will.

Another cause of backsliding is the want of waiting on the ministry of God's word. God has chosen preaching as a chief instrumentality to save men. Some fail unnecessarily—for a slight excuse or none at all—to attend the ministry of the word. Alas, some ministers fail to preach the word. Even of those who preach it in form so many fail to preach it in spirit. Ministers need praying for, and this done sincerely does not at all tend to the backsliding of the hearer.

Another cause of backsliding is failure to attend the services of the sanctuary in prayer and conference meetings. People can almost as well live without preaching as without those social meetings. Go into a neighborhood where the public altar of God has no attractions, or perhaps no existence, and you will find but little religion. It is an excellent place to backslide in if any one has enough religion there to make backsliding a matter of possibility or of magnitude.

Another fruitful source of backsliding is devotion to the world. Perhaps few would backslide over political matters if their politics had enough religion in its theory and spirit. People ought to carry genuine religion into their political theories, their political conversations, and to the polls.

Fashionable religion, or fashionable worship, or something of the sort, has caused many an individual and many a congregation to backslide. They have become too religious; but there is little of Christ in it except in name, and little Holy Ghost only that which is assumed without reality.

Personal feuds have caused many to backslide; and no wonder. For if such enemies of Christ, and so sinning against him, can be forgiven and then cherish an unforgiving temper toward their fellows for whom Christ died, they have learned the quick road to the most thorough backsliding. But alienations are a serious cause of backsliding in not a few congregations. These often arise from lack of that Christian regard for the rights and feelings of others which is characteristic of overbearing or selfish people. From whatever cause, it is a sure means of promoting backsliding.

To remedy backsliding but a few directions may be necessary. When any one is fairly awake to the necessity of a return to formerly-enjoyed measures of grace, it is not likely that he will fail to find the most effective remedy. If away from Christ (as they are) they will again draw nigh to him, and they will come with hearts of penitence. They will betake themselves to the means of grace, private and public, and one of these which has been dropped on the way is *fervent* secret prayer, the loss of which has been one of the principal elements in their backsliding. They will turn their feet to the testimony of the Lord. They will meditate on Christ, his character, his word, their duty toward him, and their relation to him. God is indeed married to the backslider, and if such seek his face they shall not seek in vain, but they will find the bread of life and the waters of salvation, and soon shall have the spirit of song instead of that of desolation.

November 4, 1874   Praying for Revival

It is a truth which has often been declared that every denomination of true Christians and every society of each denomination need revivals. But often as it has been declared, it needs to be repeated, for societies are prone to neglect seeking to supply their acknowledged and greatest need.

Revivals are possible at all times in the year, and it is the duty of the ministry and laity to seek to have them. Yet there are portions of the year better adapted than others to the promotion of revivals by long-protracted efforts. That time is approaching—or, perhaps, it would be better to say it is now at hand. Our columns have repeatedly urged preparation for revivals, but it is now proposed to urge one especial department of preparation. We refer to prayer.

The value of prayer as a means of promoting any good thing in the church is readily conceded by all true Christians. But the real strength of prayer is not fully known to many who profess Christianity. Those who pray most and with the greatest sincerity and faith best know its value. But many Christians are not fully sensible of how much depends upon it.

The Lord has evidently appointed prayer as a medium through which the divine power is obtained to help in all holy efforts of the church and of individuals to accomplish good. Christ told his disciples that without him they could do nothing; and he told them that whatsoever they should ask the Father in his name they should receive. If the blessings of God are appointed to be received through prayer, how shall we receive them in any other way. Prayer runs through the record of the achievements of God's servants in the old dispensation, and it is equally if not more prominent in the new. Evil spirits could not be cast out by the apostles except by prayer and fasting. If evil spirits could be cast out and other good works accomplished by social hilarity and feasting, or by joking and croquet playing, it is to be presumed that there would be a great stampede of devils and a wonderful outpouring of divine blessings. But for some wise reason the Savior has not so ordered it in his church.

Sometimes without much of the preparation of prayer, protracted meetings are begun and in form revival is invoked. But, alas! where there is not enough sacred awe among the people there is, in some cases at least, instituted "playing revival," which is substituted instead of real revival. This is worse than no semblance of revival; for even if a few sincere souls are drawn into the church during a protracted effort, a spurious revival leaves the church more dead and demoralized than it was before.

Real revival is in answer to prayer. It indicates that some one has been praying somewhere. Such may be hidden in obscurity or concealed from pubic notice by poverty, but the Lord knows where they are, hears their cries, takes notice of their tears, and sympathizes with their souls' pleadings for the salvation of sinners and the renewal of the spiritual strength of cold-hearted professors. Some minister who has been fattening his soul in ease may lead the revival, and professors whose acquaintance with mammon far exceeds acquaintance with the Lord may be heralded as chief laborers in the meeting, but some pious soul has been praying earnestly in faith, and in answer to these prayers it is that all this awakening is manifested.

Even true Christians are too liable as they can not see the direct fruit of prayer to lose their confidence in its efficiency, so that it is well to pass the word along the lines, "Pray, brethren, pray for the conversion of souls—for the renewal and increase of grace in the hearts of believers." This is a great need just now. Such a revival is in accordance with the longing of every pious heart. Courage, then, brother, sister; the Lord hears our prayers. If we ask anything in accordance with his will, and believe we shall have the things for which we ask, we shall assuredly have them, for such is the promise of God's word. There is then not only power in prayer but there is certainty in it; and when we ask for a revival in faith we may rest assured that the Lord will do all that can be done consistent with the economy of grace to grant our request. Now while it is true that we should labor for what we pray (and we will, if sincere), and that proper efforts to accomplish the work are to be craved and solicited, it is also true that one of the greatest needs of the church just now is the spirit of earnest, persevering prayer in faith; for such would certainly be prevailing prayer, and would result in a wonderful work of grace to bless and cheer the church of Christ.

December 23, 1874   Christmas

The annually returning Christmas-day has, in Christian countries, obtained general observance, though not always most appropriate, as commemorative of the birth of the Prince of Peace. Though the twenty-fifth day of December may not be even within the month of the Savior's birth, and though Christmas may owe its date to the fact of its supplanting a heathen anniversary festival, yet it is the only day regarded among men as commemorative of Christ's nativity.

Christmas is observed as commemorative of the most joyful event ever known on earth. It is commemorative of the coming of the Heir of Glory to the world on a mission of love, mercy, and salvation to man. His incarnation is amazing, his assumption of brotherhood to man wonderful; his sufferings, terminating his humiliation with death and inclosure [sic] within the tomb, strike us with grief for his agony, admiration for his magnanimity, and joy and triumph for his subsequent exaltation and for the hope of reigning with him as with the Lamb that was slain, who has redeemed us with his own precious blood. We, considering the import of his birth, wonder not at the story of the angelic messenger to the shepherds of Bethlehem, nor of the seraphic choir which filled the heaven with celestial notes of gladness, in words of surpassing beauty. The subsequent rapture of the venerable Simeon and the holy ecstasy of the aged Anna, in all their fullness, though matchless in appropriateness, are yet inadequate to the joyfulness of the occasion. The adoration of the sages of the East, and their "exceeding great joy," were the feeble tribute of the finite to the infinite worthiness and incomprehensible benefactions which were to jewel the crown of the new-born King.

Let our observance of Christmas be a joyful observance; let it be a holy observance; and let it be one that in good-will, remembrance of the suffering, self-sacrifice, and faithfulness to our Redeemer, shall leave behind it cherished memories. We wish a joyful Christmas to all our readers.

October 6, 1875   Insincerity

Observation convinces any one that there is a great lack of sincerity among professors of religion. It is to be regretted that this is also true of some ministers of the gospel. Not that Christians are not distinguished above all people for sincerity, nor that ministers are not distinguished in the same regard above all other Christians. Yet there is much to tempt the Christian to insincerity; and that which may spring from virtue may be carried into excess. So in this and in a thousand ways a Christian may be induced to conceal his feelings and his thoughts, even to repress them and act as if he had no such thought or feelings. How far this may be carried without sin is a difficult question. It is very certain that it may be carried so far that the professor of Christianity may sometimes seem to smile on sin and become accessory to evil. Especially is there danger of this if a tender conscience is not cherished, and if such a one become cold in his religious experience. When this is the case the want of sincerity is likely to take a further step and even do things which the judgment can not entirely approve that others may be pleased, at least that they may not be offended. There is still another step in this line. It is an effort to persuade one's own mind that there is nothing wrong in a thing that under other circumstances would be readily disapproved. This effort is not by close, candid reasoning, but by loose, sometimes cunning, sophistry to persuade the judgment to coincide with the will. This kind of success is attended with other victories of the same kind in accelerating ratio; and ere long the soul reaches that point when its own interest or the wish of others will enable it to "call good evil" if it stands in its way or to "call evil good" if it harmonizes with the poor soul's purpose. It is not necessary to say that such a soul has now lost all that constitutes genuine internal Christianity; but it may not have yet lost the form of godliness. If so, such a one may be civil, and even moral, in his life; he may be reverential in the forms of devotional service; yet where is his sincerity? He is as sounding brass and like a tinkling cymbal.

When sincerity has taken its fight from the deluded and backslidden professor, he may not yet have ceased to exert quite an influence, especially among youthful and weak disciples. The result is that a low type of Christianity is made the model of many who, if they shall not be eternally wrecked by such influence, will come far short of that type of Christianity of which the guileless Savior was the perfect example.

There is another sort of insincerity to which all classes of Christians are prone. One often sings a song full of the expression of the finest devotional sentiment,—and song is one of the grandest helps of devotion,—but after a time the attention is drawn from the sentiment of the song, and the singing, even in the church, has little realization of those sentiments which ought to stir the heart and set the soul on fire. The same, in a degree, is often true of prayer. Is it not also true of the preaching of the word, of exhortation, and of religious conversation? What terrible reading of hymns and of the Holy Scriptures is the result. What a vein of insincerity runs through the words and actions of such Christians, whether ministers or people. The world looks on and concludes that if those Christians do believe in what they sing and pray and preach, they certainly deal in such truths as if they were dull fictions. When words and services and even conduct are thus insincere in their appearance, what wonder is it that interest flags, unbelief finds entrance, and that many souls go away unfed and disheartened?

There is a remedy for all this. This remedy consists not in methods earnest only to the eye and to the ear; for these are most disgusting if they reveal their hollowness, as is often the case. But the remedy consists in well-cultivated habits of close attention to the reality of all our words and worship, that, so far from a listless habit being contracted, we may form habits of reality and simplicity and sincerity. If any are floating toward insincerity they would do well to bestir themselves and resolutely break its delusive influences.

December 22, 1875   Moral Independence

Independence of character is known to fewer than many suspect. All are more or less subject to the influence of others. This dependence with many amounts to almost absolute servility to some person or persons, and not less complete subjection to community on the part of others. It takes an oaken, discerning, or conscientious character to avoid this; and great numbers possessing these qualities yield before influences which test the weakness of human nature, and circumstances which put it upon exhibition.

A few persons have appeared in history in support of the possibility of something higher than mental enslavement to personal or collective influences. Among these was William Penn, the son of an English admiral, born to rank and heir of wealth. Brought under religious influences, he embraced sentiments at total variance with a corrupt age, and wounded the pride and disappointed the ambition of a stern father. He is sent to France to imbibe the gayety of its society, and he returns accomplished and gay, the delight and glory of his father. But a renewal of his convictions brings him again to his loyalty to conscience, and again, through much of his earlier life, alienation sits in the paternal home. He is cast into prison for faithfulness to his convictions, and months does the highborn son, the philanthropist and statesman, spend in confinement. He pleads his right to liberty of conscience before a court which endeavors to starve an acquitting jury into acquiescence with its views, and is at last set free, a relenting father paying his fine. This man in subsequent years endures proscription for conscience' sake, and at last, with broadness of views and wisdom worthy of such a mind as his and such a character, founds a commonwealth and a city which is soon to witness the celebration of the centennial of a free nation—not all Penn could have wished, but the freest nation on earth.

Penn may have erred in some of his views; but his errors are small compared with the prevailing errors of his age. If in some things he went to seeming extremes, these are few compared with those of others of his day, and even these lean toward virtue. Broad-minded, sweet-souled, clear-headed man he was, and all this crowned with an independence unlike asperity or stubbornness. Few have been his equals, and few have been permitted to do so much as a pioneer of freedom of conscience and of peace, and as an apostle of that lofty independence of men which arises from complete allegiance to God.

Taking a survey of the situation of modem society, what shall we say of the prevalence of an independence lofty as that of William Penn. We can find enough of austerity, asperity, and stubbornness. There is enough of ambition to lead against this current or that, if it will give a popular following; but, alas, how few simply regard the questions of truth and right. It is easy to many to reason themselves into the belief of this or that if inclination, applause, or other reward is before them.

To exemplify what we have said: Does a wave of popular opinion sweep over the land with regard to any measure or event, domestic or foreign, secular or ecclesiastical, and how few in their sentiments and actions do not bend before it as weeds before the gale or shrubs before the rising current. So it is in politics; so in religious opinion. It is so in social maxims and fashions. No matter how objectionable their origin or tendency; no matter how foolish. Few even among the good do not succumb rather than appear singular or encounter that intolerance which abhors and persecutes all independence that consults reason and conscience.

Who is it that did not despise the simplicity of the rough altar of God's choosing when there were arrayed against it the court of Ahab and the priests of Baal and Ashteroth? Thousands still in the presence of the influence and splendor of men's forms and inventions do not turn their faces to the simplicity of Christ. Before popular influence many are ready to do the most foolish thing if it is current and popular; and much more do they regard the clamor of the multitude than the voice of reason and common sense or the example and precepts of Christ and his true followers. Those who rise in wealth and popularity are prone to this; those who aspire to distinction tend that way; and even those who find the measure of their aspirations in fancied greatness common alike to all ranks of society do the same. Go to the great centers of wealth and show and worldly refinement, and what will you see in the conflict of the spirit of Christ and that of the world? With the great mass of the church the spirit of the world will prevail. Do any seek the simplicity of Christ; they will meet sneers and frowns, not only from the world but also from those of the church who tend to worldly conformity. Few there are who, like Penn, ask of any theory or practice, Is it right? and if it is found so to be, pursue it as they would heaven; or if found to be wrong shun it as they would the ways of Satan. One age under the special influence of the Spirit of God and under the leadership of shining lights of moral independence and piety break away from follies, and the next age garnish the sepulchers of those who broke the chains of folly, and return themselves to the very same follies, despising in others of their own times the very principles they celebrate on the monuments of the dead. Follies discarded by one age, like effete fashions of former times, are resurrected to fill their place in cycles of vanity and foolishness. This is what some call progress.

December 22, 1875   Remember the Poor

Compassion is one of the loveliest moral beauties of earth. Its exercise is the duty of each and all. In its higher and holier forms it is a fruit of the divine Spirit. True compassion is discriminating, but not overmuch so. It distinguishes between the pain or woe brought on and retained by moral delinquency and that which is guiltless and unavoidable; but it does not pass by the unhappy child of folly and sin.

Well might many of us contrast our situation with that of numbers around us. How many live on one half or one fourth of the means which we regard as hardly sufficient for our comfort; and how often are even these scanty means beyond their possible reach. Under what disadvantages do many struggle. What hardships do they endure. What is a common place blessing to us may be an inestimable joy [to] them. What do we know of their longings and of their repressions of heart emotions? Some know not because too busy to consider the poor and the unhappy. They lose the blessing: "Blessed is he that considereth the poor: the Lord will deliver him in time of trouble. The Lord will preserve him, and keep him alive; and he shall be blessed upon the earth: and thou wilt not deliver him unto the will of his enemies. The Lord will strengthen him upon the bed of languishing: thou wilt make all his bed in his sickness." Job considered the poor from the very depths of his heart, and found as a fruit of such consideration "that the Lord is very pitiful and of tender mercy." Jesus exemplified it, and is now crowned by heaven and earth with ascription of "blessing and honor and glory and power." Howard tried it, and dying with a soul full of heaven, chose a humble spot for his grave, charged that there should be no funeral pomp at his burial, and said: "Bury me there; plant a sun-dial over my grave, and let me be forgotten." Benezet tried it, and when thousands of the grateful poor had gathered with tearful eyes around his bier, an American soldier, with a heart full of the sorrow and of the grandeur of the occasion, exclaimed, "I had rather be Andrew Benezet in that coffin than George Washington with all his fame!"

Some regard themselves as of a superior order, and the poor and afflicted as inferior. Yet to a great extent the children of these despised ones will furnish the instructors and leaders in community, church, and state. The blind whimseys [sic] of rank are most ridiculous, often appearing more like burlesque than the fruits of rationality.

But, it may be inquired, what can be done for the poor? With many, employment and its legitimate wages are the chief wants. Others in straitened circumstances only need help till they can arrange to help themselves. Some need advice, and others little less than constant superintendence. Many want, above all earthly help, sympathy.

Benevolence is an excellent preface to any needed advice or reproof; but it should be in deed rather than in word. The advice or reproof should, however, be so delicate and judicious as not to make the beneficence seem an insulting excuse.

Benevolence is far from bad economy. Its fruits, deeds of beneficence, afford the purest joy and happiness to the giver. The gifts bestowed are not generally so much subtracted from one's means without an equivalent; but he who gives with pure motives is, in consequence, the better balanced for planning his financial affairs. Propensities tending to recklessness or extravagance are superseded or measurably subdued by it presence. Besides, it often opens to us the channels of success in business or otherwise. Providence also gives that favor to the benevolent which assures prosperity. Above all, benevolence is duty to God and promotes riches toward him.

Benevolence is one of the best recommendations of Christianity. What does it, whether in reality or in forms alone, do for the Roman Catholic Church? The sisters of charity and other orders of beneficence become a power. Rome's level of the rich and poor in its worship—a commendable feature of benevolence, as also a right—carries a power, though its poor are taxed almost as much as the wealthy are in Protestant churches. We need not wonder how their costly temples are built. Their poor communicants are taught that their souls' salvation depends on their meeting the exactions of the church. Yet a consideration in other respects for the poor gives power to that church. What a recommendation, then, is pure beneficence wherever it is fully practiced by Christians.

Those who open up the channels of beneficence for others do a good work. There are many articles of produce, clothing, and other things which are to those who have them of little use. It is better that they should be employed in beneficence; and those who can tell others how to do so are doing a good thing for the giver as well as for the needy. Many articles not strictly keepsake, though partaking of this nature, might without dishonor to the departed be better used in doing good than kept as a prey for moth or rust. What a work can be done by prompting and regulating visits to the sick, and providing for, caring for, and comforting them. Persons in grief, strangers, the homeless, and the churchless, all furnish excellent objects of beneficence.

There is plenty of work for Christian associations, church associations, and individual enterprise. How much better it would be to substitute real and direct beneficence for fairs under various forms, with their silly maneuverings and flirtations. All should be made to feel that Christians are not endeavoring to seem to be, but in simplicity of heart are doing Christ's work. The opportunity at this time to do good is great. The heritage of opportunity to the benevolent is unusually rich now, especially in the cities.

December 29, 1875   Pleasure in Our Work

A real pleasure is to be found in our daily duties and employment if properly sought. The opposite to this often arises from needless opposition to things necessary. It is sometimes from a cherished disinclination, like that which prompts the stupefied to delay in arising. It is painful postponement of that which would bring almost immediate pleasure. Much would be saved by tearing away from enchantments. Much to mar the pleasures of our pursuits arises from longings after the forbidden, the really undesirable, or the impossible. There is much art

in finding the wisely pleasant in our employments; but it takes heart-genius to
do so, and to appropriate those pleasures. Some love the object but hate the road
which leads to it. Those who hate the road and long for the destination are in
continual conflict. They know not peace, and how can they be happy?

Illustrations might be given of the needless discomfort felt by many in their
pursuits. Why is it that people are so wonderfully affected by showers against
which they are protected; with a little mud, when their shoes are good; at the
glow of summer, when they are in cool retreats; or at the breath of winter, when
they are within doors beside a burning grate? People usually magnify such in-
conveniences tenfold and make them burdens on their lives. So it is with toil,
necessary cares, sacrifices, martyrdoms, etc.

The same is true in mental pursuits. Many do not learn to associate pleasure
with their thinking, reading, study. So it is also in morals. Some learn not the art
of taking pleasure in moral treasures, in efforts and sacrifices for the right. There
ought to be as much pleasure in moral exercise as in rowing a canoe, driving a
sleigh, or skating on a smooth field of ice, and a great deal more. In Bible reading, in holy meditation, in prayer, and in public worship, abundant streams of
pleasure ought to be found; and they *can* be found of those who make the most
out of them. So it is also of charity, of pastoral labor, of preaching, and of every
department of Christian effort.

The want of pleasure in one's pursuits is greatly against success. Those who
find no pleasure in their employment rarely are accomplished in it. Neither are
they likely to be diligent or fruitful in their work.

Those whose pleasure is not in their pursuits, sacrifice their strength. There
is friction, wear, and tear in their labors, averse to health and the growth of their
faculties. Theirs is a fretting, wearing out, breaking-down process. It brings unhappiness, and by it pleasures are driven away.

The children of God are evidently intended to find pleasure and joy in their
labors. They may extract pleasures from them as the bee finds honey in the
flower-cup. But this will never be done till men learn to thank God for their labors and pursuits, taking pleasure in their daily prosecution. This is possible to
the child of God, and especially is it so in the case of those enjoying a high degree of sanctification. Such can realize, not only that it is a duty, but a precious
pleasure to do whatsoever work God has given them to do. Such is the privilege
of those who realize God's continual presence, love, and approbation.

March 29, 1876   Christ Condemns Secretism

Some are disposed to inquire after the particular passages of scripture which
declare against secret societies. They ask where Christ and the apostles have
declared those organizations to be wrong. If they wish to know the chapter and

verse in which secret societies are condemned *by name*, we may state that these will be found in close proximity with those scriptures which name with censure gambling, horse-racing, theaters, balls, bull-baiting, papacy, the Spanish Inquisition, nunneries, Jesuitism, Mormonism, spiritualism, Darwinianism, free-loveism, simony, and a multitude of other sins and institutions concerning which there ought to be no difference of opinion among enlightened Christians. If any one can find the places where these sins are condemned by name, it will not be difficult to find the scriptures condemning in like manner secret societies. Shall all things not specifically condemned by names current in our language be approved by the church of Christ, and tolerated among Christians? It takes an elastic conscience to indorse, or even to fail to condemn, all evils not specifically reproved by Christ and his apostles.

If it be asked, "Wherein are Christ and his true follower, and their principles and practice, averse to those who love darkness rather than light and revel in the wiles and shades of secretism?" many scriptures can be cited in answer to the inquiry. Christ said to the high-priests concerning the openness of his teachings: "In secret have I said nothing." (John xviii. 20) He also said to the chief-priests, and captains of the temple, and the elders, when they came with Judas to arrest him (contrasting their character and plotting practices with his own guileless spirit and that of his disciples): "When I was daily with you in the temple, ye stretched forth no hands against me: *but this is your hour and the power of darkness.*" (Luke xxii. 53; Isa. xlviii. 16-18) He strongly condemned the spirit that revels in shades of concealment when he said: "And this is the condemnation, that light is come into the world, *and men loved darkness rather than light, because their deeds were evil.* For every one that doeth evil *hateth the light,* neither cometh to the light, lest his *deeds should be reproved.* But he that *doeth truth cometh to the light,* that his deeds may be made manifest, that they are wrought in God." (John iii. 19, 20, 21.) What a contrast between true Christianity, which is as open as the sun, and the darkness of secretism. How well does the great Teacher state this contrast in the foregoing.

In the sermon on the mount, Jesus taught openness of life as proper for his true disciples, and condemned the opposite as unparalleled folly. He said: "Ye are the light of the world. A city that is set on a hill can not be hid. Neither do men light a candle, and put it under a bushel, but on a candlestick; and it giveth light unto all that are in the house. Let your light so shine before men, that they may see your good works, and glorify your Father which is in heaven." (Matt. v. 14, 15, 16.) No wonder, then, that Paul said: "Have no fellowship with the unfruitful works of darkness, but rather reprove them." "Ye are all the children of light, and the children of the day; we are not of the night, nor of darkness." (Eph. v. 11; I. Thes. v. 5; Prov. iv. 18, 19.) With what ponderous force do Paul's words apply to that fellowship of darkness in

"A temple where no narrow creed
Protects a chosen few;"

But "holds alike deserved meed
To Christian, Turk, or Jew,"
(see *Odd-fellows Pocket Companion*, page 291.), when he says: "Be ye not un-
equally yoked together with unbelievers: for what fellowship hath righteousness
with unrighteousness? and what communion hath *light with darkness?* And what
concord hath *Christ with Belial?* or what part hath he that believeth with an infidel?" How loud, then, is the call of the apostle—in the same connection—to
believers: "Come out from among them, and be ye separate, saith the Lord, and
touch not the unclean thing; and I will receive you, and will be a Father unto
you, and ye shall be my sons and daughters, saith the Lord Almighty." (II. Cor.
vi. 14, 15, 17, 18.) What a glorious thing to thousands would deliverance from
lodge idolatry be.

Truly might Christ say of himself: "Wherefore if they shall say unto you,
Behold, he is in the desert; go not forth: behold, he is in the *secret chambers*;
believe it not." (Matt. xxiv. 26.) This is true of other than of Christ's second
coming.

Of the open-souledness of the true Christian, Jesus said, concerning Na-
thaneel [*sic*]: "Behold an Israelite indeed, in whom is no guile!" The guileless
spirit of that Nazarene apostle and the guile of the lodge have "a great gulf
fixed" between them. Well would it be for all Christians to "lay aside" "all
guile" as the Lord commands, and to imitate the Savior, in whom no guile was
found. (John i. 47; I. Peter ii. 1, 22; Rev. xiv. 5; Psalms xxxii. 2.) Paul says he
had "*renounced the hidden things* of dishonesty, not walking in *craftiness*, nor
handling the word of God deceitfully,"—which last thing (as also the former
ones) the lodges do not renounce, but practice.

The lodge is a *conspiracy* against those outside of its limits, to secure ends
by secret plottings, instead of manly, open methods. Conspiracy, so far from
being approved of God, is condemned in the Old Testament as well as in the
New. The Bible tells us of a "conspiracy" against David by Absalom, and another against Amaziah, the good king of Judah, by men of Belial. It tells us of
the "conspiracy" of the men of Judah and Jerusalem, which led to their serving
other gods and breaking Jehovah's covenant—even as it is in the profane, deist-
ical worship of the lodge; its expurgations of Christ's name from scripture quotations; and its perversions of other scriptures, mixing them up with mythical
stories. Such conspiracy is reproved of the Lord by the mouth of Ezekiel; especially are the professed ministers of Christ rebuked for conspiring to show no
difference "between the holy and profane," nor "between the unclean and the
clean," as it is in the brotherhood of the lodge. (II. Samuel xv. 12; II. Kings xiv.
19, 20; Ezek. xxii. 25, 26.)

Forty Jews entered into a conspiracy, covenanting with an oath and curse
that they would neither eat nor drink till they had killed Apostle Paul. (Acts
xxiii. 12, 13, 21.) Herodias and her daughter conspired together to take the head
of John the Baptist, which they obtained through the wicked oath of Herod.

(Mark vi. 24.) The sin of wicked oaths is in taking them, not in failing to carry them out.

But the great conspiracy, the parent of all other conspiracies, is that of Satan against Christ, which is mentioned in the second psalm, as also in the fourth chapter of the Acts of the Apostles. "The kings of the earth set themselves, and the rulers *take counsel together* against the Lord, and against his anointed." For of a truth against the holy child Jesus, "Herod, and Pontius Pilate, with the gentiles, and the people of Israel *were gathered together.*" (Ps. ii. 2, 3, 4; Acts iv. 26, 27.) Truly "the Lord shall have" conspiracies "in derision;" and against his church "the gates of hell," pouring forth their hosts, "shall not prevail."

Composite photograph of the Milton Wright family. Left to right: Wilbur Wright, Katharine Wright, Susan Koerner Wright, Lorin Wright, Bishop Milton Wright, Reuchlin Wright, and Orville Wright. Image courtesy of Special Collections and Archives, Wright State University, Dayton, Ohio.

Chapter 3

The Church of the United Brethren in Christ

November 3, 1869   Our Troubles

Our publishing agent, Bro. W. J. Shuey, Bro. W. McKee, Mr. R. Allison, of the
Franklin Type Foundery [sic], Cincinnati, and M. Chamberlain, an engraver, also
of Cincinnati, were arrested by a United States officer, week before last, on the
charge of making internal revenue stamps with the *intent* to defraud the Government out of revenue on matches. They were to have a hearing before the commis-
sioner of internal revenue in this city on last Friday, and were ready to meet the
charge; but the prosecuting witness failing to appear, the case was postponed to the
8th of November. Until they have a hearing it would be improper to give a detailed
statement of the facts, lest it should be taken as an attempt to prejudice the case in
their favor. The secular press has given this matter such wide publicity that we are
constrained to say this much before our time, for the satisfaction of our own people. The matter grows out of a small job of printing, done in our establishment
nearly four years ago, of match-labels, which, in some respects, resembled the ten-
cent internal revenue stamp. The establishment received four dollars for the job.
The cut was engraved and electrotyped by the gentlemen associated with our
brethren in the charge, and the whole transaction was done by them without the
least intention to wrong any one. The engraving, electrotyping, and printing were
done for a party in this city who was engaged in the manufacture and vending of
friction matches. The gentlemen from Cincinnati are Christian men of unimpeachable moral character and business integrity, and they, with our brethren, will be

able to show, to the satisfaction of the court and an intelligent public that they are utterly guiltless of the grave charge brought against them, and that they stand, as heretofore, without a spot to blemish their good name. In the meantime we bespeak for them the prayers of God's people.

December 15, 1869   United Brethren in Christ and the Evangelical Association

The *Evangelical Messenger*, in a recent number, indorses the sentiments of a correspondent who had suggested that two denominations can accomplish organic union only by meeting each other half way, which he thinks is not likely to be done, unless those denominations are about equal in numerical strength. The *Messenger* apprehends the impracticability of the proposed union between the Evangelical Association and the Methodist Episcopal Church, because the larger denomination is not likely to concede much, nor the smaller one to yield all for the privilege of being swallowed up by the larger, thus losing its identity. The *Messenger* suggests that two denominations, akin to each other in faith and usage, and nearly equal in numbers, would be more likely to form a desirable union. It instances the Evangelical Association and the Church of the United Brethren in Christ, and mentions some of the advantages which would be likely to result from a union of those churches, such as avoiding a hurtful rivalry, consolidating the German congregations of each, as also their English congregations, and strengthening their educational and publishing interests. All this the *Messenger* suggests can be done without sacrificing long-loved usages or self-respect, and without either denomination making unbecoming demands or accepting humiliating conditions. It expresses its long-cherished belief that such a union can be effected, forming, on terms of equality, a harmonious compact. The *Messenger* finally responds to the inquiry, "How about the secret-society question?" by saying that the two denominations could meet each other half way, which it suggests would "be equally satisfactory, favorable, and advantageous to both."

The *Messenger* estimates the numerical strength of the Evangelical Association at upward of sixty thousand members, and the United Brethren Church numbers twice as many, so that if a complete union could be effected the united body would constitute, as the *Messenger* suggests, a membership of about two hundred thousand. Some, at least, of the advantages suggested by the *Messenger* would surely follow if a complete and harmonious union of the two churches could be effected. We shall therefore consider the practicability of such a union.

There seems to be a sufficient oneness in general doctrine and mode of worship to present no especial impediment to the proposed union. Although the differences of the workings of the two organizations might involve greater difficulty, this, too, could perhaps be overcome. But on the secrecy question the *Messenger* has evidently mistaken the spirit of our people. With the far larger portion of the United Brethren ministers and membership freedom from connection with secret societies is a firmly-established principle of church polity.

In many of our conferences there is not one fourth of our people who could be transferred to an organization composed of two former ones, uniting with a compromise of this or any other cherished principle. If forty thousand members of the Evangelical Association could be induced to enter such a united body on such terms, it is not probable that an equal number from the United Brethren Church could be induced to go in with them; and this would not form either a strong body numerically nor one half so well established as either of the two bodies now is.

On the secrecy question there is an irrepressible conflict in America, and we have no doubt but antisecrecy principles will finally prevail. But it may be said—and has been intimated in our paper since we were elected to our present position—that the sentiment in favor of a modification of our rule on secret societies is a growing sentiment in our Church. We will also show our opinion. It is not hard, when efficient means are employed, to bring out in any denomination an element in favor of any plausible change of church law. In our opinion the movement against our rule on secret societies, which carried with it for a time many who yielded simply because they regarded resistance hopeless, culminated at least a year before the sitting of the last General Conference, and has been on the descending scale ever since. We suggest that any who think of revolutionizing the sentiment of the Church on this question have a large job before them.

The attempt, a few years since, to form a strong non-episcopal church out of the non-episcopal denominations, is a lesson for us. The fragments of the attempted union have been gathered to a considerable extent into other churches, and some of the denominations which were represented in the movement have not only been depleted in numbers, but for a time at least were left in a dangerously unsettled condition.

In conclusion, we reciprocate the fraternal spirit which the *Messenger* manifests toward the United Brethren Church. We for many years have regarded the denomination of which the *Messenger* is an able exponent with warm fraternal feelings, praying for her purity and rejoicing in her prosperity. A complete union of that denomination with our own, without any sacrifice of principle on the part of either, we should hail with delight.

January 12, 1870   We Must Educate

We do not propose in this article to say much respecting our institutions of learning, but to urge our people to educate their children. It is not to be hoped

that all parents will succeed in giving their children a collegiate education; but
there are few families that might not be better educated than they are. It is a sad
fact that comparatively few properly appreciate the advantages of mental culture. If God has given us minds capable of great improvement is it not our duty
to cultivate them? Is it not the duty of parents to give their children the very best
possible opportunity to attain to intellectual excellence? There are some hinder-
ances [sic] in the way, but are these not comparatively trifling? What are a few
dollars—what is a little of luxury, or the splendor of this world, compared with
the development of those mental powers which distinguish us from the lower
creation. It would greatly increase the happiness and usefulness of our youth if
they could be better educated. And they can, if their parents will take that interest in the matter which it is their duty to do. They ought to remember that with
the present years of their children's lives is passing the golden opportunity.
Would it not be a great deal better for parents of limited means to withhold from
their children a portion of those luxuries and unnecessary expenditures of various kinds, which are now afforded them, than to allow them to reach manhood
and womanhood with their mental powers undeveloped? Why should we suffer
the growth of the immortal intellect to be retarded and stinted by allowing other
interests or other enjoyments to take precedence of its welfare? Should there not
be a thorough reformation of our people in their practice respecting the education of their children? We are not now pleading for an academical [sic] or collegiate course, but for the general education of all our families. Give us the thorough education of all our youth in those branches taught in our best common
schools, and the advancement of many to a greater degree of learning will certainly follow, as it ought.

If parents would daily manifest to their children an interest in their advancement in education, the children would feel that their improvement was a
matter worthy of their own interest and effort. A new life would be felt by many
a one who now is passing through what he supposes to be the dull routine of a
school-room prison. A little tact and a great deal of interest on the part of parents
in the education of their children would increase the advancement of those children to an astonishing extent.

Let them allow no trifles to hinder their children from regular, punctual attendance at school; but let them give them a sufficient length of time in the best
schools which can be provided for them; let them encourage them, and assist
them in acquiring habits of home reading and study; and let them furnish suitable periodicals and books, and a generation hence we shall have a degree of
mental culture which will increase our happiness and usefulness as a people, and
render us, if we live up to our spiritual privileges also, worthy, according to the
clemency of the kingdom of grace, of the continued favor of Him who requires
us to use the ability and opportunities which we possess, with due reference to
his will and his glory. It is highly important that there should be a general awak-

ening of our people to the necessity of a more thorough education of all our children.

April 13, 1870   The General Conference Misrepresented

Among the propositions respecting which the action of the late General Conference has been misrepresented was one to submit to a vote of the people, throughout the Church, the question of a change in the constitution of the Church on the subject of secret societies. It would have required a two-third majority to have affected any such change. It may be justly presumed that very few members of the Conference believed that one half that number were in favor of any change of the constitution on the subject. The paper did not propose to submit the question at once to the vote of the people, but proposed the most effective method of securing continued agitation and strife for three years to come by thus long putting off the vote—until 1872—and still enjoining it at last. It also proposed by a conference edict to close the columns of the Church paper on the subject for more than two years and a half, which would doubtless have been claimed by many as a prohibition of the publication of anything against secret societies during that time.

Surely it is not customary for ecclesiastical bodies to submit propositions to a vote of the people with a view to future changes in sentiment which they thereby invite to occur. The mover of this proposition had, a few days before, objected to putting off a similar vote on lay representation till the year 1872, because the subject having been already thoroughly discussed, he did not wish that we should be afflicted with this agitation for two or three years longer. This was an excellent argument at least against the proposed action on secrecy.

The proposition on secrecy was introduced several days after the previous debate and action of the Conference on that question, and after several prominent members of the Conference had been compelled to leave. It was introduced, too, on the eve of the contemplated adjournment of the body when there was a general feeling that with the discussions which must necessarily attend any proposed changes in the paper, the Conference could not properly spend enough time to adapt it to the views of the majority of that body; hence the proposition to lay it on the table was carried, but with a bare majority. Some who would have favored a submission of the vote to the people at an early day voted with the majority to lay the paper on the table, while others who regarded the proposition [sic] as having, however unintentionally, a mischievous bearing, yet believing that the Conference had better spend some time in putting it in the right shape, voted against tabling it. We voted ourself against the tabling of the paper, though if it had been passed in the form in which it was submitted by the mover we then felt that we should have forthwith declined the position to which we had been elected a few days before, that of editor of the RELIGIOUS TELE-SCOPE. Whenever it is believed that there is anything like the necessary two-thirds majority in favor of any change in the constitution of the Church, there will be no difficulty in getting a vote of the people on the subject. Meanwhile the advocates of measures strategic in effect if not in intent, should not assail the action of the General Conference.

Since this has been broached in our columns by others we deem it our duty, as conductor of the Church organ, to make this explanation, as we shall consider it our privilege and duty to do whenever the action of that body is unjustly as-sailed from any source, though otherwise we should have felt justifiable in maintaining silence with regard to the action of the conference on this and some other measures respecting which there may be a dissatisfied minority.

August 3, 1870   Action of the Board of Education

The Board of Education appointed in accordance with the directions of the last General Conference, by the bishops at their meeting last January, met at this city last week. Six members were present and four absent. Those present were L. Davis, D. Shuck, W. C. Smith, E. Light, E. B. Kephart, and M. Wright; the ab-sentees were S. Weaver, W. S. Titus, D. Eberly, and P. B. Lee. An organization was effected by electing L. Davis president and E. Light secretary.

The session was mainly devoted to the consideration of the subject of the founding of a biblical seminary—a work specially committed to them by the General Conference, and to accomplish which they were clothed by that body with ample powers. The members all seemed deeply sensible of the magnitude and importance of the task assigned them. After lengthy, careful, and patient deliberation they agreed upon a plan, to be submitted to the Church for their financial co-operation. It was agreed to locate the institution at Dayton, Ohio, and that an appeal should be made to the Church for donations amounting to one hundred thousand dollars for this purpose; sixty thousand dollars of this amount to be appropriated to the endowment of four professorships, thirty thousand dol-lars to procure a site and buildings, and ten thousand dollars to procure a suit-able library. It was also provided that when thirty or forty thousand dollars should be secured, measures should be taken to put the institution into practical operation. The corporate name chosen for the contemplated institution is Union Biblical Seminary.

Great harmony and unanimity of sentiment prevailed as to the necessity of providing such an institution, and a remarkable oneness with respect to the action finally taken was characteristic of the meeting. The minutes of the meeting and the address of the Board to the Church will be given next week.

The want of an institution under the control of the Church, where young ministers seeking a thorough course of sacred learning preparatory to entering upon the regular work of the ministry, has for years been felt by some of the most ardent and judicious friends of the Church. The General Conference, in its session five years ago, recommended to our institutions of learning measures intended to partially and temporarily supply this want. So great has been the increase since that time of the sentiment favoring a regular biblical institution that at the last session of the General Conference there was no manifest opposition whatever to taking measures to provide such an institution under the control of the whole Church, where a thorough course of theological study could be pursued by those seeking such preparation preparatory to the work of the ministry. This work was committed to the Board of Education, and the proposed plan is the result of their first meeting.

In the past, graduates of our literary institutions desiring to study divinity have been compelled to resort to the theological schools of other denominations to accomplish that purpose. Some have done this in the past; others are at those seminaries now; and the number who will pursue a course of theological study is increasing every year. It is not a question as to whether graduates contemplating the ministry in our Church will take such a course of study. Some have done so, others are doing so, and still others will, and we rejoice to note the fact. Our denomination has its share of the finest and most enterprising minds of the country who are preparing for the ministry. They value ministerial education, and they will have it in the institutions of other churches if not in our own. If we do not furnish them an institution in which they can have the coveted influence and associations of the denomination of their choice they will go where they will be brought under the influence of doctrine and church economy averse to ours. Some will come out little affected by those influences; others will be molded measurably by their associations and surroundings, but not enough to carry them from us; and others, still, will be lost to the Church sooner or later. It is time for us as a people to inquire whether it is best that we should throw the finest talent and culture of the Church so far from its direct influence. Do we not need all of these to assist us in our mission as a Church? We have lost much by not earlier pushing forward our literary institutions, by so long delaying the organization of a general missionary society, by neglecting for so many years the German work in the West. Shall we take lessons from the past and avoid the consequences of future neglect to provide for the thorough culture of our ministry?

But little could be done until the Board should take measures to secure a charter under the general law on charters in this state. So it was necessary to select a corporate name. Considerable time was given, and a commendable degree of patience was exercised in selecting a name for the institution. Union Biblical Seminary is in many respects a desirable one. It is convenient, euphoni-

ous, and expressive. It is desirable to unite the whole Church for perhaps a half
century to come on one institution of the kind; hence, in this respect, as well as
in its general popularity, *union* is rather a desirable component in a title. Biblical
is comprehensive in its meaning, the Bible furnishing, as it does, the ground-
work of natural as well as revealed theology. Seminary is a part of the title
commonly given to institutions of the kind. It is euphonic and tasteful. The
whole name is a good one, and, we trust, will meet with general acceptance.

The Board, trusting in the liberality of those in the Church who have the
means, has devised the plan, and will appeal to our people to furnish the necessary funds to carry forward this desirable enterprise. If that response which
should be expected is given to the appeal, it will not be long until we shall have
the Union Biblical Seminary in successful operation. We doubt not that if God
has a future mission for us as a people he will raise up friends to plead for the
cause throughout the Church, and especially that he will put it into the hearts of
the liberal, having the necessary means, to donate largely to found and establish
this much-needed institution. We feel it in our hearts to earnestly pray that he
may graciously grant so to do.

August 31, 1870   The Missionary Work

Some have been found—and we may rejoice if the number is few—who, while
professing Christianity, have been opposed to missions. It is indeed strange that
any one knowing the value of salvation, and who is moved by the love of Christ,
can fail to be an earnest friend and advocate of missions, and, if possible, directly or indirectly, a worker in the field. It was to save the world that Jesus gave
himself. It was for this he commissioned his disciples. It is for this he reigns, and
for this he sends out his Spirit. His intercessions and his providences tend to this
end.

The missionary work contemplates man's enlightenment. Darkness envel-
ops his mind and broods over his heart. His way is dark. Christ, who is the light
of the world, has chosen to communicate that light through the medium of human instructors—not alone, but in part, and that part essential and important.
"God hath chosen through the foolishness of preaching to save them that believe." Though substitutes have been found, yet preaching, if to be discarded, or
lightly esteemed, at the suggestion of human wisdom, has never been repudiated
by the Savior, who sends out chosen ones to preach the gospel "to every creature." Some suppose it has lost its power; but if genuine, it is at once foolishness
to the unbeliever and "the power of God unto salvation" to such as believe.
There is a want of faith in its power which must greatly account for the want of
success in missions.

Missionary support has its example in the apostoles' [sic] days. Paul received support of another church while he preached to the Corinthians, as he informs us. The love of Christ must constrain every live Christian to pray for the salvation of the world; and how can any one sincerely pray for that for which he will not labor? What kind of people are those who will say, Be ye warmed, be ye clothed, and be ye instructed, and yet will not give for these purposes? Are they not of the number who say and do not? On what kind of a foundation do those people build? What shall attend the descending of the rains and the beating of the floods? An unmissionary heart is surely an unregenerate heart. In what infinitesimal doses do some persons of respectable means imbibe the missionary spirit. Can their indifference be excused? or shall we file for them the plea of gross ignorance? If the latter plea fails, it will go hard with them at the bar of God. Are their souls lean? No wonder, for their gifts are unnecessarily lean, and so must be the hearts from which they proceed. They sow sparingly and reap accordingly. If men of several thousand dollars of property can content themselves with a dollar each, contributed annually to the missionary cause, their consciences must be easily satisfied provided their pocket-books are not too closely pressed.

The field is a large one. The frontier, the overlooked neighborhoods, the foreign field, are all white to the harvest. Millions upon millions, which have hitherto seemed shut out from it, are annually becoming accessible to the gospel. The necessities of various sections of our own country, as well as of distant foreign fields, call for our interest, our prayers, and our action. The openings in Asia, Africa, Europe, and in the minor American countries, to say nothing of the new settlements of the West and the destitute portions of the older states, demand that Christians should be wide awake, and that they should prove themselves in the strength of grace equal to the occasion.

Before the press began to throw off books and periodicals; before steam began to navigate the rivers and seas, and propel our machinery; before the telegraph and railroad was known; before commerce had penetrated every port, and brought every nation into communion with us and with each other, there might have been some excuse for tardiness in the cause of missions, but with these and with the demonstrations which the past half century have afforded of the utility of missions, he must be asleep who dreams that a few pence will meet the demand of the Lord on the comfortable means entrusted to his care.

While our Church has been increasing rapidly in numbers and wealth, there has not been that increase in missionary contributions which might have been justly expected. Some way we have failed to properly keep the missionary cause before our people and impress them with its importance. Perhaps a share of this neglect is attributable to our periodicals and a part of it to a failure to have them circulated as much as they ought to be. No doubt a considerable share of the delinquency rests with those who have failed as pastors and ministers to instruct and exhort the people to contribute. Some, perhaps, have failed to thoroughly comprehend the importance of the work, and hence they fail to make others believe what they do not realize themselves. But a very large share of the blame rests with those of greater or less means and greater or less ability to earn means, who have withheld their material support. They even pass by on the other side when the cry for help is heard appealing to their consciences. These incur a fearful responsibility. Their wealth becomes an occasion for the hardening of their hearts. Their danger is imminent. What shall be their reward! Thousands upon thousands need a thorough reformation on the subject of missions. A missionary revival is greatly needed. Perhaps few of us do not need a reconsecration to this work.

October 19, 1870   United Brethren Church in Indiana

We called attention some time since to the statement of "Lozier" in the *Western Christian Advocate*, that a considerable defection in the United Brethren Church in Indiana had caused valuable accessions to the Methodist Episcopal Church, especially in Indianapolis and vicinity. As this kind of a statement has been circulated by some of our exchanges, we will give what "Lozier" says in order that what we have to say of the matter may be the better understood. We quote from his letter to the *Advocate* of August 17th.

> Methodism in Indianapolis has made a big haul of good fish out of the United Brethren net. There was a weak place in said net, and it sustained an extensive and still-extending rupture, and the Methodist net being close beside them, and, withal, much like theirs, save the weak place, they came over to us. In short, the United Brethren Church of Indianapolis has come over bodily to us, including several prominent ministers and congregations in and adjacent to the city. Already a new church—'Massachusetts Avenue'—is projected by our new "brethren," and they will be found abreast with any of us in every good word and work. The cause of this defection is the extreme measures adopted at their last annual conference touching secret societies. It has already added a number of earnest and efficient ministers to our ranks in other parts of the state, together with hundreds of excellent people, and the end is not yet.

We shall make a statement of facts connected with this case that all impartial persons who may see this may form a correct idea of the matter referred to by "Lozier."

A small minority of the ministers of the White River Conference had flattered themselves and persuaded some others that at the (then) approaching General Conference, the law of the Church forbidding connection with secret societies would be repealed. Of the reprehensible means they used to accomplish their purpose we shall not now write. When they found themselves disappointed in the action of the General Conference they promptly called a convention at Indianapolis and passed resolutions favoring nullification and rebellion. Though this convention was small in magnitude pains were taken, by lying dispatches to the Cincinnati *Gazette* and colored statements in the Indianapolis *Journal*, to produce the impression that it was a convention involving a large portion of the minister and people of the White River Conference in its support; and these reports were widely noticed in the religious journals, many of which are under the dominion of secret societies. The convention appointed the time for another similar one, sent out circulars extensively, seeking to stir up to resistance and nullification, if possible, all, throughout the Church, who were favorable to a change of the rule on the subject of secrecy. The most ambitious among them evidently anticipated quite a general movement, of which they by superior pluck and enterprise expected to be chief leaders. Such a spirit of falsehood as accompanied the national rebellion characterized this movement from the beginning to its final collapse.

The next annual conference dealt mildly yet firmly with those engaged in the rebellion. It was a clear case, in which law and persistent rebellion were at issue. Three were expelled, and two withdrew. These, in connection with some three others who had previously voluntarily severed their connection with the conference, now undertook to organize what they styled the "Liberal United Brethren Church." They took with them the larger portion of the society at Indianapolis, and held the keys of the church-house there, refusing to allow the minister appointed to the charge to preach in it. Again dispatches relating to this conflict were telegraphed to the Cincinnati press, as before, abounding in misrepresentation. To false representations made in Indianapolis, the loyal members of the Church in the city made an able and candid reply, in the Indianapolis *Journal*, arguing with much force the justice of their claim. They also entered suit for the possession of their house of worship, which, after a number of months of delay, was voluntarily given them by the secessionists before the trial came on.

The new church held another convention, also a diminutive affair, appointed evangelists, projected a church periodical, and went out for the conquest of the world! Before a year had passed the leaders became sick of the enterprise, and ashamed of their organization, which had been baptized as the "Liberal United Brethren Church." They joined the Methodist Episcopal Church, claiming, we suppose, as Lozier has, that they came as ministers of the Church of the United Brethren in Christ, forgetting, we fear, to state that their transit was really from the defunct, abortive "Liberal United Brethren Church," of which they were now heartily ashamed. Lozier's draft of "good fish" was from that collapsed denomination which for the magnitude of its aspirations, the swiftness of its race, and the magnificence of its failure, ought to take the foremost rank among the prodigies of 1869-70. Lozier seems to say that several societies, in and adjacent to Indianapolis, from the United Brethren Church, have gone over to the Methodist Episcopal Church. This is true of only two societies, and they are of the defunct "Liberal" organization of which their spiritual fathers are ashamed. One of these is a small country society at a place where the United Brethren have about as strong a class as they, and a neat house of worship.

It is not true that the United Brethren Church in Indiana is disintegrating, or likely to do so. Such an attempt as was made by the "Liberals" to destroy the Church is not likely to be entirely unproductive of embarrassments, for the time being, in the regions where such wicked attempts are made; but large revivals have characterized the year in the White River and other conferences in the state, promising young ministers are being added to their ranks, and the future is bright with promise to the Church there. Indiana, according to late statistics, contains more than one sixth of the whole membership of the Church, being second to Ohio only in this respect. The movements in favor of rebellion have tended, in the White River Conference, greatly to the unification of the Church. At a future time we shall notice some references by out contemporaries to this matter, some friendly and some unfriendly to the Church.

March 1, 1871   Native Talent and Education

Some assume the native talent of men in general to be about equal. This illusion is easily dispelled by observation and discernment. Yet the difference between the intellect of the genius and that of the mediocre may be less, in sound sense and real knowledge, than many would suppose. Facility in bringing certain faculties into operation, agility in their action, and capability of their continuous exercise, to which these faculties seem to almost require superhuman inspiration, make the great difference between ordinary and extraordinary men.

Men of good perception, sound judgment, and extensive information, often fail to manifest extraordinary genius, while others, no more than their equals in these respects, shine as brilliant lights in their respective spheres. Perhaps we can not better illustrate this intellectual phenomenon than by presenting a corresponding physical one. We observe a man of good physical proportions. He is strong, is supple, and even graceful in his action; and yet, in the use of his nerves and muscles he is neither a good mechanic nor an accomplished artist, though he has spent years to become the one or the other. He possesses as fine physical qualifications as Apelles or Phidias, but his lack of faculty to put these into skillful and harmonious action, would in a line drawn or in a curve turned exhibit to the discriminating eye the marks of a bungler instead of the graceful touch of the hand of genius. Just so may a mind be strong and agile, and yet want the faculty of bringing itself into the most graceful and fruitful action. It may possess fine powers without the capability of bringing these into that operation which will be most fruitful in elegant and brilliant results.

It is the province of education to develop those faculties of the mind, and to bring them into skillful and fruitful operation. Some departments of science and literature may be mainly instrumental in producing strength, others in developing order, others in cultivating taste, others still in increasing the power of connected, symmetrical thought; but all, more or less, tend to discipline the mental powers and to bring them into patient and harmonious action, and to give them a strength before which the creations of ignorance vanish, and the intrenchments of sophistry become futile. If there is genius in the mental composition, education arouses it, and teaches its possessor his capabilities. It is astonishing that Christian parents should content themselves with but little effort to give their children facilities for mental cultivation. This neglect may be a sin of ignorance, but sin it is nevertheless. It is within the power of any Christian church, with the native abilities which it possesses in its membership, to move forward to the very front rank in talent and intelligence, if general, persistent effort be made to accomplish that end. We as a church ought to realize this; and, while the humility and simplicity of the gospel, and its precious spirituality, ought to be adhered to with the greatest care, we as a people are under obligations with our hearts and prayers and contributions and patronage, to seek the prosperity of our schools, academies, and colleges. *It is now full time that we were moving along the whole line in favor of our educational enterprises.*

June 14, 1871   Need of Missionary Zeal

In the past few years our Church has evidently made some advancement in the missionary cause; but there is still a great want of that zeal which should inspire us as a people. We do not so much want system—for ours is pretty good; nor management in the prosecution of our missionary work—for, in the main, our missionary affairs are well managed; but we need, as a people, a greater degree of missionary fire—more of burning zeal in the cause of Christian missions. This spirit we must have; and while we look to the great Head of the church for the outpouring of his Holy Spirit to produce it, it is proper that we should be such means as comport with scriptural precepts and example seek the baptism from on high, and proper enlightenment with regard to our missionary work. We should employ some means by which the great body of the Church shall be aroused upon the subject. It is not enough that a few officers of the missionary board should be warm in the cause. If these must warm the whole Church, their capacity for radiating missionary heat as well as light may be severely taxed. Some plan must be devised to reduce the number of icebergs on the subject of missions in the Church, or they will prove highly detrimental to the zeal of those who would otherwise abound with missionary warmth. While it is true that a few must kindle the missionary fire as far as human instrumentality is concerned, it is from the great body of the people that the warmth is to come which with intense heat is to melt opposition before it and mold the world in accordance with the will of God. We have been too long depending on fires on a small scale. The zeal of our Board of Missions and that of a few of our most earnest preachers and people, is something calling for devout thankfulness to the great Head of the of the church; but some means ought to be devised to make that zeal more universal among our people. Reserving for a future article the duty and influence of the press in this direction, we shall endeavor to urge the necessity of missionary meetings and anniversaries looking toward the awakening of our ministers and people to the importance of the cause of missions.

We have disciplinary provisions for the holding of annual meetings on all our fields of labor. These meetings, we think, are generally held by our itinerants; but they are not usually made what they ought to be, nor what the General Conference designed they should be. They are generally in a great degree inefficient; yet they are far better than nothing of the kind. It is well that our bishops so carefully inquire whether the itinerants perform their duties respecting the holding of those meetings. Would it not be time well spent if our worthy superintendents would give a half hour during each conference session to the instruction of the itinerants as to the best method of making those general missionary meetings a success? It can not be doubted that it would be beneficial. The object of those meetings should not be so much to raise funds directly, on that particular occasion, as to kindle the missionary fire in the souls of our people. To this end the meeting should be composed of the most efficient members of the whole circuit, together with such others as can be drawn together with them. It will tax the organizing capacity of the preacher in charge to the utmost to make arrangements to secure a general attendance of the efficient working members of his charge at those annual meetings; but he ought not to yield until the most complete success is insured. He ought not to rely mainly on public invitations and exhortations, to secure such attendance; neither should he be satisfied with equivocal assurances from members respecting the prospect of their being present; but he should have positive promises from dozens and scores of his best members to be at the meeting. These promises ought to be just as reliable as ministerial appointments. And when the meeting has assembled, not more than two or three good sermons ought to be provided for—and these should be full of fire—but the rest of the time should be employed in prayer and speaking by the members, including, also, remarks from exhorters and preachers, but brief and after the same style as those of laymen. If exhorters and preachers would throw off the ministerial style, and tedium, too, in social religious meetings, and just be laymen, they would cease to be regarded as detrimental to the success of those meetings.

Missionary anniversaries held after the style above indicated on each field of labor, would, in a few years, effect a great advance in the Church with reference to missions. Without being tedious, we can not in this article enlarge with reference to those anniversaries, but in the future we may treat of other meetings greatly needed to quicken the souls of our people, to stir the hearts of our itinerants, and to give more animation, faith, and efficiency to our Board of Missions.

August 9, 1871   Union Biblical Seminary

In the present number of our paper will be found an abstract of the proceedings of the Board of Education, which held its second session in this city last week. It was mainly occupied with the subject of the biblical seminary projected at its last session. Agents were chosen, professors were elected, and it was determined to open the contemplated institution, Union Biblical Seminary, in West Dayton, the 11th of October, 1871. Two traveling agents well and favorably known in the Church were chosen to solicit permanent funds for the seminary. These are Revs. Daniel Shuck and Wm. McKee. For the general financial agent, Rev. J. Kemp, who has himself donated $10,000 to the institution, was re-elected. President L. Davis, D. D., of Otterbein University, was chosen as senior professor, and Rev. G. A. Funkhouser, A. B., a classical graduate of Otterbein University and also of Alleghany Theological Seminary, was chosen to the second professorship. Both have accepted their appointments. We doubt not that the election of these will give general satisfaction, and we trust that the Church will enthusiastically come up to the support of its biblical seminary.

To sustain such an institution will require means and effort, but we believe there is a determination that it shall succeed. Though it must necessarily make but a humble beginning, yet it is to be hoped that, as it is an institution belonging to the whole Church, it will receive a support which will insure its rapid progress in its mission of usefulness. Probably some have not realized, as others differently situated have, the processing necessity of such a school of divinity. Without it we would be likely to lose much every year. Supplying other theological schools with students from among our graduates, we would, in some instances, by the associations and influences in which they would be thrown, lose them entirely, and in others, have them returned to us with such views and customs imbibed as would militate against their success and influence in the Church.

But there are a number who will attend Union Biblical Seminary who, without its opening, would not avail themselves of the benefits of a course of instruction the theology. It is not to be expected that for years a very large per cent of our ministers will be theological graduates, but we will doubtless have a respectable share of these who will at once be the means of assisting others in gathering biblical instruction, and serve to meet a want which every conference has of well-disciplined and well-stored minds, which are able to meet every influence which may be brought to bear against the cause of Christ. We have no sympathy whatever with the idea that only a very learned ministry is to be relied upon for efficiency in maintaining the honor of the Church and advancing the Redeemer's kingdom. We believe that men of little opportunity for leaning but of fine natural endowments, whom God has moved to labor in the ministry, will ever be successful in the use of the weapons mighty, through God, to the pulling down of the strongholds of Satan. The church of Christ on earth will never fail to have efficient and even accomplished men whose opportunities of attending schools, either theological or literary, will not be very good. These will do a large part of the work of the Church, but they should not and will not despise the advantages of which they by circumstances have been deprived. They will be zealous to afford others those opportunities which they have craved in vain.

It is true that by the increased efficiency of our common public schools the rising generation will in general be as well educated as many of those of previous ages who have been reverenced for learning by less favored associates; and hence few of good natural capacity will be unlearned, in the same sense attached to that term in ages past. But increase in the knowledge and intelligence of the masses will demand a similar advance with those who labor in word and doctrine. While the efficiency of ministers depends only in part on high training in science, literature, and theology, yet it is due to the character of Christian enterprise that the Church should have her full share of those possessing those accomplishments which add to their capacity and usefulness. In every age the most of those who have been great reformers in the church have been either theological professors, theological graduates, or fully qualified to rank as such. We may instance Luther, Melancthon, Jerome, Calvin, Bezza, Wesley, and Otterbein as among a host of theological professors and scholars who have blessed the world.

The United Brethren Church needs a biblical school, and if we move as we ought it need no go crippling in feebleness for years to come, but may be speedily raised to a degree of efficiency and respectability in which the Church may rejoice. Shall we not have a vigorous, earnest, general move for the support and advancement of our biblical seminary?

September 11, 1872   Our African Student

Such of our readers as have read the proceedings of the Board of Missions, as reported in the TELESCOPE, have observed that the policy of the Executive Committee to assist a young native African, D. F. Wilberforce, in obtaining an education preparatory to his return as a missionary to his native land, was approved by the Board, and a small allowance made to assist in his support the coming year. As this youth has been thrown under our care in a manner apparently providential, we can not see how we, as a church, can properly refuse to assist him in preparing for the work to which the Lord seems—it may be only seems—to have called him.

The father of young Wilberforce, hearing of the arrival of the Mendi missionaries in Africa, said that they were what he had long been desiring to see; and he at once repaired to the site of that mission, at Good Hope, and, though a heathen, was employed by them, to whom he proved a very trusty and valuable servant. This son, born at Good Hope, he named Daniel Flickinger Wilberforce, as an expression of the warm affection which he bore to Rev. D. K. Flickinger, our first regular missionary to Africa, who was at that time, as a temporary supply, preaching for the American Missionary Association, at Good Hope. Since that time the father has, we understand, become an experimental convert to Christianity.

When the child had grown to be a sprightly lad of about fifteen years of age, he accompanied a sick missionary of the Mendi Mission to America as a waiter, and after his arrival in New York was employed at the mission-rooms of the association for some time as an errand boy, in which capacity he proved not only very orderly and trusty, but extraordinarily expert. Last fall when the missionary secretary, Mr. Flickinger, was in New York making arrangements for our missionaries, Mr. Evans and Mrs. Hadley, to sail for Africa, he one day felt impressed with the duty of saying a few religious words to this orderly but active colored boy, whose good offices had for some days attracted his attention, but whose name, parentage, and native land were to the secretary entirely unknown and unsuspected. He introduced his homily by asking the boy his name. The reader may judge of Mr. Flickinger's surprise when they are told that the youth quickly responded, *Daniel Flickinger Wilberforce.* This led to inquiries and answers which developed the fact that this was the same child born at Good Hope, Africa, when Mr. Flickinger was there, but of whose birth and name Mr. Flickinger had become almost oblivious.

The youth expressing an ardent desire to obtain an education, and having already made considerable progress in the elementary branches, Mr. Flickinger, after earnest prayer and thought, and counsel with the officers of the American Association, proposed to the Executive Committee of our missionary Board to take the youth in care on trial for the purpose of educating him in hope of his becoming a Christian teacher, and perhaps a preacher in his native country, and in his mother tongue, for he well understands the Sherbro language, which is that used among the people where our African mission is located. The suggestion was adopted, and the youth came to Dayton, and was placed in a pious, intelligent family, members of our colored church here, and sent to the colored school, where his good deportment, devotion to study, and good progress elicited the highest praise from Mr. Solomon Day, the accomplished teacher of the colored public school. He is orderly, modest, polite, intelligent, and cleanly, and has a high place in the affections and esteem of the family in which he lives, the members of the colored church where he is a regular worshiper, and of our prominent brethren in this part of the city.

Last winter, at a revival meeting held by Rev. J. Nicholas, pastor of the Third United Brethren Church, one evening when the editor was present, young Wilberforce was soundly converted to God at the altar of prayer, and the next evening we had the pleasure of receiving him into the Church. Since that time his life and devotions have been such as become the religion of the world's Redeemer. Few American youths excel the pattern set by this native African; and we have just reason to hope that he will prove very useful somewhere, and probably in his native land, to which he proposes returning as soon as he has attained to age and culture sufficient to labor efficiently there.

We hope that the whole Church will pray that he may be kept by the power of God unto salvation, and that he may become a mighty instrumentality for the elevation and salvation of his race. Born in Africa, well versed in the Sherbro language, and possessing good mental endowments, he gives just occasion to hope that God intends him to do very valuable missionary work for the Church into whose care and communion he is providentially thrown. By race identified with his countrymen, (being a full-blood African,) having spent his youth among them, thus becoming completely identified in patriotic feelings with his native land, and being acclimated both by race and residence to the malaria of the western coast, it does seem that this youth, now about sixteen years of age, is peculiarly promising as a candidate for the African mission. Though we could not ordinarily approve of such an experiment as the Board is making, yet, as the cost is not large and the promise is so great, we can not but approve its action in this case in continuing for the present the education of this missionary, as we ardently hope he may prove to be. Will the Church pray that God may be glorified in the life and labors of this young native African.

September 11, 1872   Presiding Elders

That the office of presiding elder in the Church of the United Brethren in Christ has been a useful one in the time past will hardly be called in question. Some think, however, that its usefulness is mainly of the past, and are therefore in favor of abolishing it, or rendering it optional with conferences, fields of labor, and congregations. It is argued that the office involves an unnecessary expenditure of means, withdraws too many valuable laborers from the pastoral work, tends to exaltation on the part of elders, as it also does to envy among their co-laborers, and often unfits ministers for other work to which they may be returned after a term, or terms, in the presiding elder's office. It is true that it takes valuable men from the pastoral work; but the Lord intended that there should be some evangelists as well as pastors, and none are so well calculated to perform the duties of the former office as those who are most likely to be elected presiding elders; and that congregation which has no desire to have the preaching and other services of a presiding elder each quarter can not be presumed to be overflowing with either spiritual life or love for the ministrations of God's word. The cost of these ministrations, for which a very liberal equivalent is rendered, is a burden to no field of labor—nay, it is a very trifle compared with self-imposed burdens borne by professors in general without any valuable returns. If men are liable in the presiding eldership to spiritual pride, it is also true that many pastors are not less exposed, and that men who can not bear elevation may be spared exaltation either as to the presiding eldership or as to conspicuous pastorates. Envy will never fail, with or without occasion, to exist among weak, unspiritual ministers; and perhaps the best method of securing its destruction is by plain rebuke and direct suppression rather than by pandering to its whims or yielding to its dictations. If a term, or terms, in the presiding eldership spoils any minister for a future pastorship, either the mode of presiding elders' labors needs correction by the conference or a mistake has been made in electing a man to a very important position who should have been retired from the pastoral work and from the ministry as being too poor timber for profitable service.

There are certainly some good reasons why the office of presiding elder should be retained. Without general officers overseeing the affairs of a church, there is a want of unity and concert in doctrine, polity, and operation. The office unifies, concentrates, and binds the various charges together. It diffuses information as to church affairs through the various fields visited by the presiding elder. By him as a messenger the ministers and people of each charge are informed of the labors, trials, and successes of those of other charges. Plans and modes, as well as information, are thus extended far and near. If the presiding elder be a live man he will circulate life through all the fields of labor, and often stir up an interest at quarterly meetings—if they be properly attended—which will not subside without accomplishing much in the different congregations of the charge as well as among individuals. His plans and labors are also calculated to foster and promote the general enterprises of the church.

If a presiding elder possesses the tact and talent essential to the office, he will not only do much to secure the pastor's salary, but much also by planning, instructing, and working, to advance church building, the missionary and publishing interests, the Sabbath-school cause, and every other enterprise of the Church.

If a presiding elder be such a one as will adorn that position, he will consider all the interests of the Church, but especially the more important or most neglected ones, and he will labor in conversation, in quarterly conferences, and perhaps in the pulpit also, for their advancement. If he does this he will be very useful; and he may prevent many an error in doctrine or irregularity in discipline or practice which otherwise might terminate in schism or scandal.

It would be useless for a large army to expect any great efficiency without a system of general officers that would give it unity of purpose and action, and throw its force in full power into any and every general movement in which it should engage. Just so, it is folly for any itinerant system to attempt to accomplish the most complete success without general officers; and of these presiding elders are not less essential than bishops. Believing that the itinerant system is the best evangelizing plan known to the Christian world, we can not but favor the continuance of all those offices necessary to its complete success.

November 13, 1872   Visit to Otterbein

The writer of this article was permitted to have the pleasure of a visit, the third and fourth days of the present month, to Westerville, Ohio, the seat of our oldest institution of learning. A walk of three miles in the fourth watch of the night was invigorating preparation for the services of the next day, though so much could not be said of the watching and loss of sleep which preceded and attended this wholesome pedestrial exercise. By evening, the next day, the energies of the visitor were almost wholly consumed, but the Westerville church and Otterbein generally were all the same to themselves, only a little inflicted. The disadvantage of being off the railroad will pass forever from Westerville and Otterbein when, a few months hence, it shall be placed within twenty minutes' distance, by rail, from the rapidly-improving capital of the great State of Ohio. We can only add our testimony to that of all who have seen, as to the beauty and desirableness of the location of the village of Westerville. To our mind it will, with its railroad, be one of the most desirable locations possible for a college. It is beautiful, central, rural and yet very convenient to an important railroad center. Otterbein, with all its struggles and its fiery trial, has been exceedingly fortunate. The village, with its cherished institution, never had so fine a prospect before it as now. The co-operating conferences and the Church may well be proud of both the character and location of Otterbein University. Doubtless they do appreciate the institution, and we trust they will patronize it to the fullest extent and pour out their gifts freely in its behalf.

Westerville has a good citizenship; the Church there has a membership of two hundred and fifty; and all are united in zeal for the success of its public schools and college. The town is largely under United Brethren influence, and among other good things is the exclusion of drinking-saloons from the place, which means more liberty than free whiskey ever does. May the influence of the churches of the place, combined with that of all good citizens, preserve very jealously the good name and well-being of this moral town from the encroachments of the liquor traffic.

The Church at Westerville has been for nearly three years under the pastoral care of Rev. E. S. Chapman, of the North Ohio Conference, one of our most gifted and highly-valued correspondents, best known to the readers of the TELESCOPE as our "Washington correspondent" a few years since. His labors have been blest here at Westerville, the gospel yoke fitting him even better than that of the politician.

Otterbein is finely attended, better than at any period since the war, and its operations are proceeding at once vigorously and harmoniously. It could hardly be otherwise with such a president and corps of professors as Revs. H. A. Thompson and H. Garst, Messrs. Haywood, McFadden, and Guitner, and Mrs. L. K. Miller, all of whom, without exception, seem to be laboring earnestly to advance the students and to help each other in the common cause as educators and Christians. Indeed we regard it as one of the especial beauties of the institution that it has a faculty fully worthy of the name, and that counsel and co-operation instead of personal dictation control and advance all its internal operations.

The earnestness and skill of the faculty were apparent in the management of the recitations which we were privileged to hear. These were the class in natural philosophy, Prof. McFadden; logic, Prof. Thompson; Latin (Caesar), Prof. Garst; Grecian antiquities, Prof. Guitner; astronomy, Mrs. Miller; geometry, Prof. Haywood. We were pleased at the simplicity of the manner and methods of instruction on the part of the professors, and with the mental qualities evinced by the students. We believe that Otterbein, in instruction and class of mind to be instructed, should justly rank among the first-class colleges of the state. That our people should prefer it to all others is as much the dictate of interest as it is of church patriotism.

Otterbein is now furnished with an excellent building. Its site is fine, and the architectural proportions are good. It is commodious, convenient, well lighted, and well ventilated. The recitation-rooms are convenient and neat. The literary-rooms are being fitted up in beautiful style—worthy of comparison with those of the wealthy institutions of learning.

Without attempting an enumeration of the wants of the institution, it will not be amiss to say that it must have, in order to its continued success and advancement in unison with other first-class colleges, a very large addition to its endowment. Without large endowments the colleges of the coming century will be cast in the shade. The demands of the age for liberality in educational donations will not permit our people to be content with the day of small things, though that period in our past was not only legitimate but highly honorable to those who heroically struggled upward despite almost crushing discouragements. Theirs was the glory of the pioneer; ours shall be that of those who have inherited the fruit of their toil with the obligation to make improvement comporting with the enlarged opportunities afforded by the inheritance and the promise of the age to come.

Another want of Otterbein University is that of a library. What the institution had previously was destroyed when the old college edifice was burned. The friends of the institution have done well, thus far, considering the limited time and the feebleness of the effort put forth to this end, in replacing it. But the nice library-room in the college building is almost empty. Here are the well-protected shelves, but alas! where are the books? The patrons of the institution ought not to allow the college library to be rivaled and excelled, another twelve months, by the private library of President Thompson, though wealth has never lavished her smiles upon him. It is time that Otterbein should no longer be compelled to invite her readily obtained throng of students to empty shelves, and to refer them to professors and periodicals to supply a place which only books can fill. Otterbein must have an endowment, and her Board of Trustees and earnest agents mean she *shall* have, but an ample library, not less easily obtained, is equally indispensable.

Our visit to the town, church, and school was highly agreeable to the visitor, and while our previous impressions of the place, society, and school were good, they were decidedly improved by more intimate acquaintance. We firmly believe that Otterbein has a career before her which would, if realized, quicken the zeal of all her agents and enlarge the liberality of our beloved people of the patronizing conferences.

December 18, 1872   Our German Mission

Three years since, our missionary Board sent out to Germany Rev. Christian Bischoff and wife, as missionaries of the Church. They located and commenced their labors in the northern part of Bavaria. Bro. Bischoff met with considerable success the very first year of his labors; but the work was somewhat embarrassed by the fact that none but the denominations authorized by law have any legal claims in that country. This is common in the German states generally. Bro. Bischoff succeeded, notwithstanding opposition and some persecution, in gathering into the Church some sixty permanent members. Being advised by his brethren here not to break off all connection with the established church of Bavaria, for reasons which are best understood by those acquainted with the situation there, he did not organize a separate church, though otherwise his people were, to all intents, United Brethren. Within the past few months some twenty-six members have been added to the Church there, and the opening appears fair for accomplishing much good.

The prevailing religion of Bavaria is Roman Catholic; but the Lutheran Church is also recognized by the government. From the latter Bro. Bischoff has been of late making arrangements for legal separation, which perhaps ere this has become an accomplished fact. But, though the harvest is great and the opposition strong, Bro. Bischoff has heretofore been without ministerial aid. The Board has desired for some time to re-enforce the mission; but it seemed impossible to secure efficient missionaries to send to Germany, owing to the fact that our work among the foreign Germans in this country is also in need of more laborers. But this want of the German mission is now to be supplied.

Saturday, September 7th, Rev. Jacob Ernst and his family left New York on their way to Germany, to reinforce the mission there. Within a few weeks we hope to hear of his safe arrival in Bavaria. He is quite an intelligent and lovely man, and has an amiable wife and pleasant family. They will, we trust, well represent our Church in that country. We know them well personally, and though regretting their separation from the work here, we rejoice in prospect of what they may accomplish in the fatherland. Bro. Ernst was for some time pastor of one of our German churches in Cincinnati, and was engaged in his first year's labors in Toledo when he consented to go to the foreign work to which it appears the Lord has called him. He is a native of Saxony, from the town or vicinity of Schleitz, which has furnished some among our most efficient German preachers, as Rev. G. Fritz and A. Krause, of the Ohio German Conference. Bros. Bischoff and Ernst and their families will, we trust, have the prayers of our people generally. Oh, that the Lord would give them an open door and crown their labors with great success.

February 5, 1873   Death of Bishop Markwood

The hearts of thousands will be pained, as in the perusal of these lines they learn of the death of Ex-bishop Markwood. He died on the 22d [sic] of last month, at his father-in-law's residence, a few miles from Luray, Page County, Virginia. We learn this from a letter received by Bishop Glossbrenner, which does not give particulars, though it states that his funeral was to occur on the 24th instant. He had been sinking for five days, and seemed to be aware, the evening before, of his approaching death.

Few in the Church have had more or warmer friends than he. Certainly few have had more enthusiastic admirers. Having spent his life in the ardent labors of the itinerancy, and several years of his ministry in the office of bishop, he was not only well known in the Virginia Conference, of which he was a member over thirty years, but had thousands of personal acquaintances and friends in other parts of the Church. Thousands doubtless have sympathized with him in his six years of affliction, and very many will shed tears of sorrow over the news of his death. Warm-hearted, genial, brilliant, and abounding in the Christian graces, he was well calculated to be a favorite wherever he was known. But his earthly career is ended, doubtless not without that divine Presence in his last days which had been his support and comfort under several sad years of affliction, affecting, part of the time, both body and mind.

Ex-bishop Jacob Markwood was born in Jefferson County, Virginia, (now West Virginia,) December 25th, 1818, and consequently was at the time of his death in the fifty-fifth year of his age. In his tenth year he became the subject of religious convictions, and in his fourteenth year was converted to God, being filled with inexpressible joy and peace while kneeling at the altar of prayer at a revival meeting. At the time of his conversion he was an employe in a woolen-factory. He soon felt impressed with a call to the ministry, but want of opportunity for suitable preparation and a sense of his unfitness for the responsible duties of the sacred office kept him back till June, 1837, when he received license to exhort, which was exchanged the following September for quarterly-conference license to preach. He was soon traveling with the circuit preachers, rendering them most acceptable assistance upon their large fields of labor. The following March he was received into the Virginia Conference, and the next four years he spent traveling on the Hagerstown and South Branch circuits. In 1843 he was elected presiding elder, to which office he was generally re-elected until he was elected bishop at the General Conference held at Westerville, Ohio, in the year 1861. He has been a member of General Conference every session since he first took his seat as a delegate in 1845.

In the office of bishop, Mr. Markwood displayed the zeal and untiring energy and activity characteristic of the former portion of his itinerant life. Mental and physical exertion sufficient to impair the strongest constitution was his practice and delight. The rebellion having broken out and his native state having seceded from the Union he so dearly loved, about the time of his election as bishop, he could not in safety return to his former home. During the war he made a number of addresses on the state of the country; and these were always characterized by patriotic zeal and enthusiastic devotion to the cause of the nation. During his term as bishop his services as a presiding officer were satisfactory, and his pulpit efforts in general exceedingly popular. In 1865 he was re-elected bishop, but his health soon broke down so completely that he was never afterward really able to preside or preach, though his ardent temperament led him to preach whenever he possibly could; and we believe that the people were generally much interested in his efforts. All hope of his recovery was vain; and after nearly four years more of continued affliction he died in peace, and is now enjoying his everlasting reward.

Provisions were made by the General Conference for his support; and though the plan adopted was regarded by some as objectionable, all will feel the better for having contributed for his support—and, as we believe, all were heartily willing to do so.

Truly a great and good man is fallen in Israel. He was confessedly one of the brightest lights of the pulpit of the Church. In the zenith of his brilliancy and strength, he was arrested in his career of usefulness by disease; and he who had cheered thousands by his words of sacred eloquence was called to pass through many weary days and nights of earthly gloom, but never forsaken of his heavenly Father. That Savior whom he had preached to others with such marvelous power was with him to make his bed in all his sickness, to soothe, to sympathize, to comfort and strengthen. The evening before his death he remarked that he had done the work which the Lord had given him to do.

His wife, whose devoted love and tenderness during all the years of their union increased when affliction settled upon him, most tenderly cared for him whose care for her in others years, when ill health long threatened her life, had been such as few husbands are capable of manifesting. She undoubtedly has the sympathy of the whole Church; and may God's grace abundantly comfort her in this the hour of her sad bereavement.

February 12, 1873   Lay Representation

Some of the organs of other denominations have lately referred to the position of the United Brethren Church on lay representation, in a manner which indicates that they do not very well comprehend our church polity. At this we have no right to take umbrage, through perhaps they may have some right to complain that our church paper has not more clearly defined the real relation of the Church to this subject. In truth, there is not perhaps any church maintaining an itinerant system which has so direct and effectual a representation of the laity in its councils as has the Church of the United Brethren in Christ. In order to show this, some comparisons will be essentially necessary.

First, let us examine lay representation as lately instituted in the Methodist Episcopal Church. Its general conferences will hereafter be composed of a minority of laymen. But these laymen are chosen by an electoral college which is elected by the quarterly conferences; and these quarterly conferences are largely composed of the appointees and nominees of the preacher in charge, as he is also an appointee at the absolute discretion of the bishop presiding at the annual conference. The stewards and trustees, composing a large part of the membership of those quarterly conferences, though elected by the conference itself, are all nominees of the itinerants; and the class-leaders are the direct appointees of the preacher in charge. So from the foregoing it appears that while laymen compose the electoral college that chooses lay delegates to the General Conference of the Methodist Episcopal Church, the laymen of the quarterly conferences are mainly the appointees and nominees of the itinerant preachers. So that while that church has a good portion of lay delegates in its General Conference, it has little or nothing of lay representation in the true sense of that term. The great body of the people of the Methodist Episcopal Church have almost no voice at all in the selection of those who compose the quarterly, annual, or general conferences of that denomination. Those delegates are the representatives of a chosen few, not of the masses of the Methodist people. Then let it be remembered that the majority of delegates to the General Conference of the Methodist Episcopal Church are ministers elected by the annual conferences, which are composed exclusively of the itinerant preachers.

In the United Brethren Church, every member has a right to vote in the election of delegates to the General Conference. These delegates are chosen by a vote of the laity throughout the annual conference districts. These are clerical representatives of the laity, instead of being lay representatives of the clergy, as in some other churches. If the people prefer, they can elect every one of those delegates from the local preachers of the conferences—and it will be remembered that all preachers except itinerants are specifically defined as laymen in the discipline of the Methodist Episcopal Church. So every one of the delegates to the General Conference of the United Brethren Church might be laymen in that sense of the word.

It will not be necessary to say much of lay representation in the Methodist Protestant Church. The composition of the quarterly conferences of that denomination is less from direct election by the laity than in the United Brethren Church. But the polity of the Methodist Protestants is quite liberal,—perhaps more liberal than effective. Yet, though the delegates of that church to its general conference consist of an equal number of ministers and laymen, these are chosen by an electoral college in each annual conference, composed of about one third laymen, one third itinerants, and the other third local preachers,—the local preachers and laymen being elected not by a popular vote of the laity, but by the quarterly conferences. We believe the Methodist Church (composed mainly of what was once the Methodist Protestant Church in the northern states) is quite similar to the above in the composition of its conferences.

In the Wesleyan Methodist connection, the delegates to General Conference, consisting of an equal number of ministers and laymen, are elected by electoral colleges in the annual conferences. These electoral colleges consist of an equal number of laymen, local preachers, and itinerants. So, General-Conference delegates in that church are chosen by electoral colleges, of which about two thirds of the members are local and itinerant preachers.

While we do not regard the United Brethren Church as behind other churches in real representation of the laity, we are favorable to such measures as will give laymen a seat in its higher ecclesiastical bodies. It would bring our ministers and people into closer sympathy. It would increase the interest of the laity in our church enterprises. It would increase their sense of responsibility. It would give the Church the benefit of more of the financial skill and means of the laity. The laity would be pleased with such representation. Those outside of the Church would better comprehend the reality of our liberality in church government. It would give us increased prestige among the friends of free church governments. In conclusion, we may add that the United Brethren ministry are so far from a domineering spirit that they will most readily yield to the wishes of the people whenever they call for lay delegates in our conferences.

April 23, 1873   Our Day of Fasting and Prayer

The bishops, in the TELESCOPE of March 5th, announced the appointment of the last Sabbath in April as a day of fasting and prayer, to be observed throughout the Church. While designed as a day of prayer for all needed blessings, it was announced for the special purpose of invoking the blessing of God on the deliberations and acts of the General Conference, which is to assemble in this city the 15th of May. It is fit that the day should be appointed. It is highly proper, too, that it should be observed by all our people. The quadrennial sessions of our highest ecclesiastical body carry great importance with them. Measures are to be adopted which will affect the Church in one and more generations. These will tell in time and eternity. Evil measures, or mistakes, involve consequences of incalculable importance. Good measures will bring inestimable benefits to God's people. How fitting it is that the conference should be made the subject of prayer to Him who alone can guide his church aright.

The bishops ask the people to pray for the *purity* of the Church. This is in accordance with what the Lord teaches us in the words placed on record by the Apostle James, "First pure and then peaceable." Peace and harmony—also subjects for the prayers of that day—can not be hoped for unless we also have purity. Many ecclesiastical bodies have been sorely rent by attempting to harmonize the God of heaven and the god of this world. That surely has not, in the past, been the policy of the United Brethren in Christ, however, much they may have failed in attaining to that measure of purity to which the holiest men of the Church have aspired. We have no occasion to boast, but rather to humble ourselves in fasting, prayer, and supplication before God. He has done for us far above that which we have deserved. We ought to be very thankful that he has preserved us from those serious divisions that have afflicted many of the sister churches. We must confess that as a church we have been very far from being as pure as we should have been; but the aim and policy of the Church have ever been toward uncompromising purity.

The people are called upon to pray for the peace and harmony of the Church. As David prayed for the peace of the holy city, so should we pray for the peace of our Zion. That peace may be within her walls and prosperity within her palaces, are most appropriate objects of prayer. None but those who have seen God's people involved in dissensions and torn by distractions know how much of happiness and prosperity is lost by these. Well may such a church put on mourning. It is as the days of David when his own son stirred up Israel to civil war. The moral heavens are darkened; strife takes the place of prayer; the enemies of Zion rejoice in her self-consuming commotions. If our Church would have peace, subordination to the regularly constituted authorities of the Church must prevail. To do otherwise is to involve confusion and anarchy. But while the proper authorities of the Church should be firm in maintaining the right and rejecting the wrong, their rule should be free from harshness, vindictiveness, and tyranny. Firmness for the right, soundness, and spirituality are most favorable to permanent peace and harmony. Our people will not, we trust, fail to earnestly pray for "the purity, peace, and harmony" of the Church.

The prayers of the Church are also especially directed by the bishops to three great interests of the Church: the publishing, educational, and missionary interests. We do not all know the magnitude of these interests. Perhaps none of us estimate them as highly as we ought. Probably one of the especial objects of prayer should be for a more thorough enlightenment of those who may have these interests under their management, and for a more general diffusion of the light which should enable them to aid in the enlightenment of others. God can stir up our people to a better appreciation of these interests; and he is a God who hears and answers prayer. All our people surely ought to have some appreciation of the value of these interests,—enough to really pray for them, and prayer is an excellent means to open the door of the soul for the reception of that light which the Lord can give by his grace and instrumentalities. A real, heavenly baptism on these subjects would prove most efficacious in the promotion of these interests, and with them would follow a train of blessings over which our children and children's children might sing in ages to come.

But there is one thing that must be remembered. Without faith it is impossible to please God. Our people and the members of General Conference should trust in God. Man sinks; the flesh fails in his sight; but the spirit is meek, reverent, strong, when pervaded by a living, purifying, loving faith. God clothes the man of faith; God takes care of a people who trust in him. Like Mount Zion, they can not be moved.

God has raised us up. He has guided our fathers, and prospered us. If we are true to him he will not suffer our candlestick to be removed, nor our light to grow dim or cease to shine. God rules. This is our comfort and strength. If he takes pleasure in us, he shall make us to rejoice in the sunshine of his face. He is more than a match for all our foes. If he take not pleasure in us, it were better that we should, as a people, be wiped from the earth. But God is our sun and shield. In him is light and safety. Let all our people pray unto him and put their trust in him.

May 14, 1873   General-Conference Deliberations

We propose just a little talk about General-Conference proceedings. In so doing, it is just to remark that precept is much easier than practice. All general rules of propriety must have exceptions. This world abounds in anomalies. We merely desire to modestly make a few suggestions.

More than half the delegates elected to our present General Conference have served before as members of our quadrennial assembly. Of those who have not, a large number, by experience in other deliberative assemblies, have a respectable knowledge of parliamentary proprieties. What we may say will be only the utterance of thoughts not new to the body in general. Nevertheless it might be well for all to have them fresh in mind.

Every member who understands himself will feel that he should attempt no great display. It is well known by those of experience that attempts to distinguish one's self are likely to result in an *extinguishment*, even if fellow-members have mercy enough to leave all to the care of the self-inflicter [*sic*]. Perhaps in a few instances men of ability and worth, accustomed to exercising a potent influence at home, do not entirely comprehend the fact that the magic power they possess there can not be, in one day, transferred to a general conference. Assumption and presumption spoil everything in such cases, and the victim finds, too late, if he is teachable at all, how much he has lost by indiscretion.

Yet every member should feel that when he really has something to say, on any question before the body, no apology is needed for his expressing his views. Apologies for being a new member and all personal allusions, quite natural, especially when laboring under embarrassment, are to be carefully avoided. It is the subject, not the speaker, which should engross his own mind as well as the time and attention of the assembly. Time is very precious. Others, perhaps, have equal desire, as well as right, to be heard on the subject. Therefore apologies, preliminaries, etc., are very much out of place. They try the patience of those who desire progress and dispatch in business. They consume time on trifles and leave golden thoughts unuttered.

Again; much that members feel like uttering must be voluntarily suppressed. All can not be said. No one should claim the privilege of being heard simply because he feels like speaking. Too many good utterances make a surfeit. Enough is enough on any subject. Yet it is a hard precept to apply to one's self, though we may see that others should not persist in protracting discussions.

Many injure their cause and disgust an assembly for lack of making a personal application of these truths to themselves.

Generally, a few remarks will tell more, if well directed, than a long speech, and reflect more credit on the speaker and the assembly. Remarks too much extended are tiresome and repulsive, though they may be otherwise good. They become dull as lead, though far less weighty.

Some persist on being heard on almost every subject. They are too obtuse to perceive the affliction they perpetrate, and their persistence becomes most observable and repulsive. Nothing but inflexible good nature would permit any one to refrain from wishing them out of the assembly. Their unpopularity becomes well-nigh unanimous. They do not even admire each other.

The parliamentary tricks sometimes practiced in political or other secular assemblies should certainly have no place in religious bodies. We believe they usually do not with us. Unusual stickling for certain ideas of parliamentary law is rather pedantic than profitable. Usually the rulings of the chair are quite correct, and, when rendered, should not be questioned without weighty reasons for so doing. It is scarcely necessary to add that no Christian gentleman will fail to treat a presiding officer with respect, and even deference, and conform to his decisions until duly reversed by the assembly.

In order to make the public proceedings of a deliberative body most efficient, committee work must be well done. This can not be unless committeemen, outside of the committee-room, give their best thoughts to the subjects referred to them for consideration. If they will duly consider the questions when at their boarding-places, talk with those informed on those subjects, note and arrange their thoughts, they can truly add efficiency to committee work; and they ought to be ashamed to be mere appendages to any committee. Well-done committee work saves time, prevents confusion and humiliating public exhibitions.

It is said by old members of some ecclesiastical bodies that cases of attempts to spring propositions upon an assembly at a period so late that a considerable part of the members have gone home, or when there is not time to duly discuss the questions raised, are not very uncommon. In all such cases a rebuke is deserved. If such untimely propositions are made, the prompt tabling of them is but just, and any other course is but a question of expediency. Fair, magnanimous dealing is all the kind tolerable in a grave, religious assembly.

Those whom our people have sent to represent them in the General Conference, as a general thing, do, without doubt, understand the value of divine aid and the efficacy of prayer. Their prompt attendance at the daily services of devotion, during the session, will not only profit them and further their work, but it will exercise a most wholesome influence on all who may be in attendance as visitors. A general conference ought, in spirit and in truth, to be a very devotional body.

June 18, 1873   Camp-meetings

The children of Israel were required annually to spend a season worshiping in booths or tents. It was doubtless good for them spiritually, and perhaps equally good for their physical well-being. Retirement from their ordinary dwellings and occupations, and continued attention to worship and spiritual themes, were eminently calculated to favor a devotional frame.

Perhaps camp-meetings in this latitude are also good for Christians. With proper sanitary regulations, they are certainly excellent for physical health. Indeed, to those shut up in close dwellings during most of the year, they are a delightful change. Those tired of house life will know how to appreciate them, and perhaps at their close will know better how to value the homes, of the monotony of which they had grown tired.

That camp-meetings, properly conducted, are good for spiritual health will not be denied. Shut out from the fastidious luxuries of home, the lungs inhaling the free air of heaven, all hearts finding a common utterance at the altar in public worship, and the voice of song and prayer measurably freed from the cramping forms and restraints of the regular church-service, the humble disciples of our Lord will acquire a devotional frame and enjoy seasons of spiritual feasting such as will ever afterward be sunny spots in in [sic] the memory of their pilgrimage toward their heavenly home. Christians of different neighborhoods and of different denominations meet and form acquaintances, and by mingling together in worship are bound by ties which connect neighborhoods and kindred denominations more closely together. Thus the cause of the Master is more unified in their souls, prayers, and efforts. Their hearts become warmer, stronger, and larger.

There is the greater need of camp-meetings because without them there is likely to be too little special effort during a large part of the year for the salvation of the unconverted and for the building up of converts in the faith of the gospel. If protracted efforts are mainly or wholly confined to the winter campaign, will not the result be a tendency to make our religious growth periodical rather than continual. Protracted efforts in other forms than camp-meetings may to a great extent obviate this difficulty, but it is doubtful whether annual meetings "in booths and tents" will not prove a most valuable agency for good to such as have the will and enterprise to organize them.

Camp-meetings should be put under close police regulations, such as the laws of most of the states allow, and the ordinances for the preservation of sobriety and order should be firmly enforced. Two regular policemen, in full uniform, will be worth more than a score of unauthorized, unskilled patrolmen. Order can be had by ample provisions for it, and the meeting will thus be saved from harrowing conflicts with the disorderly.

It is true that there are difficulties in the way of carrying on these meetings. One of the chief of these is a tendency in a class of church-members to make enterprises out of them instead of spiritual meetings. The class of members alluded to are too likely to be allowed to seize upon these undertakings and organize them—perhaps conduct them too—without much heart in the real work to be accomplished. They suppose such enterprises could not be run without them. They do run church enterprises indeed, but run them far from Christ and heaven. Camp-meetings should be placed under the most pious and judicious management. Piety and spirituality should be the great objects, and everything else should be subordinate to them.

In some sections of the Church camp-meetings are common. In others they are almost wholly unknown. Is it not worth while for our ministers and people to inquire whether such meetings can be made useful in places where there is now little concentrated effort in behalf of the salvation of sinners and the edification of believers, during the long, weary seasons of labor and care? May it not be well to inquire whether the difficulties which have caused camp-meetings to go into disuse are such as are insuperable? We do not believe sufficient difficulties necessarily exist to destroy the utility of these meetings; and while we do not hope to bring all to see as we do, we do hope to add a mite of encouragement at least to those who are now using those meetings for spiritual good in the sections of the church where they are laboring for Christ's cause.

December 24, 1873   Our Centennial at Hand

Our Centenary year is near at hand. It is to us, as a church, the year of jubilee. We have little more time to prepare for it. We ought to do a great and good thing, in the year 1874, for God and the Church. Duty and gratitude call for a thank-offering to the Lord. From a handful, he has within a century, increased our numbers to one hundred and thirty thousand souls. We have been saved through all that time from any schism of serious magnitude. God has given us grace, through a hundred years, to stand together. He enabled us to stand firmly against human bondage,—a system that entailed guilt upon nearly the whole continent, that rent asunder many Christian denominations, that drenched our land in blood and almost rent in twain our nation—our country. God has vindicated the righteousness of the great principles of humanity, justice, and liberty which he taught our fathers by his word and by his Spirit, and which they and their children, through obloquy, defended until, in his providence and in his judgments, he overthrew slavery and planted liberty, and the rights of freedmen to citizenship, among the guaranties of our national Constitution. God has been with our fathers, and with us, when dark clouds overspread our skies, when deep waters were before us, when enemies howled against us and gnashed with their teeth, when the strength of man was feebleness and human comfort was cheerless. He has been our light in darkness, and has given us grace notwithstanding our unworthiness. Christ has opened our way, fought our battles, and crowned us with victories. He has strengthened our hearts, enlarged our borders, and given us increased facilities for happiness and usefulness. He has caused us to sing in the valley and to shout from the top of the mountain. The Lord has done great things for us whereof we are glad. Notes of praise, works of love, and offerings of thankfulness ought to distinguish the year one thousand eight hundred and seventy-four, in the Church of the United Brethren in Christ. Where is the conference, the field of labor, the society, the family, or the individual, in the Church that has not abundant occasion to praise the Lord for mercies and blessings, past and present.

Standing on the borders of our centenary year, let us retrospect the time of our conversion, those precious seasons of grace, those holy transformations by which friends and relatives have been made companions with us in the heavenly way. Our thoughts may be in part of tears, of wrestling prayers, of sainted farewells, of distance or years of separation; but they will also be of joy unspeakable, of hope full of glorious anticipations, and of a heritage transmitted to us by those who have crossed over death's stream, committing to us, as a sacred trust, those interests for which their tears had fallen, their prayers had ascended, and their toils had been given through many years that deeply tried their faith and constancy.

As we think of the history of our country—of its trials, its victories, its heroes, its statesmen, its laws, its institutions, what it has done for us, and what we have suffered or sacrificed for it,—how our patriotism is kindled within us. Our hearts swell with emotion; our souls are on fire. When we talk of the days of our childhood, when we remember the loving looks, words, and deeds of a father, of a mother, remember the caresses of brothers and sisters,—some of them far away, and some of them sleeping death,—when, in retrospect, we travel from youth on to manhood and womanhood, and recall innumerable, precious memories that come from the nursery, from the playground, from the hearthstones, from the chamber of affliction, from the scenes of toil, from all the departments of our dear old home, clustering around the old family tree, how sweetly and closely are our hearts drawn by the ties of kindred to the parent stock in all its branches. Others, no doubt, had homes and friends as precious to them as ours to us; but to us, no other home and no other family are half so dear. So when we go back over years of life in our department of the Christian church, when we call up its history,—think of its trials, its victories, its ministers, its heroes, its institutions,—consider what it has done for us and what we have sacrificed for it,— remember the prayers and longings and labors we have invested in its behalf— then our affections and enthusiasm are drawn out toward our dear church-home. Its precincts, its institutions, its people its history, its monuments, are ours, and our feelings are not a little akin to those of the patriot who says: "This is my country—my own dear, native land." And, when we recall the shining countenances, the sweet words, the loving deeds of fathers and mothers, brethren and sisters in the church; when with them, we in memory, sing over again the songs which were like harmonies from the borders of the land of Buelah; when we, in memory's vision once more float together on prayer till we bathe in the holy atmosphere which gathers around the foot of the ineffable throne; when we remember how we were with them enveloped in a cloud of glory, or how we first mingled our tears for mourners in Zion and next shouted victory together in sympathy with their newfound joy; when we think of our mutual instruction, comforts, and affection; when we think of the dead gone to heaven before us, and the far-away living whom we hope to meet also in the better land; when we remember the funeral services, the communions, and all the sacred memories which gather around the church of our choice, we feel our affection to our church-home rising with strong desire, and all feel like having some part in the thank-offerings of our "year of jubilee" the most we need, after all, to make our centennial a success, a harvest unto the Lord, is a heart full of love to him and to the Church.

December 31, 1873   Our Next Year

To-morrow the Church of the United Brethren in Christ shall have entered upon the hundredth year of its existence. Our jubilee is not divinely appointed in the strict sense of that term, though semi-centennials, called years of jubilee, were enjoined upon the Israelites. They were required to hallow the fiftieth year, the second of which would be of course a centennial. But our observance of the hundredth year is not divinely enjoined. It is purely voluntary. Yet it seems fitting, and will no doubt call forth the enthusiasm of our people in a large degree, and their devout thanksgiving and liberality with great unanimity. It is not a small debt of gratitude that we owe to Him who has been with us and prospered us during one hundred years.

One hundred years ago a band of converts, after the endurance of reproach and persecution from formal churches which abhorred the life and power of religion, had the satisfaction of seeing a little church organized which recognized and enjoined evangelical piety of heart and holiness of life. They were few in number, and possessed little influence, except at the court of heaven. They had sought for years, not division, but peace; yet they were put far away from formal Christians on account of the love and zeal they exhibited. Little could they then have thought of the spread of their organization from sea to sea, and that theirs would become among the most numerous in membership of the Christian denominations of some of the great states of the Union. Little could those fathers in the Church have thought of such a situation as is now that of the Church which they were then organizing. Now the representatives of the Church gather within a few days from the Atlantic and Pacific states in our generalcouncils [*sic*], and after adjournment, are in a few days again at their homes ministering as usual to their several congregations. Our prosperity and our privileges have certainly exceeded all their expectations. What prosperity and what changes shall the next hundred years bring us? God only knows. But if we are faithful to him, there need be little doubt that, if time continue, a hundred years will bring changes that would seem as marvelous to us, could we in vision contemplate them, as our present would be to the fathers if they were to come up from their graves and look upon it.

But what are to be the objects of our contributions during our centennial year? The fact that about one third of the present membership of the Church is the fruit of our missionary efforts, and the fact that its facilities for success have been, and still are, far less than they should be, will sufficiently recommend that arm of our church service. The command to go and "preach the gospel" will still be our marching orders, we trust, and with the assurance of Jesus, "Lo, I am with you alway, even to the end of the world," will be our cheer.

When the homeless condition of many of our churches on the frontier and in destitute places is considered, and the great good that can be done with a few thousand dollars, to be loaned, returned, and reloaned, to help in the erection of churches, is appreciated, surely there will be no lack of heart and liberality for our church-erection enterprise.

Our biblical seminary, an institution delayed too long, but at last auspiciously begun, and now doing great good, though so inadequately supplied with means, will be appreciated by those who are awake to the necessity of increasing the qualifications of the ministry of the Church, and to that of educating our own most gifted and enterprising young preachers, instead of consigning them to the schools of other denominations. This enterprise will doubtless receive its full share of our people's liberality.

Our colleges which are more and more appreciated by our people every year,—those institutions which have greatly added to the membership and influence of the Church, and which have blessed so much those who have attended them—will, we are confident, receive large additions to their funds. Their endowment, their libraries, and their indebtedness will be looked after with the most earnest care by the people of the several patronizing conferences. Large contributions to increase the funds of those institutions ought to be expected during the centennial year. Our college interests are among the most precious in the Church.

There are also local interests, such as building churches, parsonages, etc., that should receive large sums. Not that these interests should be allowed to absorb contributions due the general interests of the Church. Yet extraordinary efforts for local interests (all of value to the general cause) ought to be encouraged, and reckoned as part of the centennial offering to the Lord. Large funds in some cases can be had for such purposes that can not be obtained in any other way.

Our donations should be largely in cash. For some purposes, notes of a large denomination will be in place. The centennial year ought also to be one of large bequests. Many could bequeath thousands of dollars, and die at last the happier for so doing. This branch of benefactions is too little looked after by our ministers, and too little considered by our people.

Our aim in our centennial offerings should be God's glory and the welfare of the Church. What do these require? should be our constant inquiry. Let us inquire of the Lord and our brethren, and act accordingly. We ought to remember, too, that the example of each one will tell much toward promoting the liberality of others or retarding it. Let not our acts this year leave memories desirable to be obliterated, but such as will cause the mention of the name of many a donor in coming years to be as the pouring out of precious ointment. Let all our various church interests be in the most harmonious fellowship this centennial year. It will be best for all, and acceptable to God. May God put into the hearts of our people much unanimity and great liberality.

January 21, 1874   Has the Church a Constitution?

Thirty-three years ago, our fathers adopted a Constitution for the Church. Under its operations eight general conferences have been held; the territory of the Church has been doubled, its membership tripled; a missionary society with considerable endowment, with large annual collections, and with extended operations has been founded; a church-erection society has been called into existence; our Printing Establishment has changed location, acquired considerable funds, and become a power in the Church and in the land; seven colleges have been established, and several academies; a theological institution has been founded and put into practical operation; the Church has acquired property worth about three million dollars, and has become one among the leading denominations in numbers and influence in not a few counties and in some of the best states of the American Union. Under the provisions of this Constitution, far more than nine tenths of the members of the Church have been received, and to the authorities constituted by it have been committed by departed worthies bequests of no inconsiderable sums. If our Church Constitution is not of binding force, as all our provisions for electing delegates, etc., are in it, we have not held a legally-constituted general conference for thirty years past; we have no legal bishops, nor other general officers of the Church; our annual conferences have no legal boundaries, if indeed they have at all any legal existence. Indeed, it may be questioned whether the Church itself has any legal existence. Either we have a constitution or it is a fiction. It is either a real constitution or it is no part of our ecclesiastical framework. If it is not a real constitution, it is a fraud—*a fraud huge and unprecedented.* But some may be ready to exclaim, "What Rip Van Winkle has awakened from the slumbers of a quarter of a century to call in question a Constitution not only desired by our people, but which they have eight times, by general vote under its provisions, impliedly reaffirmed and sanctioned, and the validity of which their representatives, in the highest judicial as well as legislative body in the Church, have again and again affirmed by overwhelming votes?" Be not too fast; it may come from a source honored and even official. Let this be the apology for an editorial defending the validity of our Church Constitution; for our official duty requires the repellance [*sic*] of any attack on the organic law of the Church.

It may seem that our centennial year is unsuitable for the raising of such a question. Grant it. Yet some may consider the overthrow of a constitution as an end so desirable as to justify whatever sensation the proposition to treat it as a nullity may produce. Indeed, were not such a proposition from a source of characteristic gravity, and were it not known that the idea has been broached seriously, though rather timidly before, it might be regarded by some as a joke of rather huge proportions. Probably it is better that such a proposition should be above-board than in an undercurrent, and perhaps it is best that the proofs of the validity of our Constitution should be clearly presented.

There is no specific, universal rule by which a constitution is to be adopted. Generally it is done either by the requisite majority of the people who are to be governed by it, or of their representatives. The Constitution of the United States is ordained in the name, not of the states composing the Union, but of the people,—"We, the people of the United States," etc.; yet it was never submitted to a popular vote, but ratified by the legislatures of the different states composing the Union. We believe that while the constitutions of some of the states—probably most of them—have been submitted to a popular vote, some of them never have. The State of Rhode Island held, for sixty-six years after the formation of our national government, the charter granted by an English sovereign, as its state constitution. The *Magna Charta*, the ground-work of the English Constitution; was, by force of arms, extorted from King John, at Runnemede, in June, 1215.

Yet who calls in question the validity of our national Constitution, those of any of the states, or that of the English nation? Those who would do so would not be likely to obtain much consideration in any national or state legislature, or in any supreme court in christendom [*sic*]. It would be regarded as bare-faced absurdity.

The circular published by order of the General Conference of 1837, claimed that if general notice had been given to the Church previous to the election of delegates, that there would be a memorial presented to the General Conference, praying that body to adopt and ratify a constitution, it would have had full power to do so. Such notice was given in that circular four years previous to the sitting of the General Conference of 1841, and that body after discussions, which, from the published reports, did not appear to call in question the legal right to ordain such a constitution, decided, by a vote of fifteen to seven, to adopt one; and so they did. As the form framed in 1837 was confessedly of no binding force, they acted on the well-known wish of their constituents and adopted a constitution, embracing—but in a much improved form—the essential provisions of the former, adding the clause on slavery and secrecy (those twin sisters), and making all future amendments impossible, except, when requested by two thirds of the whole society.

We shall now show that this constitution was so generally and universally approved by the people that their representatives, elected by a direct and popular vote, have promptly and repeatedly reaffirmed its validity. And let it be remembered too, that this body, including its presiding officers, is the highest authority in the Church on any question of legality, and so it was from the very first organization of a general conference in the Church. These decisions on the validity of the Constitution form a line of precedents that no intelligent court in Christendom would attempt to set aside or reverse. The whole history of jurisprudence will sustain this remark.

Early in the session of the next General Conference after the adoption of the Constitution (that of 1845), action was taken incidentally affirming its binding force in a paper adopted excluding two persons of Indiana Conference, who claimed to be delegates from the same. During the same session a resolution, moved by J. J. Glossbrenner, was adopted, affirming it to be out of the power of the general conference to make proposed changes in the Confession of Faith, *because the Constitution forbade it.* This resolution was adopted by a vote of *fifteen to eight,* even those who voted in the negative explaining that the changes proposed were merely intended to make the meaning of the Confession of Faith clearer, and not to change the sense, and hence, in their view, not in violation of the Constitution.

In the General Conference of 1849, owing no doubt to some feeling against the clause on slavery and secrecy, a resolution was offered affirming that the Constitution was illegal. The reason then urged in favor of the resolution was the same as is now urged against the validity of the Constitution. But this resolution was *rejected by a majority of more than eleven to one*—thirty-four voting for it, and only three in its favor—*two* according to the conference journal. One, at least, of those in its favor had voted the reverse four years before, and it is well known that he in after years earnestly maintained the binding force of the Constitution. After this vote a quarter of a century ago, the question of the validity of the Constitution (questioned by few before) seems to have been regarded as settled beyond dispute.

A report on the subject of lay delegation was adopted by the General Conference of 1857, incidentally but fully recognizing the validity of the Constitution. Also in the debate on secrecy, the same session, the binding force of the

Constitution was fully recognized by the ablest speaker among those favoring modification of the law on that subject, and we believe that not one who voted with him expressed an opposite view on that point.

In the General Conference on 1869, a resolution moved and seconded by delegates very hostile to the clause on secrecy, incidentally but positively affirmed the validity of the Constitution.

The late General Conference, by its action on lay representation, fully recognized the binding force of the Constitution.

If in the face of proofs so abundant and so conclusive we were to deny the binding force of the Constitution of the Church, it might be charged with some show of justice that intensity of prejudice, partisan feelings, and nullification proclivities had overcome our better judgment. Surely we could not resist the conclusive testimony of facts confirming the validity of the Constitution of the Church.

Another argument of great force, and clearly legitimate, but not really necessary in the abundance of other evidences, is found in the well established principle of law and jurisprudence, that any contract or compact generally acquiesced in and almost universally approved for a long period by those who are affected by it, is recognized by all respectable authorities as of binding force, even if all the legal technicalities had not been strictly observed in the original making of it. This is true as regards titles, and in a still fuller sense as to marriage. It is most clearly proved that the Constitution was valid from the very day of its adoption; yet if this were unproved, the general acquiescence of the Church in its provisions, and its well-known general approval for a third of a century, would alone be conclusive as to its validity.

We conclude, then, that the plan of Constitution framed in 1837 was confessedly not regarded by its framers as binding, and hence was not a finality; that it was evidently regarded by the people and by the general conference of 1841 in the same light, though its essential provisions (some of which are omitted in the quotations on our third page) are incorporated in an improved form in the Constitution adopted in 1841. This view was taken in discussions in the general conference of 1849, and affirmed by a majority of more than eleven to one—if not really of seventeen to one, as the conference journal records.

The validity of the Constitution is affirmed repeatedly by papers adopted in the General Conference of 1845, and it does not seem to have been really questioned by any. Since that time it has been—down even to the present year—repeatedly reaffirmed by the highest authority in the Church on questions of legality. All our General Conferences for over thirty years have derived their existence and legality from its provisions; hence, also all the institutions and titles to the property of the Church. Nearly all the membership have been taken into the Church in accordance with provisions made under its legal authority. It has stood without any open and general dispute, concerning its validity for a third of a century—almost wholly without question for a quarter of a century, thereby deriving unquestionable authority by age, acceptance, and continued uninterrupted operation. The legality as we have intimated of nearly everything in the Church, hangs on its really unquestionable validity, and we fail to see the wisdom of attempting to put flames to our whole ecclesiastical compact to get clear of some constitutional provision unacceptable to some, just as we fail to see the wisdom of a free-holder in burning down his mansion to get clear of a sky-light which his fancy leads him to dislike.

This editorial has been induced by views expressed in an article on our third page setting forth the other side of this question. The discussion of one or two points mentioned in that article we omit to notice, intending an expression of opinion at no distant date, though from a sense of propriety we have hitherto carefully abstained from any expression while the final action of the bishops on the question submitted is not yet given. We have regarded general discussion (and, we might suggest, conference action) as premature, until that decision has been rendered. But our view of this matter has not, of course, governed in the case. We are yet of opinion that the decision of the question will be made by the bishops, and will prove satisfactory to the Church in general.

April 5, 1876   Rights of the Church

There is a specious proposition that, "Whom Christ receives, the church *must* also receive." This may be true in a certain sense; but, as it is not true that every member of Christ's church is bound to receive into his family every one whom Christ embraces in the kingdom of grace,—at least, unless such a one conform to the regulations of that family,—so it is not true that any church is bound to receive persons into its visible organization unless they will conform to those regulations of that church concerning which the majority of its lawmaking body must decide; and that in harmony with its organic law, or constitution.

All organizations, churches included, must have regulations. The church is not a liberty-hall, where liberty is to be perverted into license, anarchy, and evil. The idea of discarding the imperative obligation of the members of an organization to conform to its regulations is *anti*-organization; and ecclesiastically it is *anti*-church; for a church is an organization, and organization implies regulations to which its members *must* conform. Organization is for harmony and strength; not for anarchy, internal collision, and the weakness which these inevitably produce. The church *must have* some authoritative regulations; and if it is its duty to receive all converted persons, it is its duty *only* on condition that they conform to its regulations. If the church has obligations, so have its members; if they have prerogatives, *so has the church*.

The idea that the church is bound to receive all whose claim to conversion it can not disprove,—without any conditions of conformity and obedience on the part of those claiming membership,—may be plausible and popular; but it is very absurd; and if baldly stated it would appear exceedingly silly. It allows men to claim the benefits of organization, and repay these with disorganization. It proposes to allow men to enter upon the benefits of order by bringing in disorder and confusion. Such a theory may do in cases requiring no regulation or authority, just as quaker-guns may do excellent sham service in time of peace; just as open carriages may be as good as any in fair weather; and as ducks and fish and clams are independent of floods. It will do only for sham service; and no church, whatever its professed theory, carries it, in all things, into practice.

Some say that a church is bound to receive all who give evidence of being Christians. Yes; evidence in part by conforming to the regulations which their brethren deem necessary; not by trampling order under their feet and disregarding the rights of the church, and the Christian judgment and feelings of those composing the denomination whose privileges and endowments they crave. But to sit in judgment on the internal religion of the professor is not the prerogative of the church. We can not authoritatively read the heart. We are not set to judge men's religion, as if on the final throne. We deal only with men's conduct; nor can we reject some whom we do not regard as genuine Christians, till they, by immorality or disobedience to regulations, subject themselves to discipline.

There is scarcely a disorder or sin which has not had some respectable advocates—advocates who in other respects might pass for Christians. Let those who clamor for "liberty" (license) in the church, try it as respects slavery, Sabbath-breaking, polygamy, and the use, sale, and manufacture of intoxicating drinks. There have been, in other respects, some pious slave-holders, Sabbath-breakers, distillers, and dram-drinkers. Shall the church refrain from disciplining sins and evils because these have befooled some good men? Is there not the more need that the authority of the church should be brought to the rescue of men from such sins and evils? Whenever the church places its moral standard so low as to exclude no sin or evil which any man, reputedly pious, indulges in, it lowers it very near to the borders of perdition.

Some things, not in themselves sinful, can not be tolerated in any church. Singing is not in itself sinful; yet if indulged while the pastor is in the midst of a discourse, or when a deliberative body is in the midst of its proceedings, it would subject the disorderly person to discipline; and persistence in such conduct would warrant his expulsion. Churches have rights—not only in this but in other respects—greater rights than some have imagined.

The Scriptures teach that the spiritual Jerusalem is the mother of us all. They teach us to reverence, obey, and harmonize with the church. The uncircumcised are not to defy Israel in the church of God. The member of church must refrain from the sin or evil which the voice of his brethren condemns. He must not assume the right to practice that which they deem wrong or injurious.

He must not be like the juryman who taxed his eleven fellows on the panel with contrariness, because they would not substitute their judgment for his.

God has ordained governments, not only civil, but ecclesiastical. He that is disobedient to either resists the ordinance of God. And it is the duty of governments to require conformity. Errors in this regard have proved disastrous. The laxity of our federal government ripened into "states rights," secession, and sanguinary rebellion.

If the church claimed the right to compel all within a given territory to be in its communion, and the right to enforce by corporal penalties its behests, then the claim of anarchists to exemption from its regulations might seem more reasonable. But the church is a voluntary organization. No one is compelled to take part in it; and hence it is inexcusable if any bring disorder and contempt of law and regulations into it. Ecclesiastical looseness has, at certain periods in church history, run into great excesses: in the Church of England, in the Lutheran, and in the Reformed Church. It is now running wild in some of the churches of this country. If we would escape the shoals on which others have been stranded we must have some enforced regulations. If some say, "We must have no law obnoxious to even a minority," how long will it be, on this principle, till a multitude of minorities shall raise the cry against every measure not approved. They would simply cry out, "We can not bear it," and thus compel the majority to yield.

The very idea of entering into or remaining in an organization to antinomianize and anarchize is either nonsense or deviltry. And of those who refuse to conform to the regulations of a church, by refraining from a forbidden evil, it will be found that in nine cases out of ten their religion will finally prove not to be genuine. Few gentlemen,—even if not Christians—can consent to occupy so dishonorable a position. Some do not rightly consider this matter, and there are no doubt a number of exceptions; but in general those who persist in trampling under foot the regulations of their church are not, in any true sense, valuable members. The disobedient sin against peace, order, the spirit of charity; against their brethren, and thus against Christ.

May 31, 1876   Reception of Our Missionaries

Last Thursday evening the Sabbath-school of the Third United Brethren Church (on Ludlow Street) gave a reception, in expression of their love and esteem for our returned missionaries, Rev. Joseph Gomer and wife, whose labors have been so successful in the Sherbro country, West Africa.

Among those present—for the house was full, mainly of colored people— were Rev. W. J. Shuey and wife, Mrs. Lanthurn, Rev. D. K. Flickinger, J. W.

Hott, D. Berger, S. M. Hippard, W. McKee, G. S. Lake, and others of the United Brethren Church, and Drs. Webster and Bradley and others of other churches. The tables, containing cakes, etc., were very nice, the ice-cream of the most approved quality, and the floral decorations neat rather than profuse—the colored people always ranking high in good taste. We presume the missionaries had not often been feasted on ice-cream in Africa. Bro. Gomer is probably fifteen pounds weightier than when he left for Africa five years ago last December. His wife, though she has suffered some in health, now looks as if a tropical climate has proved healthful to her.

After songs by the Sabbath-school, the pastor of the church, Rev. G. S. Lake, led in prayer. Mr. Solomon Day, the superintendent of the school, in a very neat address, welcomed home the missionaries, saying that the present demonstration was little else than the spontaneous outgoings of the feelings of the teachers and scholars of the school; that they claim the missionaries, in some special sense, as their own. He recounted the sacrifices of the missionaries briefly, spoke of their worth, and concluded by again expressing the warm feelings with which the Sabbath-school welcomed their former superintendent home.

Bro. Gomer responded, saying that this was to him and his wife a happy occasion—one of the happiest of their lives. He said that it was a great trial, five years ago, to leave them and his aged father, who had since fallen asleep; but after they had fully consecrated themselves to God and the work they were happy. He said that they prayed all the way over to Africa, and God was with them. They had been discouraged by assurances that the work of bringing the heathen to Christ was slow. Truly, it was slow; but when some came to Christ they rejoiced. When first they arrived in Africa they were gazed upon by the heathen natives, who wondered to see a colored man and woman dressed as white people. They had sometimes been, while at Shengay, very sick, and sometimes felt that death was near; but God had preserved them, and they were glad, now, once more to meet those who in former years had preached the gospel to them and those who had attended Sabbath-school with them. "We have tried," he said, "to please those who sent us and who have supported the work; but above all we have tried to please God." Not a murmur had he heard from his wife's lips while there, nor had *he* felt to complain. Some whom they had won to Christ has passed in triumph to their home on high, and others were still serving Jesus and witnessing for him. He felt that God has been pleased with their labors, as his blessings have plainly showed. He said he was glad to be appreciated of his brethren; yet he feared he might be tempted of pride. The Scriptures abounded in condemnation of this, one of the most hateful of all sins. In a list of hateful sins, a proud look is mentioned first by an inspired writer. He read the scripture beginning with this sentence, "Take heed that ye do not your alms before men, to be seen of them: otherwise ye have no reward of your Father which is in heaven." He said: "We are the weakest instruments ever used of God to promote his cause." He said he feared pride, and remembered that Herod, when he took to himself the glory ascribed to him by the people, was smitten of God.

He related some incidents of travel and labors in Africa. One evening the missionaries visited a native village. Truly, the people gave them a *warm* reception. Having traveled all day, and being goaded by the flies as they had passed along, they desired to retire, as early as possible, to rest and sleep. But around them gathered a large number of young women, to whom they preached the gospel as best they could for half an hour, and, telling them they had told them as much as they could remember, they ceased to preach. But the girls expressed impatience and eagerness to hear, and cried out, "Talk more," which the missionaries were constrained to do, for some time longer. Having been assigned a mud hut—the best the natives had—as a sleeping apartment, they assayed sleep; but here the rats interfered and kept nibbling at their toes, not even wholly shielded by the protection which their country cloth afforded. And soon after the men of the village surrounded their hut with drums and other rude musical instruments, making a din which was kept up till midnight, as a demonstration in honor of the "big strangers." When the men retired the women of the village also got up a demonstration in honor of the "big strangers," which lasted till seven o'clock next morning, giving the missionaries little opportunity for sleep.

Bro. Gomer also gave some account of a visit which the missionaries recently made to Turtle Islands, which gave glimpses of the terribly degraded condition of the heathen natives.

After Bro. Gomer had concluded, Rev. D. K. Flickinger made some remarks on the work in Africa, and on the elevating influence of Christianity as it is demonstrated in the lives of some of the early converts of Sherbro Mission. He also mentioned the fact that Brother and Sister Gomer had agreed to return to their work in Africa after spending a few months here, the time of their return to be about the first of next December.

The songs, the refreshments distributed, and the conversations of this reunion were the closing features of a very enjoyable, and, we trust, profitable occasion.

June 14, 1876   Bishop David Edwards

A truly great man in Israel has fallen. Bishop Edwards is dead. Nations mourn their great; how much more may the Church mourn her worthies, only she weeps not as those who have no hope. Bishop Edwards is recognized by thousands, throughout the Church to which his heart and life-labors have been given, as living still. He was a Christian; he now lives with Christ, whose image he bore for so many years. He was a moral hero; he mingles now with kindred heroes of all ages, in the presence of their peerless Captain. He was a servant in the Church, but a kingly one; he is a servant still, but glorified, a kingly priest at Christ's altar on high.

A native of North Wales, his heart was too large and his mind too strong to embrace in his love and heart's sympathies less than two continents, or less than two worlds. All races were near his heart; Christ's servants everywhere were his brethren, the dearer in proportion to the closeness of their conformity to his precious Savior's image, and the identity of their footsteps with those of Jesus of Nazareth. His fellowship was broad and full and tender; but he could fellowship no sin or wrong. Integrity was his staff; righteousness was his garment, but it was emphatically the righteousness of Christ, accompanied with peace and joy in the Holy Ghost.

With talents which would have been conspicuous in any of the lucrative learned professions, with financiering abilities of no mean order, he gave his years, his labors to the Church he so much loved,—himself a friend and jewel in the general church of Christ; he lived economically and even frugally, dispensed liberally and died not a beggar nor a pauper, but not rich as to earthly possessions. He counted himself happy to spend and be spent for Christ's cause, and especially for that branch of the church to which was given the vivacity of his youth, the strength of his manhood, and the treasures of his experience and age. Indeed, he lost not with years the freshness and clearness of his mind, the warmth and courage of his heart, nor the charm of his voice of sweetness and melody. His eye (mentally, morally, and physically speaking,) dimmed not with his threescore years; but his last years were his best and strongest—we had almost said the brightest of his life.

Few men ever loved the church of their choice as he loved his, as those most intimate with him, and who knew him best these many years, could abundantly testify. To his people he could truly say, "For what is our hope, or joy, or crown of rejoicing? Are not even ye in the presence of our Lord Jesus Christ at his coming? for ye are our glory and joy." We almost hear from his lips, now mute in death, the apostolic language: "Now we live if ye stand fast in the Lord." It was no ordinary sense in which he loved the Church of the United Brethren in Christ. During his last most painful sickness, when too weak to hear anything taxing his attention, he called for and heard with the intensest interest and solicitude anything relating to the operations and prosperity of the Church. Her bishop of twenty-seven years was all that time, and to his last conscious moment, her bishop in heart and spirit. From his youth a fearless champion of reform, of Holy Ghost religion, of the higher Christian life, he closed his eyes upon this world full of these grand, heaven-approved principles, and rose to that blessed realm where these are never unpopular, but ever approved of the Master, and of all around his throne.

In his friendships, the bishop was warm and constant; nor did his love and appreciation of men depend mainly on personal intimacy. He read men's character and qualifications with great discernment, and appreciated their gifts and qualities of mind and heart almost irrespective of personal association with them, and entirely without regard to personal support to be received from them; and whatever of disesteem he might feel toward certain qualities of any it did not prevent his doing justice to any good quality which such might possess, nor prevent a tribute to their gifts and usefulness. His judgment of men was, in a remarkable degree, tempered with charity and generosity, even toward those not in harmony with him in policy or in personal feeling.

He had great influence, wherever he went, with ministers, not from personal friendship purely, but from their appreciation of his piety, integrity, impartiality, and honest devotion to his convictions of truth—for his masterly intellect, his greatness of soul, and his moral heroism.

He was as firm as he was clear in his convictions and positions—and time has demonstrated that he was rarely wrong; yet he was eminently practical and ever ready to reconsider and even sometimes change his positions, or radically change his methods.

As a preacher, Bishop Edwards was always clear, manly, able, and instructive. He was generally spiritual and powerful, exerting a remarkable influence on his audience, and not unfrequently, especially on great or peculiar occasions, his eloquence was, almost beyond comparison, overwhelming. Often have we seen him hold audiences spellbound for an hour, and many times carry them to the very heavens in enthusiasm, or completely melt their hearts with tender emotion. His best efforts in these last-mentioned respects we have never seen surpassed, and rarely have we known anything which would compare with them.

He was a model presiding officer, a rigid disciplinarian, nor would self-seeking ever come in to induce him to relax wherein duty and conscience demanded strictness, though his administration often displayed all the leniency of a spiritual father. In order and discipline he exerted a wonderful influence in the conferences and in the Church. We could not say too much of his eminent and faithful services in this regard.

In his remembrance of fields of labor in a conference and of any information he ever gathered concerning them, and in his knowledge of itinerants, their characteristics, their history of successes and failures at each particular point of labor, the bishop was simply marvelous. In most of the conferences over which he presided he seemed to know more than the presiding elders in this regard. And, while on a stationing committee he was far from being a dictator or an impracticable, his conscience and his loyalty to Christ's cause would not permit him to be indifferent as to whether the assignment of itinerants to their fields were in harmony with the will of God and promotive of the prosperity of the Church.

The bishop was the early, life-long, and outspoken friend of the oppressed slave, the equally open enemy of intemperance, and not less so of the secret lodge, and all clans; and as such he was recognized fully by the friends and adversaries of great evils. He gave the trumpet no uncertain sound on these questions, however much hated or menaced for his noble principles.

We write these things having had many years of intimate acquaintance with Bishop Edwards and his labors, and for a considerable part of that time having sustained the most unreserved personal relations with him. What we write are the sentiments of years, and we suppress eulogy rather than color anything we write in exaltation of one whom hundreds of ministers, with ourself, venerate as a spiritual father in the gospel. Of him the beloved and sainted Bishop Markwood said, many years ago, to Rev. J. W. Hott, in personal conversation, speaking, it may be, somewhat strongly, as was his wont, in the warmth of his heart, when eulogizing those whom he esteemed and loved: "I have looked at Bishop Edwards upon every side. He is the best man this Church ever had. It never has seen his like; it will never see it in the time to come."

Of course this if not to be understood in its most literal sense as to the dead or the living, or as to the future, expresses well the esteem and love of a warm-hearted colleague.

Bishop Edwards filled, in his life, nearly every office in the Church: class-steward, class-leader, exhorter, pastor, presiding elder, editor, bishop. Besides he has been a member, officer, and active worker in nearly or quite all the important boards of the Church; and he has presided in important bodies not denominational with marked ability. Seven times has he been elected bishop, generally by a decided majority, and the last time by the largest majority given to any for that office. He has filled every position he occupied, faithfully and efficiently.

The bishop is taken away at a time when human wisdom would say he is much needed. His district and the whole Church mourn for him. Even those who differed with him in some points of policy were in other respects under his influence. His personal influence disarmed hostility.

The memory of Bishop Edwards will live green in the hearts of those who have been associated with him at any time during his long years of eminent public service. We trust that measures will be immediately taken to raise a fund thoughout the Church to erect a suitable monument to his memory, on the beautiful spot beneath which he rests in Woodland Cemetery. We trust, too, that persons having knowledge of interesting facts relating to his life and labors will write out the same and send them to this office, to assist some suitable person to whom they may be in the future intrusted [sic] to write his biography.

Like all saved by grace,—the only method of salvation,—the bishop realized all the more as death drew near that Christ was all his plea; and he felt that all his desire to live would be "to preach salvation by faith in Christ alone." Much did he preach Christ while he lived; but in his death he felt that more of Christ, and especially of salvation through the merits of Christ alone, would be the burden and delight of his sermons if he were permitted again to preach the gospel to his fellow-men. Well might hundreds of our ministers heed these dying words of Bishop Edwards, and not merely talk, but *feel and preach salvation by faith in Christ alone.* May the spirit of our blessed Savior give us as ministers to appreciate those words of our bishop beloved, as he neared the confines of immortality.

December 27, 1876   Separatists

In the history of the Christian church, there have been two classes of men who have separated themselves from established ecclesiastical organizations. The one does so for greater purity; the other, to be less pure. The latter class often claim to be reformers. They are retrograders—ecclesastical backsliders. The former class have a noble record; the latter, always an ignoble one. The latter generally fall, perishing of their own principles, or being swallowed up by the world, or by some ecclesiastical organization quite earthly in its spirit and affiliations.

Among those who have separated for purity's sake, the Vaudois are an example. Their testimony to pure doctrine and pure faith and life is a treasure in the history of the Christian church. The same is true of other Italian reformers, as also of the Swiss. The Huguenots are a noble example, shining in France, as papacy and infidelity have there only cast shadows. The Lutherans struck, also, for greater purity, and made a noble record. So the Reformed Church of Holland.

The Presbyterian Church of Scotland and the Episcopal Church of England are examples of striking for greater purity than before possessed; the Quakers and Puritans likewise. All these have made noble records. The Wesleyans struck for greater purity, and their record is no longer in dispute. The United Brethren in Christ organized for greater purity, and it stands as one of the churches of the Lord's planting. So did the American Wesleyan Connection, and exerted a powerful influence by its testimony against the cruelty, fornication, and robbery of American slavery.

But there have been separatists whose principles and proclivities have been adverse to purity. They have generally been failures—many of them ignominiously such. Among these the Methodist Episcopal Church South, the southern Associate Reformed Church, and the southern Protestant Methodist Church may be instanced as the most honorable and successful of those which have gone off as anti-puritan separatists. Baptizing slave-holding, slave-breeding with its concubinage and its sham marriages, its slave-trading with its auction-blocks, coffles, slave-pens, and slave-hunting, does not constitute a glorious record for churches. Neither do the inciting of a rebellion to overthrow a free government and establish one based on the corner-stone of human bondage, and preaching and praying for the success of the rebellion, add to the glory of those anti-puritan separatists. Neither does their glory sparkle to-day in the whippings, mutilations, rapes, and murders which southern pulpits ignore, or cry, "It is naught."

The Evangelical Christian Union, which came in counter to the struggle to put down the slave holders' rebellion, and to comfort sympathizers with the Southern Confederacy, has not been either glorious or successful as an organization; but now "its shade still stalks on some dread cost," etc. And descending to notice separatists of less magnitude, the "Republican United Brethren Church," which was organized in Indiana about the year 1853, on the corner-stone of toleration of slavery and secret societies, has proved to be far from a heaven-ordained church. A similar organization in Pennsylvania has, in success and enviable history, nothing more to boast. A similar anti-puritan separatist movement in eastern Indiana, in 1869, culminating in the organization of the "Old United Brethren Church," the holding of an annual conference, the election of presiding elders to go out with gifted helpers to evangelize the world,—and especially the United Brethren Church,—on the basis of toleration of Freemasonry and other secret societies, has neither laurels, success, nor long life; and its surviving friends desire no chronicler of its achievements. As in the case of a similar movement in West Virginia years ago, (nipped in the bud, thought it actually attained to the possession of a newspaper organ,) those then connected with it little boast of their relation to it, though some connected with the incipiency in the mountains of the then "Old Dominion," now call, like revolutionists, for their followers to get their *ultimatum* ready.

When men labor for anti-puritan reforms or as anti-puritan separatists claiming to be reformers, they do but ignore all the lessons of ecclesiastical history. They attempt what Christ would not authorize, and what Satan has never accomplished except by lulling the church into slumber or beguiling it, as Balaam taught Moab and Midian to over-come Israel by stealthful temptation instead of violence. There is a singular uniformity in the history of the anti-puritan separatists and "reformers" of all ages. "He that sitteth in the heavens shall laugh: the Lord shall have them in derision."

April 18, 1877   Does God take Pleasure in Us?

The psalmist declares that "the Lord taketh pleasure in his people." All scripture indicates and affirms that our heavenly Father regards his people as his "portion" and his "jewels," and keeps them as the "apple of his eye." And in the New Testament Christ is represented as loving the church as his bride, even to the shedding of his precious blood for her cleansing and salvation. What is true of the church in general is especially true of such portions of it as are most faithful to him,—to such as are "faithful witnesses," such as "*love* righteousness and *hate* iniquity," "hate evil," "hate every false way," and "keep themselves unspotted from the world."

The Lord may suffer his faithful ones to be afflicted and tried for a time, as he did Joseph and Moses and David and Daniel and Job; but if he take pleasure in them he will show them his favor at last. Joshua and Caleb said that if the Lord took pleasure in Israel he would give them victory over their enemies and bring them into "a land flowing with milk and honey." David, retreating before the rebellious Absalom, said to Zadok, the high-priest, "Carry back the ark of God into the city: if I shall find favor in the eyes of the Lord, he will bring me again and show me both it and his habitation; but if he thus say, I have no delight in thee; behold here am I, let him do to me as seemeth good unto him." What a precious faith and spirit is that of David as an example to the church of trust and resignation at any time when afflicted by those within it, and beloved of it, though erring and rebellious in spirit. M noah's [sic] wife reasoned well when her husband was affrighted at the sight of the angel which conveyed a gracious message to them, and whom they saw ascend toward heaven in the flame of the altar of their sacrifice. She said, "If the Lord were pleased to kill us, he would not have received a burnt-offering at our hands, neither would he have showed us all these things, nor would as at this time have told us such things as these." So the church, in evidence of the Lord's favor in the past and present, may find reason to trust and hope for the time to come.

It may be a question of some interest to many in our church, "Does the Lord take pleasure in us as a people?" We have just reason to trust that he does. Have not the people of our church from its origin been "faithful witnesses" of the vital truths of God, and against abominations which the Lord abhors? When unregeneracy, formality, worldliness, and sins prevailed in the German churches of the East, in the midst of which our Church had its providential origin, were not our fathers faithful witnesses of the necessity of the new birth, of the value of vital religion, and examples of godly lives? It may be a small thing in the eyes of many, but not so in the sight of God. They also bore witness against abominations prevailing around them. While other churches tolerated and apologized for human bondage,—which necessarily included in its train the slave-whip, the auction-block, the slave-coffle, the slave-ship, the slave-market, the slave-pen,—our fathers refused to sanction or fellowship it, and when we came to have general rules they forbade it among our people—even so early as the year 1821. All this was done when all the churches, except a few, passed the abominations of slavery unrebuked. And we, it must be observed, have with those few excepted churches stood shoulder to shoulder in battle against other popular evils. So early as the year 1821 we also adopted a rule against the great evil of intemperance, which, though it would be sanctioned now by nearly every church of the land, was then far in advance of any of the popular churches of America. This faithful testimony against an evil, the magnitude and ruin of which is beyond all estimate, does not indicate that the Lord takes no pleasure in us as a people. Our testimony against secret societies, and refusal to tolerate the lodge, dates back to some months prior to the Morgan murder being made known to the public; and our General Conference of 1838 adopted a stringent rule forbidding our people from connection with the lodge. Other churches have approved temperance principles when these became overwhelmingly popular, and condemned slavery when universal disgust cried out against "the sum of all villainies," and they will do the same on secrecy when it again falls into disrepute, as some of them did in the days of its former disgrace. Will God not remember the church which has stood faithful, through evil report as well as good report, against the three great evils of our age and country—slavery, intemperance, and secret societies?

No doubt many who have long prayed and labored for the welfare of our Zion feel deeply afflicted with the spirit and words and acts of those who apparently aim to compel our Church to affiliate with secret orders, as, years ago, some strove to persuade our people to affiliate with American slavery, and with the manufacture and sale of intoxicating beverages. But no devoted friend of the Church ever saw so trying an hour as Caleb and Joshua experienced in the presence of demoralized Israel, nor as bitter as David realized before the threatening hand of the unfilial Absalom. Yet those holy men of old, relying on the Lord's pleasure in his faithful people, could have the strongest faith in the ultimate issue. Nor need any fear that the Lord who has raised up, preserved, and blessed our Zion, will give her over to the triumph and derision of her adversaries.

April 18, 1877   Pro-rata Representation

There are two principles of representation known to political and ecclesiastical governments. The one is representation according to organization; the other, according to population. The former is seen in conventions of national governments, in legislative bodies (as the United States Senate), in many if not in most ecclesiastical councils—as presbyteries and synods. The latter is seen in our national House of Representatives, in one or more branches of state legislatures, and in a degree in some church councils. The common sense of mankind has in all ages and in all countries where representation is known recognized both of these principles of representation as well founded. We believe there is something, and that not a little, in both of these principles. Therefore, while we believe in pro-rata representation in degree, we do not favor it in the absolute.

We heartily sympathized with the pro-rata principle when the question was raised at the General Conference at Western, in Iowa, in 1865. We expressed our views in a speech in the General Conference in Dayton, in 1873, as appears in the published proceedings of that body. As we have only one legislative body for our Church, we think that the true method of representation would be found in something like a medium between that of our national Senate, which gives equal representation to each state irrespective of population, and that of the House of Representatives, which gives representation according to population.

We have never considered some conferences oppressed under our present mode of representation. We believe the cry sometimes raised of "oppression"— "taxation without representation"—is generally regarded by the most intelligent people of our Church as being for effect, like the cry of political leaders, whose arts are sometimes copied. The leader who raises it certainly risks the credit of partaking of the nature of a demagogue, and those who echo it along the line of being too easily deceived. Yet we believe that pro-rata representation in degree is right, and we feel confident it will be conceded when proposed and advocated in a truly fraternal spirit and unconnected with secondary objects supposed to be the exciting cause of its being asked. We regret when we see the adoption of a principle with which we sympathize almost hopelessly defeated, or long postponed, from injudicious advocacy.

There is hardly any church that has adopted the principle of *simple absolute* pro-rata representation. The presbytery of the Presbyterian Church is composed of all the ministers within a certain district and one ruling elder from each pastoral charge. If the pastoral charge has one hundred members its representation is just the same as if it had five hundred. The same is true of the synod. The principle of representation for organization rather than for number of people harmonizes with Presbyterian polity. The General Assembly, however, is composed of representatives from each presbytery in proportion to the number of ministers in the presbytery—each minister, as a general thing, being supposed to represent a pastoral charge of a greater or less number of members. This principle of representation of organization is substantially the same, we believe, in the various Presbyterian denominations, including also the Reformed and Lutheran churches.

The Methodist churches in general know nothing like pro-rata representation in their quarterly or annual conferences, and where anything like a pro-rata principle is found in any of their bodies it is based on the number of *ministers, not the number of people* which these ministers in any way represent.

In our own quarterly and annual conferences the pro-rata principle is entirely wanting. A class of ten members has a right to just as much representation in quarterly conference as a class numbering one hundred. A charge of one hundred members has just as much representation—if it be representation at all—in annual conference as a charge of three hundred. If anyone were to raise the cry about "intolerable oppression" or "taxation without representation" on account of lack of pro-rata representation in our quarterly or annual conferences, it is likely he might be suspected of crying for effect, or of having some other as the major object in view; nor would he have much right to complain of being thus suspected. But that does not say that a nearer approach to pro-rata representation may not be really desirable as to our quarterly, annual, and general conferences.

We might show that under the Jewish theocracy the two principles of representation we have mentioned were recognized. But not only is this true, but it is also true that a principle of clerical prerogative in councils was also divinely recognized. And what is said of these principles of representation and clerical prerogative applies also to the primitive Christian church, as appears from the New Testament and from ecclesiastical history.

We are pained when we see the pro-rata principle prejudiced in the house of some of its friends. This is done when it is too closely associated with the advocacy of the nullification of law and of the constitution of the Church; for to nullify the enactments of the legislative body of the Church is *to deny all the rights of representation,* and also *to strike at the very existence of all law and all authority.* The cause of pro-rata representation is also injured when it is associated with disrespect toward local ministers, proposing that from these shall be taken the rights of which the constitution says they shall not be deprived. Some of the best men we have ever known were in the local ministry. It is a good element in the Church. Those who heap contumely upon it evidently overlook the most worthy and fasten their eyes on those less worthy or less efficient, or on those whom they dislike because standing in the way of some favorite scheme. Many years of actual experience in itinerant labor enables the writer of this to know that this is a worthy and valuable element in our ministry.

We have said little on this subject because we have had little hope of effecting any harmonious advance toward pro-rata representation when a violent method of advocating it is resorted to, or when it is made subsidiary to some object which excites the strongest feelings of opposition on the part of our ministers and people. We think, however, that such an advancement would not materially affect any other question over which there is earnest contention. Most of the strong conferences, numerically, are devoted to all our long-established principles on moral reform. Neither could we be influenced on *this* question by any other question now before the Church or any that may arise. *If a principle is right it is safe to recognize and adopt it.*

May 9, 1877   General Conference

The session of the General Conference is at hand. As at other sessions, there is much to be done. One of the principal things is the revision of the Discipline.

This may involve some change and adjustments; but these should be as sparing as possible. Continual changing of arrangements and phraseology is to confuse and mislead both those who obey and those who administer law.

The General Conference also is to look after the various interests and institutions of the Church. Among these are the Missionary Society and the Church-erection Society, the Printing Establishment, Union Biblical Seminary, the General Sabbath-school Association, and our Sabbath-school and educational interests at large.

We as a church are carrying on missions in Africa and Germany, in the frontier states and territories of our own country, and home missions in all our conferences. Upon these to a very great degree depend the growth and prosperity of the Church.

We also have a publishing house which has now a magnitude, financially, worthy of notice, if it be not large compared with some other publishing houses.

One of the things worthy of consideration is whether, in view of the favorable condition of the finances of our publishing house, it might be advisable to order an annual dividend of the net profits of the publication of our church organ, the RELIGIOUS TELESCOPE, to be made to the several annual conferences. If this dividend should be made, so that each conference shall receive a share proportionate to the number of paying subscribers which the paper has in the bounds of its district, annually, it would furnish special incentive to each annual conference to increase the circulation of the church paper, and would prove a great blessing to the people—increasing their intelligence, their interest in church affairs, and promoting the happiness of every family receiving its visits. There is good reason to believe that this policy would within a few years *more than double the circulation* of our church paper, and increase the profits of its publication to *five times* that of the years past. We hope this suggestion will receive the favorable consideration of the General Conference. It may require some care; but it will not be impracticable to make such a dividend of TELESCOPE profits to the several annual conferences. A dividend proportionate to the paying subscribers in each conference would cause each annual conference to see that all its itinerants become live agents to circulate the church paper, thus adding to the present good-will a most wholesome incentive.

The General Sabbath-school Association has expended a few thousand dollars the past four years for the advancement of the Sabbath-school cause in our church. A considerable part of this went to furnishing periodicals to Sabbath-schools in regions rendered destitute by grasshopper ravages. This had the double happy effect of blessing destitute Sabbath-schools and keeping up the circulation of our Sabbath-school periodicals, which otherwise would have been considerably less. The TELESCOPE, in consequence of not having a large fund to give it gratuitous circulation, suffered somewhat—a fact *sometimes overlooked* in making comparisons as to circulation.

The election of general officers of the Church is a matter of much interest. The usual offices are to be filled. It is probable that four bishops will be elected, besides, possibly, the election of a bishop for the Pacific coast. So the election of one or two new bishops is almost certain. This fact will, perhaps, add somewhat to the usual interest felt concerning the election of general officers of the Church.

The general boards of the Church will also be filled by election. Nominations are made usually by committees. It might be well, perhaps, to have these nominations to include three times the number to be elected, instead of twice the number, that the choice might be more ample. It must be remembered, however, that the conference is not at all restricted to nominations, in voting, but may elect partly or wholly outside of nominations, though this would be unusual. The nominations ought in all cases to be reported at least a whole day before the election, and the list put in print, as may be done at Westfield.

The important elections, instead of bring crowded into a half day, probably ought to be more extended as to time. At least this question is worthy of consideration.

Probably, on the whole, the delegates to this General Conference are as able as those of any previous quadrennial assembly in the history of the Church. The delegations from several annual conferences are the same as four years ago, and are composed of men improving with age and experience. Some conferences have gained strength by changes in their delegations; others have lost strength. Probably the conferences will have a fuller number of delegates present than ever before. We look for two or three delegates from the Pacific coast, and most cordially will they be welcomed. The sentiments of delegates to the General Conference will, we think, on the controverted questions of the Church, stand the same, and in about the same ratio, as four years ago.

One of blessed memory—Bishop J. Markwood—was absent from our last quadrennial meeting; another, a prince and leader in our Zion,—Bishop D. Edwards,—will be missed from this General Conference. How the hand of Death lays low the heads of those loved and revered among us.

Devotion ought to characterize all our meetings during the entire session. Order and courtesy ought to mark all the conference proceedings. Secret prayer ought to be with every member. Piety ought to be increased in every family where delegates find homes.

Among the special services will be one in memory of Bishop Edwards— perhaps sometime during the first Sabbath of conference. It is expected that a memorial discourse will be delivered by the senior bishop.

Truly there is a God in Israel. The Lord reigns, and we trust that everything shall work for the good of the Church. It is by his grace that we must live and prosper. If he takes pleasure in his own right hand's planting, our Church shall triumph in his strength. May the Lord grant it through his Son, our Savior.

Union Biblical Seminary, Dayton, Ohio, in the 1880's. Image courtesy of the Center for the Evangelical United Brethren Heritage, United Theological Seminary, Dayton, Ohio.

Chapter 4

American Politics and Society

September 22, 1869   Alexander von Humboldt

The fourteenth day of this month was observed throughout the country, especially by the German portion of our population, as the centennial of the birth of
the most distinguished savant of the nineteenth century, Baron Alexander von
Humboldt. He was born in Berlin, which, after all his travels, was also the place
of his death. His father was an officer under Duke Ferdinand, in the seven years'
war, and afterward a Prussian royal councilor. Alexander was left fatherless before he was ten years of age, but was educated at home, with great care, by distinguished teachers in the natural sciences, mathematics, philosophy, and politics. In his eighteenth year he studied at the University of Frankfort-on-the-Oder,
but soon returned to Berlin and devoted himself to the study of the Greek language. An acquaintance with a distinguished young botanist, Willdenow, led
him to cultivate his taste for botany. At the age of twenty he spent a year at the
University of Gottingen, and soon after made a rapid journey through Belgium,
Holland, England, and France. He continued to add to his stock of scientific
knowledge, while he was employing that which he had already acquired for the
benefit of his country. In 1795 he made a tour through Tyrol, Lombardy, and
Switzerland, in the interests of geological science. In 1797 he passed three
months in intimate association with those two distinguished German men of
genius, Goethe and Schiller. He soon after set out with a view of visiting the
volcanoes of Vesuvius, Stromboli, and Etna. He was baffled in this, as also in

other projects of travel, in consequence of the disturbed political condition of both the eastern and western continents. He visited Paris and Madrid, however, and was treated with high consideration on account of his great learning and amiable character. With remarkable privileges granted by the Spanish government, he sailed for South America in the frigate Pizarro, on the 5th of June, 1799, and, after visiting Teneriffe, and exploring the island and its celebrated peak, he reached Venezuela by the middle of July. In this province he spent eighteen months in scientific explorations; and after some interruption he explored the Magdalena River as far as Honda. In 1801 he, with his party, made an exploration of the northern Andes mountains, reaching Quito in the beginning of the succeeding year. After exploring the wonders of Peru and Mexico, he sailed for Havana, and afterward visited Philadelphia, where he received a friendly reception from President Jefferson. After an absence of five years he again reached Europe in the year 1804. He then chose Paris for his residence. Afterward he spent a number of years, sometimes in the diplomatic service of his country (Prussia), and always in the service of science. He was alike a botanist, a chemist, a geologist, and an astronomer, and wherever he went or wherever he stayed he seemed to ever gather comprehensively from the great field of nature to enrich the various departments of natural science. In 1829, under the patronage of the Czar of Russia, he undertook an exploration in north-eastern Europe, and through a large part of Asia, exploring the gold regions of the Ural, the Altai mountains, and all the most interesting regions intervening, reaching, at last, the Caspian Sea, and returning to St. Petersburg after a journey of ten thousand miles, which had been accomplished in nine months. We can not, in this condensed account from the records of his life, mention but a tithe of his valuable services to his country and of contributions to the great treasures of natural science.

Von Humboldt was distinguished for the comprehensiveness of his intellect and observation. With a penetrating ken he looked into the various departments of natural science, and with a remarkable skill brought to light its wonders and beauties. He was distinguished especially for his ability of comprehending and presenting as a unity the various departments of the natural sciences. For this his most notable work, the Cosmos, was written. He was also distinguished for the tenderness with which he patronized every young man of scientific genius who came within the range of his notice. He was noted like great men usually are, for the simplicity of his character. It is to be feared, however, that he, in the indefatigable pursuit of science, took too little interest in its great Author. His works are not famed for piety. He died in the ninetieth year of his age, having retained in old age the vigor of his body and of his mind in a remarkable degree. We do not entertain the spirit of hero worship; nor do we approve of the vain methods by which this sinful world delight to honor the illustrious dead. But there has been no man of the past century who has added so largely to the rich treasures of science. His works still live and constitute a monument which will be fresh when marble piles shall have crumbled into dust.

October 20, 1869   The Late Elections

The recent elections in Ohio and Pennsylvania have been carried by the Republicans, by small majorities compared with those of last year. Elections in those states have become a sort of game of chance. Out of hundreds of thousands of votes, it is but a comparatively small majority which turns the scale in favor of one party or the other. A majority of one hundred thousand in favor of one party may, in a few years, be reduced to but a few thousand; or the scale may be turned entirely against that party. This fact makes those elections lively, as well as wily conflicts.

When we consider the importance of the issues which may be involved, we may deprecate this uncertainty; yet this very uncertainty keeps politicians under a continual sense of dependence on and responsibility to their constituents. They are obliged, as individuals, and especially as parties, to act with great circumspection. They are made to feel that they must answer, politically speaking, with their heads, for the general conduct of their party. Political intrigue may place them in the front ranks of their party; but that party, with those very leaders as chief mourners, may sink beneath the displeasure of the people.

No doubt the larger portion of the people of both of the great political parties of the country are firm and unyielding in their political positions, or rather in their devotion to their respective political organizations. And of this firm class in both parties, whatever of difference may be predicated of their intelligence, patriotism, and virtue, it can not be doubted that a larger portion of them are sincere in their views, and unimpeachable in their integrity and devotion to the good of their country.

It may be interesting to inquire into the nature of the elements which turn the scale in those elections.

There is one class who are not to be depended on by either party as a sure support in any election. It is composed of those who, from the liberality of their hearts, or from the coldness of their natures, or from their lack of principle, form no particular party attachments. Some of them, perhaps, consider it generous, just, and honorable to maintain a sort of impartiality in order for the maintenance of which it may sometimes be necessary to palliate the vices of one party and depreciate the virtues of another. They in this way keep the scale of parties, according to their judgment, vibrating very evenly between the preponderance of each, in merit and demerit. These glory in their impartiality, and may be regarded as the game which may fall into the hands of either political party in any contest.

Another class are those converts from the opposite political party, whose conversion has been rather superficial. These are much addicted to political backsliding, and need very careful nursing.

Another class think that the decision of the election is a foregone conclusion, and that their individual vote can not change the general result; so they stay at home.

Another class, still, think that the great issues are settled; and now they feel at liberty to vote in favor of such minor issues as they may prefer; or they feel at liberty to not vote at all.

Some are always inclined to regard political matters with indifference, and do not, unless some very great excitement has reached them, care about voting at all. Some are unprincipled, and unless they see something involving their interest or prejudices, they do not care about voting; and when these are involved they will vote with either party, and for any measure, however important for good or evil, provided their own minor interests are thereby promoted.

Among the classes upon which an election depends is that which is not yet freed from the spirit of caste which the prevalence of the slave system engendered. With them, this spirit dies slowly, and whenever any measure stirs its smoldering fires they vote with especial reference to measures against which that spirit rebels. With such the Fifteenth Amendment is an abomination.

There is still another class who are in some way tributary to the whisky-ring, and these, by the comparatively rigid enforcement of the liquor revenue laws for the last few months, are filled with venomous opposition. It would not be strange if these alone would measurably control an election.

But there is still another class who, believing that "to the victors belong the spoils," considered themselves as especially entitled to the patronage of the late incoming administration; and, being disappointed, as the majority of office-seekers must always be, they have, with their local or more general influence, as the case may be, retired like an outraged Achilles, and thus materially weakened the influence of the party to which they belong.

Among the influences which may have had an effect on the late elections we do not propose to write; neither, without occupying too much space, can we attempt a more complete analysis of the classes upon which the uncertainties of political triumphs depend. But we may, in reference to those matters, refer to the necessity of increasing the intelligence of our people. Not only is it necessary that our common schools should train our children in the sciences, but it is necessary that by the circulation of good periodicals our people should be well informed on moral and political questions. An increased degree of attention among the people to matters of public concern and political action is necessary for the safe and intelligent ordering of political affairs by the sovereigns of our nation, the citizens of this great Republic.

Again; it is necessary that the moral tone of our citizenship should be improved. It can not be denied that while the great class of our citizens are respectable in morals and in possession of a good share of integrity, there are thousands whose morals are quite low, and yet who constitute a majority in an election. There is a sense in which these hold the balance of power in any state and throughout our common country; and how important it is that every moralizing influence should be properly brought to bear to diminish this class and to improve its remnant.

While there are other agencies which may be auxiliary in accomplishing this great work, our dependence must mainly be in Him who is the Way, the Truth, and the Life. As the main instrumentality, we must depend upon His church, which is "Zion, the perfection of beauty," out of which God is shining. Its citizens are "the salt of the earth," and "the light of the world."

November 3, 1869   Regency Presidents

An anecdote has been related of Franklin that when in the convention which framed our national constitution it was proposed to give titles to the chief officers of the government, he arose and remarked that, as it was likely that the proposition would be adopted, he would suggest one for the vice-president of the United States: it was, *"His Most Superfluous Highness."* This, according to the story, ended the debate and buried the proposition. Had the philosopher lived to the present day, he would not only, in seeing the practical workings of the vice-presidency, have seen the fulfillment of his prophetic vision in some notable cases, but he also would have yielded to the propriety of its special application as a prefix to another title which has obtained currency, namely: "His Accidency."

Among the "accidencies" Tyler is first—but they have all been false to those who elected them—Tyler, Filmore, Johnson—and the last error was worse than the first, and it is to be hoped that the evil culminated in him who, with maudlin speech, "swung around the circle." Certain peculiarities seem to have been attached to all of those most unfortunate men. We have already intimated that all of them were political traitors. Perhaps the defection of Tyler was the severest shock on the nerves of his party, for by the time the author of "my policy" was lifted to the presidency, the people had begun to look upon succeeding vice-presidents as having a bias not less fatal than that which Edward Beecher attributed to the sins of a pre-Adamic state. Like a certain would-be sage who, having seen the earth robed in a mantle of snow two succeeding anniversaries of the Savior's birth, waited with confident expectancy the third coincidence, and then set set [sic] it down in his almanac that there would be snow every Christmas, henceforth and forever; so the people have learned to look on "His Accidency" as invariably meaning more than "His Superfluous Highness."

These vice-presidents succeeding to the presidential chair have been also alike famed for their vanity. A respectable share of modesty has been common, with others who have occupied the presidential chair. Perhaps this egotism of these successors of presidents has been in part owing to their inability to obtain national recognition of their talents and services, and of their utter failure to find efficient trumpeters of their imaginary fame.

All of these accidental vice-presidents have been repudiated by the people; and even when the measures they have favored have proved successful, they have not escaped the doom of national contempt.

Further, the political creed of all one of them seems to have been stereotyped before they were politically buried, and when they have risen from their graves after some political earthquake, as Ex-president Filmore recently did with his grave-clothes on, and with a funeral napkin about his head, they have not failed to read in sepulchral tones, their old political creeds freshly struck from the old stereotyped plates.

Tyler did this in the union-saving council of 1861,—Filmore did this recently in his speech in the Louisville commercial convention, where he referred to his approval of the Fugitive Slave Law, as if he had never heard the cannon at Vicksburg, or the Emancipation Proclamation, or as if the newspapers containing the reconstruction measures of Congress had not fallen like snow-flakes over his political grave. Johnson did no better in his last visit to Washington when, for a season, he essayed to quit the tombs which he had inhabited much like him of Gadara. A writer in one of our exchanges has advanced the idea that some provision ought to be made by the Government so that ex-presidents need not drag out a miserable life—shorn like Wolsey of all their former greatness. This writer even suggested something like the suttee by which the numerous widows of a rajah are enabled to join the spirit of their husband—going off in a chariot of literal fire.

We only suggest to the affectionate political friends of the surviving "accidencies" that if they would walk backward—a good course for them—and cover the nakedness of their unfortunate friends, as the pious patriarchs did that of their father, they would confer a favor on those positional magnates of the past, and save the finest sensibilities of the nation from mortification.

January 5, 1870   Women as Physicians

Various professions and employments of late years are made accessible to women. There is one which common sense ought to have opened for them long ago, or, rather, never to have suffered to be closed against them. We refer to the medical profession. That women have the capacity to become successful physicians no one can have any doubt; and that virtue and decency would place in their care the treatment of their own sex in such cases as involve delicacy, is too clear to require an argument. A number of females, appreciating the propriety of this, with commendable resolution, have encountered the prejudices of public opinion and all the obstacles which old usages have thrown in the way of their progress, and have attained to a high degree of eminence in medical knowledge. There are now even hundreds of female medical graduates in the United States. Last fall the female students attending the Female Medical College took tickets for attendance upon the clinical lectures of the Pennsylvania Hospital. The opposition felt by the male students to their attendance was expressed, as our readers know, in a manner which renders their standing as gentlemen more than questionable. No doubt, the arrangements not being as yet adapted to a mixed class of male and female students, a courage a little in advance of that best comporting with female delicacy was required on the part of the female students, in order to have the full benefit of those lectures. Perhaps this gave a good coloring to the objections of male students to the presence of both sexes on those occasions, but it did not by any means justify their rowdyish, brutal conduct. Arrangements, it appears from the latest accounts, have been made to obviate this difficulty, so that decency and utility can now harmonize in the attendance of both sexes at those lectures.

William Lloyd Garrison, in a communication published in a late *Independent*, gives a notice of an article published some months since in the *New England Medical Gazette*, written by Mrs. Dall, which sets forth in forcible language the especial propriety of having women qualified to treat the diseases peculiar to their sex. This view of the subject, so consonant with common sense and common decency, the editor of the *Medical Gazette* approved, and urged the necessity of giving women proper opportunity to obtain the qualifications required to enable them to walk the difficult path of medical science. A medical association of Boston took a different view of Mrs. Dall's article, and approved a letter written by Dr. Storer, one of their number, in which he animadverts severely but unjustly on the views set forth by Mrs. Dall. We only have this to say respecting the views of Mrs. Dall, to which so much objection is raised, that they certainly accord with facts and good sense; and we hope the day is not far distant when female physicians will abound, and to them, as a general thing, the treatment will be given especially of all cases of their own sex in which delicacy is involved. We have no doubt that they would excel in such practice; and we are sure that virtue and decency in both sexes would be not a little advanced by the accession of intelligent, noble-hearted women to the medical profession. We do not doubt that another generation will find woman filling her proper place in this profession, free from the prejudices which now beset her path with a tenacity not excelled by the spirit of caste which disputes every inch of the advance of colored men in personal and political elevation.

January 19, 1870   Political Corruption and the Press

Corruption, to a fearful extent, pervades our national councils and contaminates the various departments of our Government. The vast contracts of the war, with the opportunities afforded for supplying those contracts at a great profit, have led to the bestowment of public funds, as if they were public plunder, upon the favorites of those in power. Sometimes a consideration was the price of official favor, and hand joined in hand in secret plans to swindle the Government. Anything else could hardly be expected in time of war, when the very foundations of society and commerce are being shaken and upturned. Bad enough before, it has become worse; and now honesty is by many no longer regarded as essential to a politician's standing in public life. Dishonesty, instead of being regarded as the exception, is now looked upon as the rule, and all in public political life are regarded with suspicion. No doubt there are honest men, even Christian men, among our statesmen; but with the opportunities afforded correspondents of the press to circulate reports so perverted as to render truth and falsehood indistinguishable, it is quite impossible for the people whom these statesmen represent to know whether the allegations are just or unjust. It is hard even for the better-informed classes of society to form a very reliable opinion respecting the honesty and faithfulness of those public servants. This uncertainty as to the true standing of those who represent the people is the most subtile [*sic*] evil of all, and well may we inquire, "Is there no remedy?"

It is certain that if editors were so disposed, false reports need not to so large an extent go the rounds of the press; but they are often fond of paying sensations, and are, besides, liable also to be imposed upon. As startling, scandalous reports suit especially party tastes there will ever be found journals enterprising enough to furnish an ample supply of them.

One method by which the evil may be, to some extent, remedied is for respectable journals to require that everything of the kind be given under the real name of the writer, and then for them to hold correspondents to a strict account for faithfulness in dispensing their strictures on character. In this way journals and permanent correspondents may build up characters of their own, if faithful witnesses, which will render them standards in matters of fact. It is important that a public sentiment should be formed requiring this truthfulness of those who take in charge the public character of the rulers of our nation; and it is the best class of journalists, political and religious, which must do most of that which is to be done to abate the evil of national slander. The functions of journalism are too important and should be held too sacred to admit of journals playing the game of lawyers pleading on some minor suit—each striving to make out the best case he can for his client irrespective of his real convictions of the truth in the case. Journalism needs lifting up a little higher than it now stands; and when we contemplate the wonderful power which the press now has and is destined to have, may we not be justly solicitous for its elevation and purity?

February 2, 1870   The Fifteenth Amendment

The adoption of the Fifteenth Amendment is well nigh an accomplished fact. With it will be completed the successive measures which the events and necessities of the last decade have forced upon our nation. It will give to every citizen of the United States, not excluded by crime, the right to vote, irrespective of color or former condition of servitude. This is, indeed, a marvelous change from that phase of public law and jurisprudence set forth in the "Dred Scott Decision," in which the colored people were adjudged to "have no rights which a white man is bound to respect." Presidents were chosen, judges were appointed, and patronage was dispensed with special reference to the safety and aggrandizement of the "peculiar institution" which laid its heavy hand upon the body and drew the curtains of night around the soul of the helpless African, holding in derision all the tender sentiments common to the human heart and the dearest rights sacred even to the much degraded. Now the colored man educates his children in the public schools, speaks from the public rostrum, votes at the polls with his white neighbor, holds office in some of the state governments, sits in the legislative halls, and will soon take his place among the grave senators of America. Truly the change is wonderful. Could the champions of slavery have seen the results of their efforts to build up a government whose corner-stone should be slavery, they would have shrunk back appalled at the prospective fruit of their madness. But the change has come, and the African is furnished with a stage upon which he may exhibit his long-questioned claim to brotherhood with the white man in the ranks of literary and political greatness.

There is, however, one feature connected with the adoption of the amendment which is not so pleasant to our contemplation. It is that which bribes the lately rebellious states to its acceptance by making its approval a condition of their re-admission into the family of states, with their equal representation in the national councils. While we most heartily concede to Congress the right to fix the terms of re-admission for those states which flew away from our political system in madness like stars from their orbits, we can not but regard with grave apprehension any plan by which so important and fundamental a measure as a change in our national constitution should be affected by a constrained vote of any of the states. It is certainly averse to those maxims of government most consonant with republicanism; and while we rejoice in the prospect of the speedy accomplishment of the end which will bring most speedily peace and quietness to our nation, we can not but fear that the sacrificing of principle in adding this plank to our national platform may be the cleaving down of one of the pillars upon which rests the safety of our republican institutions.

March 30, 1870   The Piegan Massacre

Some time since, in Montana, Colonel Baker made an attack on a village of Piegan Indians, who had been suffering from the small-pox, and gained an easy victory, massacreing [sic] the weak and defenseless inhabitants—women and children receiving their full share of the gallant fire of these heroes of the regular army. These valiant knights rival the glory of the pugilistic band whose leader, when he had reached his dotage, said:

> I can mind
> When I, Hans, and one or two more,
> Beat quite blind
> An old woman, who had never seen before.

Some congressmen and some newspapers have sought to ridicule the horror which the recital of this lesson of "civilization" administered to savages, has produced among the really civlized [sic] and Christian people of the country. We have before us an article from one of the political journals which aspires to state proportions in which the attempt is made to satirize the "sentimentality" of those who can not excuse our countrymen for imitating savages in fiendish ferocity; but we are glad to know that some of the most influential of our political journals do not fail to let exposure and satire do their perfect work in making the officers of the army feel the responsibility of inflicting this dark stain on the credit of our army and the civilization of the present century. The immolation of sepoys by the British army in India has its more than equal—on a lesser scale however—in the army of the Great Republic.

Colonel Baker is excused (?) for this cold blooded butchery on the plea that he did not know the condition of the village before the attack. This does not excuse the indiscriminate slaughter of squaws, papooses, and the subsequent murder of prisoners. The report of the victory by the colonel is not even as creditable as Falstaff's furious boasting before Prince Henry. A gallant "running away" would have been highly creditable beside this murder of non-resistants and captives. Let the war department of our country take the best measures to wash this foul stain away, or at least hide it from memory by a complete abolition of the exterminating policy too popular in frontier settlements, but so at war with civilization and Christianity.

April 20, 1870   The Mormon Question

Among the incipient rebellions which have threatened the peace of our nation, Mormonism ranks only second to slavery. That an artful and ambitious leader should set up, in a once almost inaccessible region in the interior of our country, a commonwealth with institutions diverse from those of the states of the Union, and then when the hand of national power is extended, bid defiance to its every exercise only so far as it corresponds with his lordly will, is a remarkable fact. That the Government has so long brooked the insolence of Brigham Young and his subordinate sachems, and tolerated their political teachings and practices, so utterly subversive of order and so absolutely at war with our Government, is marvelous. The action of Congress has been remarkably slow. But at last the Cullom bill has dragged its slow length through the popular branch of the national legislature, and it remains to be seen whether the Senate will find some method of smothering the measure. Meanwhile, some of the leading political journals are favoring the policy of non-intervention with the domestic institution of the Mormons, just as conservatives so long advocated the same policy respecting slavery. We did deal tenderly and bounteously with slavery until it reached that power and insolence which moved it to dare defiance to the majesty of our Government, and to attempt its destruction. Mormonism is weaker, but it is isolated, and, with the elements likely to be furnished by immigration, it may assume a magnitude which will corrupt our institutions if it does not directly assault the power of the Federal Government.

That Brigham Young has ruled Utah for many years past as absolutely as the Roman pontiff ever ruled a nation in the dark ages can not be denied. The officers of the federal Government have ruled just as far as he chose to allow, and could dare go no further. They are the representatives of a great republic obsequiously governing under the dictatorship of a wily potentate who dwells in a house of polygamy, and whose secret government and punishments are, in Utah, almost as irresistible to Mormon or gentile as the behests of the Inquisition were during the papal persecutions. The crimes of Brigham Young far exceed the sum of those for which the dark dungeons of many a prison are crowded. Yet he walks forth as a ruler instead of a convict. It may be said that Mormonism if left alone will fall to pieces of itself. Will it not, meanwhile, corrupt the social life of many of our states and territories, the *morale* of which is not any too desirable now? Will it not weaken those institutions essential to the well-being of our nation? Errorists are already doing enough in undermining the sacredness of the marriage relation.

It may be said that those Mormons having thus long been left undisturbed to build up their commonwealth, the corner-stone of which is polygamy, ought not now to be restrained. Has not our nation in the past tolerated many things under a system which itself could tolerate the Government only as it yielded to the imperious will of that system. Shall we continue a repetition of the same folly? An absolute despotism in the interior of the empire of a republic is indeed a novelty, and it perpetuity would constitute an anomaly in the annals of government.

But it may be replied that war would ensue as the result of interference. This is a confession of the desperateness of the case. Will not that threatening despotism, and insubordination, with the corruption which attends its peculiar institution, breed still more war and more work for prisons and executioners? Shall the majesty of the general Government quail before a divided population all of whom do not exceed in number the inhabitants of many a city in our states?

But perhaps some one may claim that polygamy, with the Mormons, is a religious institution, and that their rights of conscience must receive proper consideration. It may be doubtful whether their conscience will require them to continue the practices of which the law relieves them, any more than the denizens and frequenters of brothels are conscience-bound to continue their orgies to satisfy the claims of their devil-worshiping. Suppose some sect should adopt murder or theft, instead of bigamy, as a part of their tenets, would the broad mantle of religious toleration shield them? Marriage is a civil as well as divine institution, and it is due that the Government regulate it so far as is necessary for the national welfare and safety. Why should Congress punish bigamy in Wyoming and tolerate it in Utah?

We are no advocates of unnecessary military interference; but cowering before the Mormon sachem will neither lessen his insolence nor detract from his prestige. The sooner we meet this foul monster of the desert and strangle it in its paradise of lust the better. If the Cullom bill is too stringent, let the Senate conform it better to the dictates of statesmanship; but let us not longer present to the civilized world the pitiable spectacle of cherishing a system of iniquity which would undermine one of the essential institutions of civilization. Let Mormons think, preach, and worship with all freedom; but let them conform to that civil institution which lies at the foundation of our social fabric. By so doing they will only conform to the teachings of the Mormon Bible, which condemns polygamy. Their pretenses to special revelations in favor of that vile institution, ought to be admitted to as little claim to rule in the institutions of one of our states as the mutterings of a wizzard [sic], to roll back the revolving wheels of material progress.

April 27, 1870   Jubilee of the Colored People

The colored people at various places have made public demonstration of the joy they feel over the passage of the Fifteenth Amendment. In some instances aged colored men, natives of the country, have recognized themselves for the first time as voters. The celebration, by our colored fellow-citizens of Dayton, on the 20th inst., was a truly interesting affair, though not so imposing in appearance as it would have been had not the rain of the day and night previous rendered it in a manner impracticable for them to have a procession of footmen. They, therefore, had to proceed in vehicles, on horseback, &c., which, of course, limited somewhat the number in the procession. They proceeded, with their banners, along various streets, making the circuit of the main portion of the city. We never saw any procession of citizens moving which so absorbed our attention and so deeply stirred the emotions of our heart. That solemnity, humble deportment, and good order which have generally distinguished those celebrations, were conspicuous in this. Their mottoes were generally exceedingly well chosen. Among these we shall mention a few, as: "Praise ye the Lord;" "It is the Lord's doings, and marvelous in our eyes;" "No social equality;" "In the midst of this, however, He from whom all blessings flow must not be forgotten."

One carriage contained four colored men, aged seventy, seventy-two, seventy-seven, and eighty years, respectively. Their banner, on one side, had, "Let us have peace;" on the other; "Just of age, politically, though born in the days of Washington."

We could not be an unfeeling spectator of the scene. Our first vote in a presidential election was cast for Hale and Julian, in 1852. We had been a reader of the best antislavery literature from our childhood, our father being one of the three voters in his township who, in 1844, supported Jas. G. Birney. We had in the past written, spoken, voted, and prayed for the great deliverance, never doubting that it would come at last; and now we feel that truly it came in a way we knew not, till a civil war was upon us. But Jehovah has brought the colored bond-men, through the red sea of war it is true, to the land of rest. With what force the sentiment of one of the banners overwhelmed us as it passed along, "This is the Lord's doing, and it is marvelous in our eyes;" and we could, with a full heart, adopt the language inscribed on another banner, "Praise ye the Lord."

A meeting at Huston Hall, in the evening, was addressed by Peter H. Clark, a colored orator from Cincinnati, Mr. R. G. Corwin, Esq., and Hon. L. B. Gunckel. All this was well enough,—but we doubt not that a regular "lovefeast" meeting would have been still more interesting. It certainly would if all the sufferers by the long reign of oppression could have portrayed the marvelous change which they had experienced since their first remembrance of the bitterness of the cup of oppression.

Henceforth, throughout the vast domain of our free republic, no one shall, on account of race, color, or previous condition of servitude, be denied a voice in the Government under which he lives. Oligarchy has run its race, and, if not decently buried, nevertheless, buried it is; and we have one people, every one of whom shall, unless disfranchised for crime, hold his place as a sovereign, reigning through the magic power of the ballot.

The enfranchisement of the colored man is an era in the history of our country, and will serve to mark an era in the condition of oppressed humanity in many a nation. The Lord hath triumphed gloriously.

May 4, 1870   Woman's Suffrage Convention

The Woman's Suffrage Convention, which met in this city last week, was a decided success. There were a good number of delegates in attendance, and they possessed a good share of intelligence and talent. The attendance of the citizens of Dayton was good, and the convention had the good will at least of most of those who assembled from time to time. The president of the convention, Mrs. Tracy Cutler, M. D., is a matronly lady of forty-five, deliberate, pleasant, and earnest in her manner of address, possessing a good share of ability. She is, in self-possession and tact, decidedly a good presiding officer.

Mrs. Livermore, the editor of the Boston *Woman's Journal*, is an honor to the cause she represents. About fifty years of age, presenting a fine personal appearance, perfectly at home before an audience, having complete command of good language, possessing an excellent voice which is at once agreeable and highly expressive of the feelings of a noble soul, she uses her information, logic, and eloquence with a most decided effect on her hearers. She would be an honor to any commendable assembly, and no disgrace to a national legislature. Her whole manner, appearance, and address is modest, chaste, and dignified; and we have heard few surpass her in eloquence. In her speech, the last evening of the convention, she answered the objections raised to female suffrage, many of which were absurd, and others really weighty. All her reasoning was plausible, some of it most conclusive, and a portion of it a little on the sophistical order. Her appeal in behalf of women in which she set forth the noble sacrifices and heroism of females during the recent war, and other worthy considerations, was irresistibly eloquent.

Miss Anthony, the editor of the *Revolution*, who has seen one half century of single blessedness, was present with her talent and her temper. A resolution complimenting her for a half century's continuance in single life was taken for an insult, and caused her to display her misanthropy and old-maidish qualities to the temporary annoyance of the convention and disgust of the spectators.

Mrs. M. M. Cole, of the *Woman's Advocate*, Miss Lizzie M. Boynton, Miss Mattie Hunt, and more than a dozen other prominent delegates, figured in the convention, receiving decided marks of approbation from the audience, and eliciting favorable reports from the daily press.

The commonly-received opinion that the women engaged in this suffrage movement are immodest in speech and deportment, and unfeminine in their characteristics, had little to verify it in the proceedings of this convention. That there are many engaged in the woman's suffrage movement who are far from orthodox in their religious views, and some—in the United States and elsewhere—who have little reverence for sacred things, is certainly true, but perhaps that very independence, irregular and erratic though it be, has led them to examine positions long considered established; and in doing so they may have not only fallen into extremes but sometimes dealt with sacred things in a manner not the most commendable. But as God used the ambition of Alexander and the Roman Senate to bring about a greater unity of the nations prior to the introduction of Christianity into the world, and used the Mohamedans to punish and overthrow the idolatry which early crept into the Eastern church, and employed the endowments of an infidel Paine and especially the wonderful genius of a skeptical Voltaire to set in motion those elements which have unsettled the foundations of national despotism in Europe, and raised up the erratic Garrison, and Philips, and Gerrit Smith, to disturb the now fallen slave-power, so we do not doubt that the most ultra and most irreverent advocates of women's rights will prove instrumental in advancing a much-needed reform in the laws affecting the privileges and welfare of women.

The laws, in many of the states, are very defective in the protection of the interests and rights of women. This agitation will at least measurably remedy this defect. It will also have the effect of calling forth the mental and moral power of women to a greater degree than heretofore, and remedying much that is foolish in their social condition. Whether it may at last prove best that women should be active participants in the use of the political ballot is a question which can best be solved by actual experiment. Already she has the ballot in Wyoming, and votes on some questions in Kansas. We think extreme haste is not warranted in settling this question; nor can a permanent settlement be made in haste. If the experiment is a satisfactory one where the question is brought to this test, woman's suffrage will soon become general. If it is unsatisfactory, the states will settle down on some other political basis. If at last it should prove all its sanguine friends hope, and there should be some state or states which should still fail to recognize its good effects, an amendment to the National Constitution would set all right.

We have no sympathy with the misanthropic tone which sometimes steals upon excited advocates of woman's suffrage, nor encouragement for the irreverence with which some of them treat the Bible and sacred things, nor respect for the ruthlessness with which some would do away with feminine modesty and delicacy, and obliterate all distinction in the lives and vocations of the sexes. We do not shut our eyes to the fact that errorists are likely to make it an occasion for mischief. We believe that the modesty, reverence, and obedience taught in the Scriptures as the duty of woman, are indispensable, that Paul was sound in his exposition of the duties of husbands and wives. We do not believe, however, that those teachings necessarily exclude woman either from the ecclesiastical or political ballot. The former has proved highly satisfactory in some of the religious denominations, and the actual experiment will test the beneficial or injurious effects of the latter. We reaffirm the opinion which we expressed eight months since that the experiment, in some state or states, is inevitable, and we may add that we are not without hope that the results will not prove as disastrous as many have apprehended. We have no hesitation in saying that whenever the majority of the intelligent women of the country desire the ballot, we have no doubt it will be readily granted by the men; and we do not think it ought to be given till there is such a general desire.

May 11, 1870   The Women Jurors of Wyoming

The women who recently sat on the jury in a Wyoming court have been the subject of considerable coarse abuse by the press of the United States. Rev. L. Hartsough, writing from that territory to one of our exchanges, defends these women from the slander heaped upon them, and sets the matter forth in a favorable light. He says the ladies were under charge of a woman bailiff, who was herself a member of the Methodist Church; that they occupied good rooms together at a good hotel, while the sheriff had charge of the men at another place. The judge approved the decision of one of the jury-women, a Christian lady, that unless a verdict was reached before 12 o'clock Saturday night, the matter must lie over till Monday. Fifteen minutes before that time the verdict was agreed upon and the jury discharged. It seems that the conduct of these women, far from being censurable, was highly commendable—perhaps more so than most of juries composed entirely of the other sex. They, from accounts, knelt every morning in prayer before repairing to the court-room, and implored Divine wisdom to guide them in the discharge of their duties. Their verdict seems to have given universal satisfaction, and the evil women of the territory are represented as alarmed, and fleeing from Cheyenne. We give the following testimonies quoted by the above-named correspondent:

"Chief-justice Howe said: 'In eighteen years' experience, I never had as fair, candid, impartial, and able a jury in court as in this term in Albany County.'"

"Associate-justice Kingman said: 'For twenty-five years it has been an anxious study with me, both on the bench and at the bar, how we are to prevent jury-trials from degenerating into a perfect farce and burlesque, and it has remained for Albany County to point out the remedy, and demonstrate the cure for this threatened evil.'"

"Chaplain White, of Fort Saunders, said: 'He never witnessed the decorum and quiet push of business and courtesy and constant respect in any court-room as this court presented.'"

It is added that none of the women on the jury were advocates of female suffrage. Perhaps it is not desirable that females should generally have the duties and responsibilities of sitting upon a jury imposed upon them, but conduct of this first jury composed in part of women seems to have been highly creditable to them; and their excellent conduct threatens to make women juries really popular.

June 8, 1870   Decoration Day

A war equal in the magnitude of interests involved with that which our country has passed through in the past decade, has rarely occurred in the history of nations. The greatest of sacrifices, the most devoted patriotism, and the most heroic and enduring valor have been manifested by the soldiers of the republic, many of whom now sleep in honored graves. Never before did such vast numbers fly so willingly and swiftly to their country's standard in the hour of the nation's peril. Never did citizens of any country voluntarily make such contributions for the sanitary supplies of a nation's armies, nor so provide for hospital relief for the sick and wounded, nor so labor for the moral and religious welfare of those in the field, camp, and hospital. Never did a greater revolution attend years of sanguinary conflict than that which has molded a nation of freemen into firm believers in the equal rights of all the human family. The principle taught by the apostle of the gentiles, that God hath made of one blood all nations to dwell upon the face of the earth, is now maintained practically in our nation in a degree that few would have ventured to predict ten years ago.

Perhaps in honors to its soldiery and in provisions for the welfare of those who came as physical wrecks out of the sanguinary struggle, no nation has ever surpassed ours. In honors, too, conferred by the living on the dead, our people have instituted a custom which, whatever scruples may exist with any against it, must be acknowledged by all as carrying poetic beauty with it. Annually our soldiers who survive their sleeping comrades come to the graves where they sleep; and relatives and citizens witness the ceremony of decorating their graves with flowers. It seems, indeed, an inadequate, yet a fitting tribute to their memory. Beautiful flowers fitly represent the fragrance of the memory of the fallen heroes, as they also so well show how soon frail mortality is cut down, and his glory perisheth as the flower, and withereth, leaving only its fragrance behind.

The ceremony of decorating the graves of the fallen heroes of the late war, seems to have been generally observed the 30th ult. [*sic*] throughout the country, though probably with some abatement, in general, of the interest formerly felt on similar occasions. In Dayton it was observed by a large portion of our citizens and those of the surrounding country with lively interest. At the Soldiers' Home several thousands of people assembled in the forenoon, and services were had, addresses were made, and the usual ceremonies were performed. General Sherman, who acted so brilliant a part in the great struggle, was present to greet his fellow-soldiers, and to give expressions of care and sympathy for their sufferings, and also to congratulate them on the prompt and unconstrained action of the nation in providing for them so comfortable a home. His brief address on the occasion was that of an accomplished soldier rather than the buncome [*sic*] of a favor-seeking politician, though it is clear enough that all our distinguished military men who have an eye to political possibilities know that the soldiers of the war carry a weighty influence to the ballot-box.

The oration of the morning was delivered by General Gibson, who is well gifted as a platform speaker.

In the afternoon a procession formed in our city, on Main Street, and moved first to St. Henry's and afterward to the Woodland Cemetery, where ceremonies similar to those of the forenoon at the Home were performed, and addresses were made by Lieutenant-governor Lee and General Sherman to the thousands assembled to honor the dead and also to see and honor the living hero of the march "from Atlanta to the sea."

While we delight to honor the patriotic dead, we look upon war, however tinseled over by ornaments of speech, as a dreadful reality, contemplating which humanity shudders and pity weeps; and we could ardently wish that what are called the glories of war may never again be known to the future history of our country or to our race. We now will have enough soldiers' graves to fill all the demands of generations to come, if they would worship at the shrine of military patriotism. May God grant us peace.

June 8, 1870   Eight-Hour Law

We do not think it generally wise in governments to attempt too much regulation of those matters which demand and supply must really govern. There are, however, some regulations which humanity calls for and which the friends of humanity should loudly demand. Among these should be an earnest effort for a law regulating the hours of labor for children employed in factories. In many places they are expected to labor more hours each working day than persons having reached maturity ought to be required to engage in toil. If their labors were out of doors, where all the wholesome influences of sunshine and pure air could be had and enjoyed this would be too much; but to confine them in close walls, amid the unpleasant and unhealthy odors of a manufactory with little to enliven the mind, and all this in the years of tender childhood, is cruel and murderous. Their minds are circumscribed; their hearts are rendered sad and cheerless; their strength is undeveloped; their days are shortened. If parents and guardians are too ignorant or too heartless—as they too often are—to avoid this evil, or if manufacturing firms are too avaricious and selfish to care for the lives and welfare of their employes, the state ought not to be indifferent to the growing treasures of the country. Everyone living in our country owes allegiance to the Government, and so does the Government owe protection to each one of its children.

November 2, 1870   Prison-Reform Congress

A convention designed to promote reform in the management of prisons assembled at Cincinnati the 12th of October, and continued in session six days. Two hundred and thirty delegates were present. They were from twenty-two states of the Union, and from Canada and South America.

Governors Baker and Hayes were present, and the latter, in the absence of Speaker Blain, of the National House of Representatives, was elected permanent president.

The convention included a large representation from the officers of the state-prisons of the different states. Ten governors were represented by proxy.

Important papers, several of them historical, were read, and the subjects involved were discussed. Several papers gave account of prison systems of this and other countries. Some treated of the philosophy of crime, the relations of society to criminals, etc.

The meeting was distinguished by earnestness, liberality, and the spirit of humanity. One of the difficulties mentioned was the influence of party politics in giving prisons into the hands of political wire-workers, and causing such fluctuations in the policy and management of those institutions as were highly injurious.

The congress adopted a platform containing thirty-six articles. These embraced a great variety of topics connected with prison discipline.

Measures were taken for the organization of a national prison association, and a committee was appointed for that purpose.

Among the delegates, and prominent, too, in the complimentary notices received from the press, was Mrs. Lydia Sexton, the chaplain of the Kansas penitentiary, who is a worthy minister of the United Brethren Church. She is described as being seventy-one years of age, and as being dressed in matronly style. Her rising hushed the assembly to the most perfect silence, and her addresses melted many to tears.

The national association, we hope, will do a great deal of good. There has been great need of prison reform; and much of it yet remains unaccomplished. We deem this convention as among the very important ones of the present year.

December 14, 1870   Senator Revels' Lecture

We last week enjoyed the pleasure of listening to the lecture of Senator Hiram Revels, delivered in Huston Hall in this city. He very far exceeded our expectations in polish, ability, and eloquence. We had supposed that his position as the first colored United States senator was almost the only ground on which his national reputation has rested. We expected to hear a man of good intellect and education, a man of sound thought and respectable speech, but we had no idea of seeing a live orator, a brilliant genius, a senator above the average of his peers in talent and statesmanship. In reading Senator Morton's compliment, in which he said that Mississippi in sending Hiram Revels to fill the place of Jefferson Davis had lost nothing in ability while she had gained much in character, we had taken it as mostly buncome [*sic*]. But after hearing the colored senator himself, last week, we left the hall believing the distinguished senator from Indiana his inferior in learning, rhetoric, and elocution, and little, if any, his superior in the intellectual power for which Senator Morton is so much distinguished.

Senator Revels is a man of medium hight [*sic*], possessing a strong-built and yet graceful physical form. His countenance is intelligent and his movements and gestures graceful. His full, grave voice possesses a rare musical sweetness, which is retained through all its variations of tone and pitch.

The modulations of his voice are most natural and elegant, in this respect entitling him to a high rank as an elocutionist. His pronunciation was noble and manly, his imagery was chaste and enlivening, and his rhetoric quite consonant with the eloquence of his delivery. Modesty, tact, and true politeness were characteristic of the lecture and the lecturer. His eloquence is graceful and enlivening, but not vehement and fiery. Not only might the intelligent colored people who composed a considerable portion of the audience be justly proud of this noble representative of their race, but the intelligent white persons in the audience might have felt honored had the senator been of their own complexion and the representative of their own state.

We can not but remark the wonderful change which a few years have wrought. A few years since, the colored people in many of our states had no rights which white men were bound to respect; now they not only vote in all the states but have one of the finest orators of the United States senate as the worthy, efficient representative of their race in America. Well may they congratulate themselves on having so pure and so talented a representative.

What an incentive does the example of Senator Revels present to encourage young men in their aspirations for high positions of usefulness. He is not only a self-made man, as the term is commonly used, but he is such despite the cruel and terrible spirit of the caste which for ages has sought to crush all the rising aspirations of the African race. Now the colored men can point to Douglass the orator and Revels the statesmen in vindication of the capabilities of his race; and besides these and scores of others the scornful persecutor sinks into shriveling insignificance. Great is the Lord: his ways are marvelous. Let his holy name be praised.

March 22, 1871   Outrages in the Southern States

The select committee appointed by the United States Senate to investigate the alleged outrages in the southern states, and to ascertain whether those crimes have been committed by organized bands of a political character, and whether persons and property are secure in those states, have reported. Had not the facts upon which their report treats been already patent to every reader of the current news of the day, this document would have produced the most intense excitement throughout the country. As it is, the statement of those facts has become commonplace, if not even stale. Like the stories of the auction-block, the slave-coffle, the slave-ship, and the slave-pen—though less than the horrid truth— these tales concerning outrages in some of the late reconstructed states, are regarded by the people as conveying only tidings of that which must be expected but which must be endured with martyr-like patience. The Ku-klux Klan,—the real name of which in its several stages has been, "The White Brotherhood," "The Constitutional Union Guards," and "The Invisible Empire,"—is a secret society with the most binding obligations, the penalty of the violation of which is death. Its efforts and outrages are directed against northern people residing in the South, against the colored population, and especially against members of the Republican party. The whipping, robbing, shooting, or hanging of citizens is determined upon in secret council, and then executed by stratagem as well as by force, the machinery of the lodge or a number or lodges being brought to bear, with all the necessary complication, and yet with the utmost precision, for the accomplishment of such diabolical purposes. Cases of violence in large numbers are occurring from time to time; general insecurity, in many localities, prevails; and in some places a reign of terror is established. By this Ku-klux organization private grudges are gratified, political sins are punished, the execution of the laws is baffled and even defeated, elections are controlled, and the principles of disloyalty are caused to flourish and triumph.

The duty of congress to devise measures to prevent these outrages is clear and imperative. The duty of the executive to bring to bear the power with which it is already clothed to give security to the citizens of the United States, is backed by a solemn, official oath. It is time that our Government should be less concerned about the perpetuity of the power of any political party or of any faction of the same and more concerned for the rights and lives of its loyal citizens.

It is to be feared that these outrages will be suffered to continue because the measures necessary to suppress them may affect unfavorably in the next presidential canvass the prospects of the party supporting them. Whether the Government has a constitutional right to protect the lives and property of its citizens, ought not to be any more a question than whether it had a right to maintain its existence against those who sought by armed rebellion to effect its overthrow. If the right of the loyal citizens of the country to protection in their persons and property against lawless violence does not exist, our national constitution, and the government it establishes, is a farce, and it is time that the nation were considering the constitutional right of its loyal citizens to live; for there are such rights in the divine law of God and the common law of mankind.

May 10, 1871   Parental Authority

There are many families in which parental authority is at a sad discount. Perhaps the father is strong elsewhere, but weak at home. A three or five year old child tyrannizes over him, though he would yield before no opposition outside of the family circle. Not that his will is not good for obedience and order on the part of his children; but his parental fondness, and his weakness or vascillation [sic] of purpose, ruins all his good plans and gives anarchy almost absolute control of that home which is nearly the sum total of all he cherishes on earth. In his great kindness to his offspring he is exceedingly cruel. By his submission to all their whims, he cherishes in them passions and dispositions calculated to make them unlovely and unhappy during life, and to ruin them beyond this present time. Their fondness, now fitful and capricious to their parents, will end in contempt and disregard; for that affection which does not carry with it a ruling desire to please its object, is based on selfishness. A filial affection which does not enjoin obedience to parental authority is of a questionable sort. Parents who do not enforce obedience in their families are sowing to reap the reproaches of their children, as well as that of their own consciences, when it will be too late to remedy disasters in which it will have involved the whole family.

Harshness may enforce obedience, but it will be outward rather than that of the heart. As soon as the yoke of absolute, unfeeling authority can be thrown off it will be done, and the spirit of recklessness will run rampant, rejoicing in its liberation from a hated yoke.

Firmness, consideration, and love will enable parents to rule in most cases with comparative ease; and those very restraints thrown around their offspring will seem like silken cords rather than fetters of iron. Affection, obedience, confidence, and happiness will reign together, and foster sweet memories for other years, when the members of the now loving family will be widely scattered. Those memories will be a power in the hour of temptation.

May 24, 1871   New Departure of the Democracy

While we do not conceal the fact that in the past the Democratic party of this country has been averse to the principles of the United Brethren Church on the subject of universal, impartial freedom for all the inhabitants of our land, we rejoice to note any advance made by it towards true principles on the great national questions of our age.

Once opposed to the abolition of slavery, resisting every effort to limit its extension into the territories of the national domain, palliating and concealing, if not positively justifying, the outrages of the slave power in its attempts to force slavery into Kansas, discouraging and almost resisting the war waged against the dismemberment of the Union and the building up of a slave-holding government upon the fairest portion of American soil, and finally contending to the bitter end against the constitutional amendments guarantying freedom to every inhabitant of the country, and the citizenship and impartial suffrage of all men, of whatever race, born on American soil, the Democratic party was hardly to be expected to accept the inevitable, to cease fighting upon the dead issues of the past, to declare in favor of the measures fought against with a tenacity and zeal worthy of a better cause, and to indorse the constitutional guaranties which have sealed the irreversible defeat of the chief measures for which that large party has contended so faithfully, and sometimes so heroically, during something like a quarter of a century. But the deed is done, or is being done. The great change is being wrought. And the movement comes from a quarter least promising for the initiation of such a departure.

On the eighteenth day of May—a day which may become memorable in American politics—in the year of grace one thousand eight hundred and seventy-one, in the city of Dayton, in a Democratic local convention, a committee, headed by Clement L. Vallandigham, reported a set of resolutions accepting as accomplished and irreversible facts universal emancipation in our country, and suffrage without distinction of race or color, affirming the validity of all the constitutional amendments adopted within the past few years to guaranty those rights and privileges, and declaring in favor of the speedy payment of the public debt, and pledging the Democratic party "to the full, faithful, and absolute execution and enforcement of the Constitution as it now is, so as to secure equal rights to all persons under it, without distinction of race, color, or condition."

We will not discuss the motives which may be imputed; we will not dwell upon the supposed unpalatableness of the utterance which may have been urged upon Mr. Vallandigham by the counsels of able, resolute, and far-seeing national leaders of the Democratic party; we will not in this connection say a word in derision of the remarkable change of base—or "new departure," as it may be called,—but we must commend the sound sense and frankness of the utterances referred to, and we do rejoice in the hope that they will be accepted, as they were in the convention in this city, unanimously by all sections of the Democratic party throughout the Union. For a few years past we have hoped that such a result would one day be reached; but for some time past the dawning of that day seemed to be receding rather than drawing near. But the time seems to have come, and Clement L. Vallandigham has arisen as the apostle, in the Democratic party, of *"the full, faithful, and absolute execution and enforcement of the Constitution as it now is, so as to secure equal rights to all persons under it, without distinction of race, color, or condition."* This is a glorious apostleship; and how strange it is that Mr. Vallandigham should be called to it! When the party, of which he is chief leader, shall have adopted, in state conventions and finally in a national one, this Vallandigham creed, and shall have stood by it till no one can retain a doubt of the genuineness of its conversion, we may set up hope as a way-mark in politics, and philanthropists may henceforth contemn despair of the political regeneration of any great party subject to the happy influences of human progress and republican government. If the great body of the Democratic party should fail to receive this creed we shall be doomed to disappointment in the early realization of the universal adoption of principles so essential to true democratic government and so worthy of the great American republic.

February 7, 1872   National Religious Amendment Convention

The national convention favoring the religious amendment of the Constitution of the United States convened at Thom's Hall, in Cincinnati, on the 31st day of last month, and closed its session the evening of the next day. The convention was largely attended by delegates and spectators, there being more than two hundred and fifty of the former. The call, which we published a few weeks since, was signed by nearly one hundred distinguished persons, including many eminent statesmen, jurists, educators, and divines. The amendment proposed is designed to acknowledge God as the author of the existence of the nation, Jesus Christ as its ruler, and the Bible as the fountain of its laws and the supreme rule of its conduct.

Justice William Strong, of the Supreme Court of the United States, the president of the National Association, being absent, Prof. O. N. Stoddard, of Wooster University, called the convention to order, and the exercises were opened with prayer by Dr. Aydellott, of Cincinnati.

Pending the permanent organization, Rev. D. McAlister, of New York, general secretary of the National Association, delivered an address of fine ability. He was followed by Rev. A. M. Milligan, of Pittsburgh, with some interesting remarks.

Judge M. B. Hagans, of Cincinnati, was elected permanent president of the convention. On taking the chair he delivered an address maintaining the principles of the National Association with the clearness and force characteristic of an able jurist.

The first evening of the convention addresses were delivered by Rev. A. D. Mayo, of Cincinnati, and Prof. J. R. W. Sloane, of Pittsburgh. These were of great excellence, both in matter and delivery, and were received by the large audience with great applause. Both were thoroughly prepared, and carried great weight in favor of the principles advocated by the convention. We hope to find room for portions of them in future numbers of our paper. Dr. Mayo was the champion of the cause of the Bible in the public schools at the time when the great struggle on that subject was agitated in the school board of Cincinnati. Brilliancy of intellect combined with the graces and power of rhetoric and elocution make him one of the finest of platform speakers. His subject was "The Relation of Education to Religion," and, having the advantage of the interest which that theme has in the past two or three years excited in the public mind in consequence of the attempts to banish the Bible from the public schools, his audience was roused to a degree of enthusiasm corresponding with the elevation of the theme upon which he discoursed. Though a Unitarian minister, he surprised some at least by the boldness of his position in favor of the Bible and the doctrines of Jesus Christ as the standard for the moral and religious instruction of the youth of the country.

Though Prof. Sloane's address was less captivating than that of Dr. Mayo, it did not possess less ability or value. Those addresses were in the main a very happy presentation of the principles of the convention.

The second day, during the morning session, Mr. F. C. Abbott, of the Toledo *Index*, an infidel publication, was permitted to state orally the substance of a written protest which he had been granted leave to present to the Committee on Business, and which they had reported upon stating that it was a candid and respectful document. The speaker proceeded to deliver, in a calm and dignified manner, an address of good ability. He said that this movement seems to have the logic of Christianity behind it, and if he were a Christian,—if he believed in Christianity,—he did not see how he could help taking his stand at the side of those composing the convention. He maintained, however, that the proposed amendment would result in preventing all except Christian believers from holding any office, civil or military, under the American Government. No honest disbeliever would be able to take the oath of allegiance required of United States officials and soldiers. The result would be to degrade unbelievers to the condition of a subject class ruled by an aristocracy of Christians. It would necessarily lead to the suppression of free thought, free speech, and a free press. He thought it would inevitably result in persecution. Every man who favors this measure votes to precipitate the most frightful war of modern times. He said that if he wished to destroy Christianity by unscrupulous means he would support this movement in every way, for it would open the eyes of millions to the fact that Christianity and freedom are incompatible. He appealed to the convention to abandon their enterprise not only as hopeless, but as most dangerous to the tranquility of the land, to make no further efforts to fan to a flame the dangerous fires of religious bigotry, which, once kindled, they would be unable to control.

Rev. D. A. Mayo took the platform and replied to Mr. Abbott's argument. He said that the gentleman who had just spoken had given the gist of the popular objection to the movement in which the convention was engaged. It is, that if in the Constitution of the United States we place a declaration that the nation is dependent on Almighty God, and bound to obey his holy law; that it is living under the rule of Jesus Christ, considered as the ruler of nations; that it is bound to conform its character and legislation to the laws of Christian morality, it will be bound to deny all political rights to those who do not believe in Christianity; will be forced into the persecution of all unbelievers in religion; will compel persons of Mr. Abbott's way of thinking to fly to arms and inaugurate a bloody war. He said that the friends of this movement ask, in substance, that the same declaration which now stands in almost every state constitution should be placed in the Constitution of the United States. He said that the gentleman who had come all the way from Toledo, as if to utter a prophet's warning, is now living under a state constitution which substantially includes every idea which it is proposed to place in the national charter. The constitution of Ohio acknowledges dependence on Almighty God as the author of the liberties it was made to preserve. It declares that "religion is essential to good government." The gentleman need not to have come across the state to find this bugbear. It is in Toledo; and, as a citizen of Ohio, he is exposed to all the danger of disfranchisement and persecution to which he would be exposed if this amendment were made. Has he ever suffered such disfranchisement or persecution in Ohio? Has his vote been challenged, his political rights curtailed, or his right to publish the *Index* or preach against Christianity denied? He said that the trouble with the gentleman and his class of thinkers is that they do not understand the practical character of the American people, or that a government is not a logic machine that takes out an abstract proposition from the constitution, and, with no regard to the genius, character, or history of a people, rides that out to chaos. He said that the American Government is practical. It believes itself dependent on God and bound to obey the great laws of Christian morality; but it does this with the most scrupulous regard to the rights of every citizen. It only forbids men to violate the laws of Christian morality. He said no government on earth had ever acknowledged the complete spiritual and political rights of man till Christianity, with its law of universal love and liberty, had inspired the souls of the people of the United States to make a government under which Mr. Abbott can denounce Christianity and even threaten a new rebellion, with no one to molest him or make him afraid.

He said it is the glory of the Anglo-Saxon peoples that they are not ridden by the logical mania of pushing abstractions out to anarchy. They mix liberty and order, worship and service, just as they are mixed in the soul of man.

The people of the United States, he thought, had done right in leaving theological creeds and church polity to the churches. But the laws of Christian morality, the highest ideal of every Christian state, he thought ought to be recognized and maintained in the Constitution and laws of the nation.

The speaker referred to the state constitution of Missouri, framed after the close of the rebellion. It contained the fullest acknowledgment of dependence on God of any state constitution, and thanked him for deliverance from the rebellion. In the solemnity of the hour, coming up out of a sea of blood, even infidelity was awed to silence, and the people cast themselves on Almighty God. Now did the convention go on to disfranchise and persecute unbelievers? Why, that very constitution contains the strongest guaranties of religious liberty that can be found in any state. It even forbids a religious corporation to invest or hold landed estate beyond a lot for a church, a school, a parsonage, and a cemetery, and specifies the amount to be so held in a city. Just what the people of Missouri did, the people of the United States will finally do. They will plant in the great charter of their liberties an acknowledgment of the nation's dependence on God, and its duty to conform to the laws of Christian morality. They will maintain this position, persecuting no man save him who tries by force to destroy that sacred inheritance of freedom bequeathed by the fathers and sealed with their own blood; and whoever tries to destroy this will himself be destroyed.

A number of addresses were delivered; judicious action was taken to promote the interest of the movement; and, after very able and well-prepared addresses in the evening of the last day, by Prof. Stoddard and Rev. Mr. Stevenson of the *Christian Statesman*, the convention adjourned. The attendance throughout was large, and the spirit of the convention harmonious and enthusiastic. The outlook for the future of this national movement is quite promising. It is likely before many years to command the attention and respect of many who now affect to regard it with indifference or contempt.

June 19, 1872   The Presidential Prospect

Though there are a number of candidates nominated for the presidency and vice-presidency of the United States, it is now pretty clear that the real contest will be between the supporters of Grant and Wilson on the one hand, and those of Greeley and Brown on the other. The recent action of the Democratic state conventions renders it apparent that the national convention of that party, which is soon to meet at Baltimore, will indorse both the platform and nominees of the Cincinnati Liberal Republican Convention. This will either merge the Democratic party into that of the Liberal Republican or swallow up the latter. In either case there will evidently be but two great parties in the field, and it rests with those who do not see fit to cast their votes for cherished principles without the slightest hope of electing their candidates, to choose between these two great parties.

The issues of the past are really dead, and the platform of principles adopted by the two branches of the Republican party, though differing in phraseology, are essentially the same. Partisan policy and prejudices will doubtless deny this, and seek to magnify the difference between the enunciated principles of the two contending political parties, but with little success among the more intelligent and candid class of voters.

As to the candidates for the presidency, it is folly to pretend to regard either Grant or Greeley as dishonest. Both have given too strong evidence of this high quality to be liable to any criticism on this point, except such as a partisan spirit, or, still worse, partisan unscrupulousness, shall dictate.

It is equally foolish to deny the ability of either of the candidates. None but a very strong, clear intellect could successfully conduct such military campaigns as those under the command of General Grant during the late southern rebellion. We never had the slightest sympathy with any disparagement of the intellectual ability of the present chief executive of this nation. An able and successful administration of more than three years attests the executive ability which any general who has successfully commanded armies, wide-spread, and composed of nearly a million of men, must necessarily possess in order to military success.

Though unpolished, reticent, and self-willed, President Grant has ability in civil as well as in military affairs. Though not skilled in political lore, he possesses keen perception and clear judgment on great national questions. That he has fallen too much into the hands of corrupt, designing politicians, we do not deny. That such is the case is too apparent from the dissatisfaction excited among able, incorruptible statesmen who have ever, heretofore, proved the truest of the true in their devotion to their country and to the cause of human freedom.

Grant was, in the beginning of his administration, a novice in governmental affairs, and that, too, at a time when the reigns of government had just been relinquished by the most corrupt "accidency" that ever disgraced a great nation. Grant's next term, if he should be re-elected, will necessarily be a great improvement on the past, unless we consider him incapable of learning either from the counsels of his friends or the chastisements of his enemies.

That the people of the country will prefer him above Horace Greeley is most probable, not only on account of his great services as a soldier and a civilian, but because they will not deem his political rival less liable to be imposed on than he, or less likely to be under the terrible pressure of politicians whose incorruptibility is not in high repute among the majority of the American people.

That Horace Greeley is an honest man has never been candidly questioned by any respectable authority. That he is a man of great knowledge and wonderful ability as a political journalist none can deny. That he is a patriot and a philanthropist is most evident. That he has performed eminent and valuable service in his department of public life all who are candid must admit. But that he is almost erratic as he is great, almost as much given to specious deceptions as he is powerful in exposing corruptions and wrongs, is too true. That his errors have arisen in part from his position as an enterprising, leading journalist is also true; for a man who would lead public thought, especially at the head of a metropolitan daily newspaper, must not wait for the fullest development of a question, nor for the most mature consideration of it; but must promptly express his best convictions according to the light in which the question then appears. It is doubtful whether any journalist who has not the courage—we might say hardihood—to perpetrate some grave blunders, is fit for the editorship of a great daily political newspaper. Prompt blundering is generally considered by the public more pardonable in such an editor than long-tarrying discretion. If we had as much confidence in the fitness of the great editor for the presidency as we have in his capacity for the editorship of the greatest political journal in New York City, or in America, we would ardently desire his election. As it is, we doubt his being as good a practical success as General Grant, and feel sure that he is not likely to be surrounded, in the event of his elevation to the presidency, by such elements as will insure a purer, wiser, or more patriotic administration than that of President Grant. We think it most likely that the great body of the American people will see the presidential question in a similar light and act accordingly.

No doubt personal disparagement of the presidential candidates will form a staple in the speeches and editorial items of the impending presidential campaign. This is lamentable. Not that men in prominent positions are improper subjects of wholesome criticism, but that style of detraction which, like the vituperation of an attorney, is intended for effect only, is contemptible. When reading the articles and squibs in our exchanges which do manifest injustice to each of the presidential candidates we feel most thoroughly disgusted. We consider both Mr. Grant and Mr. Greeley as being great men, true patriots, and eminent, well-deserving public servants. While both have faults which it is not irreverent to criticise [sic], the whole people without respect to party ought to join in doing them honor. We ought to have at least one decent presidential campaign. But we are not likely to have such this year.

December 4, 1872   Death of Horace Greeley

General grief will be felt throughout the nation at the news of the death of the father of daily journalism, the acknowledged chief of American political editors. Horace Greeley died at Tarrytown, New York, last Friday evening. His watching and grief, caused by the sickness and death of his wife, united with the labors of the late presidential campaign and the depression attendant on his defeat as a candidate for the presidency, proved too much even for his remarkable constitution. He died, it is said, peacefully, conscious in his expiring moments.

For several days general anxiety was felt concerning his condition, and for a day or two previous to his death recovery was regarded as improbable. At last the news comes that the great journalist is dead.

Mr. Greeley died at a most unpropitious time. He died just after the most decided rejection by the nation of his claims to the chief magistracy of the United States. He died defeated, slandered, and burlesqued, abused by political speakers and journals that knew their defamations and slanders could only be accepted during the heat of a political campaign. We have never approved nor sympathized with this abuse, but felt abiding disgust and a share of genuine indignation, though we did not regard his elevation to the presidential chair as at all desirable.

Yet Mr. Greeley's death was not at so unfavorable an hour. His past services are security for the future homage of those who have recently been his political enemies. He died at a time when the great mass of his previous political enemies had accepted him as their national standard-bearer. His death will doubtless result in winning the hearts of many who could scarcely forget the eminent services which he had rendered the anti-slavery movement, and the severe blows which he had dealt out to the advocates and apologists of the slave power. Greeley will live in the history of America as one of the most remarkable and eminent servants of his country.

Mr. Greeley had faults, some of them great. Though generally exhibiting good understanding in political affairs, he was sometimes remarkably obtuse in his judgment. This was exhibited in his advocacy of the formation of a people's party, in 1858, with a view to the defeat of the administration party in the presidential election of 1860. This party was to embrace such men as Bell of Tennessee, and Houston of Texas—in a word all opposed to Buchanan's administration. It was not less manifest in his extreme views on tariff, and some other national measures. But he was honest and independent, a power in favor of any national measure to the support of which he turned his brilliant intellect and pungent pen. But his opposition to the Know-nothing movement, and his prompt and generous support of the principle of amnesty toward the defeated rebels of the South, were characteristic of him. He often penetrated the future in the keenness of his vision, and boldly struck in favor of what he deemed right, and that which reluctant leaders and the masses were at last brought to approve and support.

His intellectuality, his fine memory, his ready thought and pen, his manly independence, his condescension, humanity, and generosity, combined with almost unparalleled earnestness, and a large share of enterprise, placed him at the head of American journalists.

Mr. Greeley signally failed in some of his social views, but in nothing did his unsuitableness appear more than in his office-seeking. In this he was generally unsuccessful. He held for a short time a seat in congress, but it was a weakness in him not to know that, though the prince of American journalism, he was a mediocre in legislative halls. His elevation to the presidency did not at all seem desirable, but if he had been elected, and lived to serve a term in the presidential office, there is no just occasion to doubt that he would have brought to the performance of its duties a strong intellect, great energy, a heart full of patriotism and philanthrophy [sic], and as much independence, if not more, than would have been practical, considering the parties by which he was supported. But the nation,—wisely, we think,—saved him from responsibilities such as that office would have involved, and death has relieved him of the labors which could close only with his life. If he has had weaknesses and faults, they will be less remembered than his virtues and eminent public services. Rising from obscurity without the aid of wealth or collegiate training, Horace Greeley has shown himself in the sight of the nation an intellectual giant, a true patriot, and an eminent philanthropist.

December 11, 1872   Prevalence of Homicides

Within the past two years there has been an average of about seventy homicides in New York City annually. Some of these have been committed by parties undetected, and consequently unknown. A few criminals have been convicted and punished. Many, after arrest, have succeeded in freeing themselves from the clutches of the law.

The foregoing facts indicate that the taking of human life in our day is quite common. Facts with reference to other cities and country places corroborate the above testimony as to the cheap estimate placed upon life by those who have revenge to execute, or evil designs to accomplish.

There being little occasion to doubt the increase of homicides, it may be proper to inquire into the causes producing such a result.

Crimes founded on the desire for wealth are apt to increase with the increase of wealth and the disparity between the conditions of the higher and lower classes. With the increase of luxury and extravagance there is always a tendency to increased crime of all kinds. But in our country there is no just occasion to doubt that the bloodshed witnessed and reported during our late civil war has done much to remove the feeling of horror attendant on the very mention of the taking of human life. The rule of wicked men in New York, and in some other places, has also very much promoted crime. The willingness of attorneys for large fees, to quibble long and appeal repeatedly in trials before the criminal courts, has tended to give to criminals confidence of immunity from punishment. The winking of courts at criminalities, and over-stress laid by them on the technicalities of the law,—if not the taking of bribes,—have very much encouraged the commission of crimes. Then the sentimental sympathy shown criminals has been productive of the most evil results. It is well to have true charity and sympathy for the very worst offenders; but that sort which pities the vulture while it is indifferent to the wounded dove,—that compassionates the wolf at the expense of the bleeding lamb,—is of another kind. It is highly reprehensible, though it may assume the garb of superlative virtue. The public approbation of crimes similar to the murder of Key, Richardson, and Fisk, is fruitful of homicides. These were truly bad men; but the approval of their assassination carries with it an influence which renders human life wofully [sic] cheap.

One feature of the crime of homicide demands special attention. That feature is suicide. Only last week Gen. O. C. Maxwell, of this city, almost in the presence of his affectionate wife and children, dashed into eternity at the firing of a pistol, held firmly in his dying grasp. Young, intelligent, fine looking, and highly-honored though he was, he, for reasons to us unknown, took this awful leap into eternity. This induces us to suggest a few thoughts on the subject of this kind of homicide.

Suicides are very commonly attributed to insanity, which is often the true cause. But many of the ancients committed suicide when placed in circumstances of desperation. Some pagan nations encourage and practice it as a religious sacrifice. The suttees of India have demonstrated that voluntary suicide without insanity is not only possible, but may become quite common.

It is really clear that one great promoter of suicide is the prevalent sentiment that insanity is almost its uniform cause. No doubt desperation is generally its cause; but it is doubtful whether, in a large majority of cases, real insanity is present. Men and women of extravagant mode of life, of inordinate ambition, or of consuming lust, are very liable to desperation, and many consider the self-restraint necessary to keep out of the domain of desperation as a saintly rather than an essential grace. If they run into desperation,—which is often supposed to be insanity,—it is in most cases their own fault, and highly criminal. Self-restraint and the exercise of good common sense, not to say philosophy or grace, would lead to a different result. The false notions current with regard to temporary insanity, and the pleas so often entertained by courts in its behalf, are most pernicious on account of their encouragement of suicide and other homicides. It is time that suicide should be held to be a wicked and cowardly crime.

January 8, 1873   National Liquor Law

Senator Pomeroy has introduced into congress a bill prescribing the selling or giving away of intoxicating liquors, as a beverage, in the territories. We do not anticipate its passage, though such a measure is very desirable. Not only does the welfare of the people of the territories call for such legislation, but the growth, peace, and strength, moral and financial, of the prospective states in which the whole country is interested, demand it. It may be thought strange that such legislation should be deemed proper for the territories of the United States when similar laws are almost unknown to the states composing the Union. But are not some parents considerate enough to prohibit profanity and drunkenness among their children, though they are, themselves, addicted to their cups, and not over reverent in their daily language? It is paternal to wish that progeny should improve on their progenitors. And perhaps if the states should behold the happy effects of a prohibitory law on the wards of the nation, they could be persuaded to try the much-needed remedy for themselves.

But there are other places within congressional jurisdiction, besides the territories, where a prohibitory liquor law is much needed. If such a law were rigidly enforced in the District of Columbia, and rendered doubly efficient in the capital city, the next generation might be incredulous about reports and records of the past concerning the inebriety of presidents and vice-presidents, senators and representatives, cabinet officers and military dignitaries. The maudlin speech of a vice-president in 1865 might come to be regarded as a myth, and other utterances, presidential, senatorial, etc., as being in the same category. Perhaps Johnson, Yates, Bayard, McDougal, etc., might at last rank among such fabulous characters as William Tell, Romulus, or Robinson Crusoe! The time might perhaps come when the position of congressman might not be regarded as a synonym for a wine-bibber. By extending the law so as to include our fortifications, ships of war, and navy-yards, the stigma of drunken soldier or inebriate captain, colonel, or general might cease to be regarded as of almost universal application.

It might be well to try it for the benefit of those law-makers who, unfortunately, are not a law unto themselves, and who can more easily say, "Thou shalt not steal," than avoid being drawn into some "Credit Mobilier" transaction.

As the states are the source from which national law springs, it may be questioned whether the stream will rise higher than the fountain. But rather than miss the happy effects of prohibitory laws on the territories, army, navy, and congress, we would be willing to have a *prohibitory law passed in every state,—* and enforced, too, whatever might be the effects on our legislatures, courts, city councils, mayors, or governors. We venture to suggest that all worth saving might be retained if their liquor supplies should be cut off.

It is a somewhat hopeful sign when two terms of the vice-presidency are given to such temperance men as Schuyler Colfax and Henry Wilson; and one of the most pleasurable considerations connected with this fact is another, that these men, in talent and accomplishment, well represent the temperance cause. We have some temperance men in the national government, and there is room for a great many more.

The principle of legal suppression of the liquor traffic is right; and, though there is little hope of its triumph in congress as now constituted, it is proper that temperance men in that body, as well as elsewhere, should advocate it. Such bills as that of Senator Pomeroy may produce but little apparent effect; but we trust the day is coming when temperance men shall cease to hide their light and to retard the cause by those secret conclaves which bring it into disrepute; which divert men and women from the object that temperance organizations should have in view; and divide the friends of temperance. Then, planting themselves on manly, truthful principles, the advocates of temperance will exert a moral and political power which will cause the disciples and apologists of intemperance to tremble.

Who that feels a spark of humanity can look upon those saloons where the souls and bodies of men are degraded, where their pockets are robbed of that needed to support their wives and children, without feeling like visiting destruction upon these tabernacles of Satan. There the dupe of intemperance is robbed of all that is valuable to himself, and his wife and children are visited with the unenviable name and fortune of "a drunkard's wife,"—"a drunkard's children." A prohibitory law is needed in every state. Its want is felt in a great number of cities. The confirmed drunkard needs it; the tippler needs it; the youths of our land need it. The drunkard's wife, his child, his friends, need it. Political economy calls for it. The voice of humanity, of morality, and of religion is raised in its behalf. Justice and duty imperatively demand it. May congress have a prohibitory liquor bill before it every session till a thorough one becomes United States law to the glory of God and of our common country.

January 22, 1873   Stokes' Conviction and Sentence

The conviction and sentence of Stokes by a New York jury and judge, for the murder of Fisk, took the whole country by surprise. Assassination had come to be regarded as tacit law, in the estimation of public opinion, in the great American metropolis. The current maxims, "hanging is played out," had been generally understood to include all severe punishments; so that Stokes' prompt conviction and subsequent sentence broke on the public ear like successive claps of thunder from a clear sky.

Fisk was a bad, very bad, man. He was both hated and feared, as well he merited. His fall was but the fitting end of his charlatan career. "Earth wearied of him, and the long, meek sufferance of heaven did fall." The common idea abroad was that for the murder of such a man there could be no severe earthly punishment. Besides this, there was the general sympathy prevalent in the city and abroad which generally arises in favor of a helpless culprit whose crime cannot be undone. But despite all these considerations and influences, Stokes was tried and the jury, after a comparatively short session, returned the verdict, "Murder in the first degree." This was followed by a sentence at the next session of the court, three days later, of death,—the judge fixing the time of execution at the earliest day permitted by the law.

The prisoner received it with surprise,—almost confounded. He treated the sentence subsequently as if his were a case of privileged immunity that was being grievously outraged. Though he had provided poison in his cell to end his life if such an unexpected sentence should fall to his lot, he had evidently counted on acquittal,—the common lot of criminals who had preceded him at the bar of New York justice. One almost pities him for his sore disappointment, as well as for his sad criminality and his just condemnation. But regard for the imperiled lives and peace of community forbids that pity should assume that popular, sentimental form that gives license to crimes which put on commonplace airs though horrid enough to shock the whole land.

No doubt Stokes still hopes for a new trial,—possibly for executive clemency. As to the former, all will depend on facts which we can not at this distance estimate. But though the governor of New York, Gen. Dix, is one of the mildest of men, he once commanded that any one who should attempt to lower the national flag,—in a southern port, during the rebellion,–should be shot at once. This is doubtless a fair indication of his firmness and decision. Hence we may justly conclude that a former style of indifference to law and justice has "played out" of the gubernatorial chair of the "Empire State." As Havemyer is in the mayor's office in New York City, it verily looks as if Gotham had turned over a new leaf; and if Stokes has to depend on a corrupt mayor or governor for help, his chances are very unfavorable.

We are not very partial to capital punishment; but it was anciently and in the new dispensation directly sanctioned by inspiration; and if the necessities of the times require it, it is better that its horrors should be often repeated than that the ruler should "bear the sword in vain," instead of being "a minister of God, a revenger to execute wrath upon him that doeth evil."

April 23, 1873   Our Indian Policy

The late massacre of General Canby and of Dr. Thomas, and the wounding of Mr. Meacham, by the Modoc chief and his attendants, has stirred the whole nation. So it ought. It is base treachery, even for savages. Not so much more so than, in the annals of the conflict between the races, has been recorded of some of our own people,—the massacre of the Moravian Indians, for instance,—but too bad to be allowed to escape justice.

The cry now is, "Exterminate the Modocs!" "Down with the President's peace policy!" "Return to the old policy," is the motto of not a few, and there are journals of wide circulation found to advocate it. It is a proposition to return to a policy that has been a disgrace for centuries past,—to one that has cost thousands of lives, immense sums of money, and retarded civilization with two races. It is one that has opened up fiendish scenes to the sight of angels, if little known to the people of our land. It has done more than all else besides to shut the surviving Indians down in the den of heathendom. If the exterminating policy represents our holy religion, it must require more highly-cultivated intellects than savages possess to discern its excellence for a proscribed race. If the Indian looks on Christianity as represented by the popular exponents of it, as brought before his face, his acceptance of it might seem as heroic as that of the over-orthodox Calvinist, on ministerial examination, who, on being pressed to affirm his willingness to suffer eternal punishment if the Lord so wills, responded: "I believe I had a little rather be damned than not, if the Lord is willing." It takes a degree of faith and grace for which the Indian race is not generally credited to enable an Indian brave to say, "I had a little rather be exterminated that not, if Christianity is willing." It takes more grace than should be required of mere human nature to say this for himself, his wife, his child, his race. And any Christian ought to hate such fiendish doctrine just as much as those savages are expected to do. And they ought to resist it as vigorously, though not with carnal weapons. The exterminating policy must have a father very closely resembling the devil.

If the Modocs have proved treacherous let them pay the penalty. But the proscription of the whole race, or even tribe, for the acts of a chief, or of a few, has neither the voice of Calvary nor Sinai in it. It is neither gospel nor justice. It is heartless injustice.

But some may say that the peace policy does not work well. Has any other worked better? Has any other advanced the Indian tribes in civilization as rapidly? Had we adopted this policy even a quarter of a century since we should perhaps have now had no Captain Jacks. Such as he are only the uncultivated counterparts of Tweed and Fisk and Stokes and Foster of our refined metropolis. Some of these, under the operation of the cheating and exterminating policy, might have been made at least second-rate Modoc chiefs, provided they had not expatriated themselves in order to share the spoils of the Indian agents or traders, which Captain Jack has never done.

Let the Modoc chief be captured and executed. Let his associates in the massacre of General Canby and the commission be dealt with likewise. Let the lives of the Modocs be sacrificed so far as unavoidable in vigorous warfare. But let us not imitate the demons we would punish. Let us teach them civilization rather than attempt to excel them in those traits which bad faith on our part has done so much to develop. A Christian policy is the cheapest, safest, and most effectual Indian policy. Let us remember that our own people are only a few generations removed from barbarian ancestry. We can not afford to go backward in civilization.

November 26, 1873   Thanksgiving Day

Thanksgiving day is a time-honored anniversary of New England. We might now say that it has become national. It is well; for we are too apt to forget the source of blessings and services, too apt to fail to connect these with their Author, while receiving them so bountifully.

Thanksgiving is due to our heavenly Parent for life, health, peace, prosperity. A large number of the most common blessings,—the most precious, but sometimes overlooked because were never deprived of them,—are just cause for giving of thanks. We may thank God for personal deliverances, for grace we have enjoyed, or such as we may enjoy, for our hope of heaven, for what he has done for ourselves, our families, our friends, and for others.

We may praise him for the general good health, for bountiful crops, for national peace and prosperity. We may praise him for happy institutions, wholesome laws, and exalted privileges. We may thank him for the progress of good principles in our own country and throughout the world. We may thank him for the progress of liberty among the nations of Europe. We may ascribe praise to him for the agencies employed for the evangelization of the world, and for the success he has granted us in this blessed work. We may give thanks for revivals enjoyed, or for those we may assuredly hope for if we labor to attain such blessings. Thanks are due him for our preservation from political rebellions and revolutions. We may thank God for the preservation of the Church from faction or schism, and for the degree of brotherly love and piety that prevails. We may thank him, too, for his blessed assurances, for his exceeding great and precious promises, and that he has crowned our lives thus far with loving-kindness and tender mercies. We may praise him and call on all who have breath to praise the Lord. Praise is due, and it is comely.

December 10, 1873   The Princely Convict

Every year, subjects of great magnitude and intense interest are brought before the public mind. A number of these are now engaging general attention. But the exciting events connected with the guilty career of one person who has been for many months regarded as the chief figure in the New York frauds having apparently terminated, it seems a proper occasion for some observations and reflections.

William M. Tweed, with a shaved head and the habiliments of a penitentiary convict, is now the occupant of a cell on Blackwell Island, with the assurance that, if a righteous sentence is carried out to the letter, one famous plunderer of the public treasury will not for many years tread in glittering livery the streets of New York City. The descent of this great Tammany chief from influence and power to a felon's doom is like the falling of a star from heaven. The audacity of his brilliant but guilty career only exceeds the darkness of the ignominy which is its appropriate result.

In a great city like New York, expenditure for legitimate municipal purposes is very large; hence the invitation to corruption is too strong for any who may control these expenditures, unless they be men of strict integrity. It is stronger than any that should be placed before that profession who are appropriately styled politicians, but who, like Tweed, aspire to the title of statesmen; especially if the vigilance of upright citizens, the press, and the courts, does not give full assurance that detection, conviction, and adequate punishment will almost inevitably follow guilt,—and that speedily. Not only do cities and countries need a better class of public officers than party policy is calculated to place in positions of trust and power, but they need to make them sensible of a responsibility that involves exposure, displacement, and severe punishment in the event of dishonest practices.

The Tammany ring, under the management of its great chief, entered upon a course of plunder involving millions of money, and threatening the utter bankruptcy of the municipal treasury. By bribes and by ballot-box stuffing, in addition to the ignorance of a large part of the foreign population which composes the major part of the citizenship of New York City, Tweed and his associates hoped, no doubt, to have a perpetual lease on the public treasury. They were prepared to crush any individual that should raise his voice against their crimes. They succeeded in covering up their villainy from general observation, and for some time they either eluded the vigilance of the conductors of the press or bribed and overawed those who were apprised of the real situation of affairs. Thus they fattened on corruption and daily grew more presumptuous.

But the hour of exposure came. The *Times* and the *Tribune*,—more especially the former,—with a courage, ability, and persistence worthy of the importance and magnitude of the undertaking, as well as the obligations and honor of the press, entered the lists. The strength of the better class of citizens was devoted to the carrying out of the well-begun work. A large and strong committee of investigation, composed of the best citizens of all political parties, was chosen, and the Tammany ring was pressed as closely as if the extermination policy had been fully adopted. A few months later and the very names of William Tweed and his associates were regarded as a reproach to the party with which they affiliated. The verdict of guilt was pronounced against them by public opinion on both sides of the Atlantic.

Yet it was a question whether there was not enough power in the wealth and strategy of the Tammany conspirators to give immunity from the infliction of legal justice. Long time did public expectation wait on the slow pace of legal jurisprudence. At last the final sentence was pronounced. The stroke fell upon the chief, whose conduct in the presence of an array of overwhelming evidence against him is best described by the language of Judge Davis in pronouncing the sentence against him after his conviction by the jury, who said: "Through the whole of this trial you remained, up to the very moment of your conviction, as calm and serene as though you relied upon your innocence, when it was overwhelmingly apparent to all that your serenity was only that audacity, that confidence in the omnipotence of corruption, rather than reliance upon your innocence."

For once, wealth and legal strategy had failed. Princely villainy stood a condemned culprit at the bar. All resorts failing, the distinguished convict is in a short time wearing the larceny jacket as an inmate of the state penitentiary.

Truly the career of William M. Tweed has been as magnificent as crime would permit. Possessed of talents capable, if rightly directed, of honoring and blessing the greatest city of this country, and the greatest state of the Union, the public power of which, for a time, was indisputably controlled by him, he became the very chief of public plunderers and was held up to the gaze of the whole nation, and to that of the well-informed of the civilized world, as guilty of the robbery of the public treasury of the city which had placed him in so high a trust—with all the perjury involved in such villainy—and crowned at last with a fall scarcely less signal than that of Warren Hastings would have been, if the justice which Edmund Burke so eloquently invoked against him had been duly meted out.

What is there in such an example that is inviting to the young man who is vibrating between the choice of integrity and that of dishonesty? It is well that since such examples exist they shall be occasionally held up as types of others of less note. Tweed's doom as an example ought to serve a purpose scarcely less efficient as a warning than his career has been pernicious in its corrupting influence. Restless guilt, ever on the lookout for detection, is sure of unhappiness, however splendid its decorations; and though adroitly pursuing the object of its morbid craving, it finally reaches a point of criminality beyond anything regarded as possible in the earlier stages of its career. Its audacity compels the exposure it seems to defy, stamps infamy on the face and reputation of its possessor, and entails a punishment which, by its very contrast with his aspirations, seems almost cruel in the eye of public sympathy, though ever so inadequate to the real demands of outraged justice.

What a contrast is presented in the events of the life of the great Tammany thief. Once rolling in wealth, princely in display, his favor and association courted by the *elite* of New York City, and in some degree by that of the whole land, as well as by distinguished foreigners, see him now in the custody of the wardens of a penitentiary, his head shaved, himself arrayed in the habiliments of a thief, under the restraints of a prison discipline, the denizen of a convict's cell. Truly his fall was like the hurling of Lucifer from the pinnacle of his guilty ambition to depths of degradation beyond the compass of his once proud scorn.

The story of Tweed's answer to one of the questions asked when his name was placed on the roll of the penitentiary—whatever of truth there may be in the report—is very suggestive. It is said that in answer to the question as to his religion, he said that he had no religion. Indeed, it is perhaps true in more than one sense that he has no religion. If he had really accepted the grace of God, he might have been a shining evangelical light to darkened souls, instead of an evil meteor leading a host from the path of integrity, and from the light of heaven, into the meshes of guilt and into the jaws of destruction. How awful it is that one bought with the precious blood of Christ, and once chidden by the Spirit that wooingly waits to regenerate the soul and introduce it into the family of God, should in the keenness of his anguish, as from the depths of perdition, realize and say: "I have no religion!" Religion is the great conservator of virtue and the efficient instrumentality of reformation, beside which speculative moral philosophy and theology are but as brilliant mockeries.

But Tweed is probably without religion in still another sense of that term. Probably his ideas of a supreme being are all covered with doubt, if not with positive unbelief. The efforts of infidelity in France, in England, in Germany, in the United States, have been but too successful in removing the influences and restraints of religion from many who are thus turned upon society with the practical maxim, "Let us eat and drink; for tomorrow we die;" or this other, "Let us triumph while we can, whether by honesty or by fraud; for there is not God to rule the world, and no account beyond the grave." If integrity and virtue are to be promoted it must be by the ethics of the Bible and the pure and efficacious influence of religion. Infidelity may furnish us a harvest of Tweeds, great and small, but it is the Christian religion that must furnish the Howards and Benezets, the Luthers and Knoxes, the Wesleys and Whitefields, the Edwardses, the Otterbeins, and the Finneys that are to lead the hotss [*sic*] of reformation to victory over sin and corruption, and crown the millions with present and everlasting salvation.

February 18, 1874   Ohio State Convention

A state convention will be held at Music Hall, in Dayton, March 9th and 10th, for the purpose of counterteracting [sic] the influence and taking measures to thwart the purposes of the enemies of Christianity in this commonwealth, who are working night and day, with might and main, to *infidelize* [sic] the Constitution of the State of Ohio, now being revised by the constitutional convention in session at Cincinnati. *Many thousands* of petitions have been secured—*thirty-five thousand*, if we mistake not,—by these infidels, asking the constitutional convention *to sweep from the Constitution of Ohio everything recognizing religion.*

These infidels have organized, and are organizing, "liberal leagues," wherever they are numerous enough to do so, and are, by intrigue and lobby pressure, as well as by largely-signed petitions, moving quietly, but energetically and powerfully, for the accomplishment of their well-devised plans and deeply-cherished purposes. If the Christians of the State of Ohio do not awake and bestir themselves, they will find that an enemy has sown industriously and successfully while they slept. That enemy, infidelity, is impelled by an enmity as implacable and a zeal as satanic as that which moved the enemies of Jesus of Nazareth to cry, "Away with him! Crucify him! Crucify him!" They are crying in the ears of the constitutional convention, "Away with all recognition of religion in the Constitution of Ohio! Sweep it out! sweep [sic] it out!" And it is to be feared that there are some Pilates who, against their own better judgment and the dictates of their consciences, will be disposed to yield to the clamor of these infidels and their allies, and to deliver the cause of religion into their hands to be led away to crucifixion. The infidels are pretty well organized now, and are still industriously perfecting their organization. Like some of old, they seem to have bound themselves with a curse, saying: "We will not rest night nor day till we have slain all recognition of religion in the constitution." Let not the friends of religion slumber as the disciples of Jesus did at Gethsemane, till they find that Judas, (politically speaking,) has betrayed the cause of the Master into the hands of his enemies. It is the opinion of some best prepared to judge that such is the telling effect of the quiet but powerful efforts of the open enemies of Christianity and its secret foes, that they will obtain complete success if the Christians of the state do not arouse themselves and let the Constitutional Convention know that they too have minds, and hearts, and wills, and cherished interests, and that they care for the Christian character of the great State of Ohio, and for the influence and bearings of its constitution. They can not afford to let Ohio become a conspicuous example to other states of the Union of the infidelizing [sic] tendency of the age. They can not afford to join in the cry for the crucifixion of Christ, which rung out on the air of Judea's capital in the year of grace the *thirty-fourth*. God and his Christ have done too much for the people of Ohio the past century and the past thirteen years to allow them to permit the constitution of their beloved state to be atheized at the will of those who are striving to banish the Bible from public schools, to infidelize [*sic*] the halls of learning, and to render atheistic the whole conduct of our state government. They will not permit it, we trust. They will arouse themselves, set up their banner in the name of the Lord of hosts, rebuke the infidelity which festers in venomous hostility to our holy Christianity, and plant the impress of God's truth more conspicuously in our organic compact.

Let it be remembered that it was the reference to religion in the state constitution that for a time stayed the combined efforts of Roman Catholics and infidels in Cincinnati from success in their efforts to drive the Bible from the public schools of Cincinnati. Our constitution ought, instead of being weakened in this regard, to be made far stronger than it is now. There is no just reason why a whole commonwealth should in governmental affairs be compelled to act like atheists because a minority, such as the psalmist has described, have said in their hearts, "There is no God." Their unreasonable folly and sin do not justify us in ignoring, most conspicuously, the Supreme Ruler of all nations and the Redeemer of Mankind. We must as a commonwealth act in governmental affairs either on the premise that God exists, or as if there *were no God. The latter is bald atheism.*

The convention is for delegates, which should be sent from every Christian neighborhood; but it is also intended for a mass-meeting of the people from all parts of the State of Ohio. Music Hall, in the heart of the city, on Main Street, is one of the finest halls in the west, and will contain an audience of fifteen hundred. If more room is needed, no doubt the use of some of the churches of the city can be obtained to supplement the capacity of our elegant hall. The convention which is duly authorized will begin the evening of the 9th of March, and is expected to close the evening of the 10th. We will give more information on the subject next week.

March 18, 1874   Charles Sumner

One of the greatest of American statesmen is dead. Charles Sumner died in Washington City the morning of the 11th instant. He had never recovered from the blows inflicted in 1856 by the congressional ruffian, Preston S. Brooks, a representative of South Carolina, who stole into the Senate chamber where Mr. Sumner was alone engaged in writing at his desk, and smote him down "as Cain smote his brother." The years of Mr. Sumner's suffering which followed, mitigated by partial recovery after a long time, finally terminated in his recent death after a short illness.

Charles Sumner was born in Boston, Massachusetts, January 6th, 1811. After a preparatory education in the Latin school of his native city, he entered Harvard, where he graduated in 1830. He soon after entered the law-school at Cambridge, Judge Story being one of its teachers, with whom he formed an acquaintance of great intimacy, mutual affection, and admiration. In 1834 he was admitted to the bar and soon obtained the largest practice of any young lawyer in Boston. He afterward reported the proceedings of the United States court, publishing "Sumner's reports" in three volumes. He also published a law journal, the *American Jurist*, of great reputation. Soon after his admission to the bar, he, in the absence of Judge Story, lectured to the law students at Cambridge, and at one time had sole charge of the school, in which in 1836 he was offered a regular professorship, as also in the college, but he declined both. From 1837 to 1840 he traveled in Italy, Germany, France, and England. Returning to Boston he resumed his law practice, and also edited, with annotations, "Vessey's Reports" in twenty volumes. His first public entry upon politics was in 1845, when on the 4th of July he delivered in Boston his great oration, entitled "The True Grandeur of Nations." It became famous in Europe as well as America, and was highly eulogized by the great Richard Cobden. Other addresses followed, placing Mr. Sumner at the very head of New England orators. His antislavery views separated him from the Whig party, and identified him with the Freesoil party of 1848. After Mr. Webster had betrayed the antislavery cause in 1850, and then gone into President Taylor's cabinet, Mr. Sumner was elected by the Democrats and Freesoilers of the Massachusetts legislature to succeed the fallen statesman in the United States Senate. In the Senate, Mr. Sumner distinguished himself and honored his state by a speech in opposition to the same "fugitive slave law" to which Mr. Webster had given the most servile indorsement; and in that speech Mr. Sumner enunciated the famous formula, "Freedom is national and slavery sectional." In 1856, Mr. Sumner delivered a speech on the "Crime against Kansas," in which, with logic and learning, he lashed the devotees of slavery into a fury. The speech was one of the greatest ever delivered in any parliamentary assembly. It was so able and crushing that Preston S. Brooks of South Carolina replied to it in a few days afterward by beating Mr. Sumner on the head in a most cowardly and brutal manner. For three years, Mr. Sumner's recovery seemed doubtful, but in 1859 he again resumed his duties as a United States senator, where his speech on the "Barbarism of Slavery" was as pungent as it was appropriate.

His course in the United States Senate during the southern rebellion and subsequent to it was that of a statesman always ahead of his party, not in corruption or any other form of degeneracy, but in true progress and all that is pure and manly. He has been hated, misrepresented, and abused, but he will live in history when his traducers have been consigned to oblivion or infamy. His supersedure in the chairmanship of the Senate Committee on Foreign Affairs by Simon Cameron was as disgraceful to his party in the Senate as it was servile to the personal dislike of the executive department of the Government.

Charles Sumner was emphatically the great antislavery senator—pre-eminently such. His fast labors and cares were in behalf of the civil rights of the colored man.

Hating corruption, intrigue, and everything that is little, Mr. Sumner could not easily harmonize with an overwhelmingly dominant party subject to the machinations of leaders such as are apt to rule in such a time. He could scarcely fail to rebuke an executive of rather low-toned moral tastes and maxims of policy. He was repaid by the most cordial hate of those who loved the wages of servility; and unfortunately he was driven to extremes to be regretted truly, though his rebuke of executive assumption in the affairs of San Domingo and of executive nepotism will be among the glories of his permanent record. Yet his opposition to the annexation of San Domingo may not, in the abstract, have been wise, and his almost complete severance from his party may have been as impolitic as it was impotent.

Senator Sumner was great in learning of almost every kind. As an orator he was able, polished, and grand. As a statesman he was as incorruptible and as just as Aristides. He was as broad-minded as Chatham, and as pure and philanthropic as Wilberforce.

His honesty and purity were above the reproach, or even the suspicion, of his bitterest enemies. In a corrupt age he was above the very overtures of corruption. In an age of party servility, his principles were as independent of party manipulation as they were above party in tone and grandeur. He is an example to young men in learning, in principle, in real success, and in true glory. He was far inferior to Seward as an organizer and a diplomatist. He evidently possessed but a small share of the executive wisdom and ability of Chase. He was no parliamentary leader compared to Thaddeus Stevens. He had not the flowing warmth of Lincoln's genial heart. But he was as a learned, patriotic, grand statesman second to none of his age or of any other age of American history. We can say such things with a good countenance when he is gone if we have believed and indicated them while he was living. Let honor's brightest laurels crown the memory of Massachusetts' noble son, America's grandest statesman.

April 8, 1874   Compulsory Education

The theme of compulsory education was touched upon by Miss Anna E. Dickinson in her lecture in this city last week. Indeed, that subject is quite commonly agitated in these times. For this reason and from its importance arises the propriety of its consideration. That something of the kind is a necessity has become a growing conviction in the public mind.

It would be folly to maintain that all minds by nature possess the same talents, either as to degree or proportion. Observation demonstrates a great variety of extraordinary gifts and a great disproportion in the native intellectual powers of different minds. Yet it can not be doubted that many endowed with genius have failed for want of discipline and culture. Besides these there are multitudes who, for lack of culture, grovel in darkness, while, with fair opportunities, they might have possessed respectable intelligence. The education of the feeble-minded has demonstrated what culture can do. If the born idiot can be brought to a tolerable condition, what will not mental culture do for those having sound minds?

If education is necessary to the well-being of the commonwealth, if it is a preventive of crime, if it promotes virtue, refinement, and increases the power, resources, and happiness of a nation, is it not the right of the state—and of the nation, if need be,—to require the education of all the children born or reared in its domain? Nay, more: is it not the right of the state to require of every person, old or young, that culture essential to the performance of the part of a good citizen? It is evident that such is the right of the state. Morality and the common good require it, and it is surely the right of the state to exact it.

It may be said by some that that [sic] the man or woman has not the time to go to school. This may be true, in part at least; but can they not obtain helps at home or in the neighborhood to enable them to learn how to read with ease, and for their own mental improvement?

It is too late to say that men may differ as to the utility of education. Truly a few may, either from contrariness or stupidity, deny its utility. But so do some reject the essential principles of morality. Shall we, therefore, allow polygamy, or any other form of immorality that some fanatic or knave may approve and desire to practice? Some may dispute our very existence; shall we therefore cease to treat facts as a reality? It is not a question as to whether intelligence is better than ignorance. If any are against intelligence there is the more imperative need of their enlightenment. The duty of the state to cure the fallacy is as strong as it is to furnish hospitals for the helpless sick and provide asylums for the insane.

This question of compulsory education may be hedged about with difficulties. Some are illogical or extreme in whatever they advocate, especially if it is a measure new to the country. Some may think the state has a perfect right to compel attendance at the public schools so many months each year, and for a certain number of years. But every compulsory measure should be tempered with reason and moderation. Parents of good intelligence may look upon certain schools as unfit for the moral and intellectual culture of their children. The dearest rights of parents—rights fundamental in all free governments—may be involved in the question. Instead of exciting just rebellion in the minds and hearts of good citizens, laws should be so shaped as to offend no one unnecessarily—at least so as to not oppress. Compulsory laws on the subject of education can provide that certain degrees of advancement in the branches of an English education shall be required of each child of a certain age; provided, however, that so many years or months of attendance in the public schools shall be taken in lieu of such advancement; or attendance during a certain length of time in any efficient school may be accepted as proof of the parent having done his duty in the education of his child. This would give the largest liberty consistent with the public good, and consistent with the right of each child to mental culture. It would cramp no one's conscience, violate no parent's liberty, and yet it would provide for the education of the citizen.

We have reached that point in the world's history when our responsibility to God and mankind and our welfare as a people demand universal education. It would save from a multitude of crimes; it would liberate us from millions of expenditure in dealing with the fruits of ignorance; it would elevate the character of the nation; it would increase the value of its productions; it would greatly increase our moral and military power, and it would make us mighty as the representative of republican liberty among the nations of the earth. The present prospect is that in less than a half century the United States will contain a population of one hundred millions [*sic*]. It will require great intelligence to properly direct the affairs of so great a nation and preserve its free institutions. Is it not high time, then, that legal enactments to hasten universal education should find a place among our state and national laws?

July 22, 1874   Southern Political Situation

It is not easy for an enslaved people to rise at once to the enjoyment of all the privileges of citizens of a free government without disturbing and disarranging the state of society and political affairs in general. This appears in the present situation of those states of the Union where freedmen are most numerous, though the results are far from being so appalling as was predicted by those who would have perpetuated indefinitely the bondage of the colored race.

At the close of the war the late ruling classes and the freedmen were far from being on the most fraternal terms with each other. The desire of the late slaves for freedom, the service of many of them in the federal army, and their readiness to befriend the escaping prisoners of war, all were calculated to excite enmity in those accustomed to absolute dominion over them. All the venom engendered by a protracted civil conflict was directed against those who alone were again in the power of the defeated friends of the rebellion. Soon laws were enacted and regulations made that in many of the southern states almost reduced the freedman to bondage again. This rendered absolutely necessary that course of legislation and constitutional enactment that placed the ballot in the hands of the lately-emancipated slaves, and gave them, as far as numbers were concerned, the control of the political situation in several of the southern states.

The freedmen having thus placed in their hands the ballot for their own protection and for the maintenance of loyalty to the national government, were compelled to find political representatives either of their own color or among the whites. This they could not do among the late slave-holding classes; hence they were compelled to find them among the ignorant colored men of the country or among those whites who came from the North as settlers or as adventurers among them. As a consequence, the members of their legislatures and their congressmen were to a great extent composed of those not fit to sit in the state and national councils. The general Government felt in some measure compelled to give countenance to legislatures and executives so constituted because these were the only legal representatives of loyalty in the South, and their overthrow would be the overthrow of the Government and the triumph of a rebellion defeated in battle only to be reinstated by political dominance.

The situation we have indicated accounts for those divergences of political policy which have distinguished the supporters of the war against the rebellion. Those who regarded the freedom of the colored people as an indifferent matter, were likely to regard the efforts of the late slave-holders to oppress them as also indifferent. They were ready to allow these late rebels the perfect right to rule as they had under state regulations identical with those of former years, even if that dominance was directed to the punishment of their former slaves for aspirations after freedom and its privileges and for services rendered in the life-struggle of the national Government. Hence the very existence of the party adhering to Andrew Johnson's policy was quite natural. But when the enfranchised policy had prevailed the Government was either compelled to fly in the face of its political supporters or wink at the irregularities, corruptions, and, in some cases, usurpations of the adventurers of the South who had been foisted into power mainly by the votes of an ignorant though loyal race. It is no wonder that men of the integrity of Chase, Sumner, and Greeley should have been tempted to abandon an organization which was thus so nearly accessory to political abominations which good men of all parties abhorred. They were well-nigh induced to consent to the elevation of the lately-washed sympathizers of the southern rebellion to power. Rather they hoped to raise up a party composed of the better class of all parties. Their hope was vain, and they risked the cause of freedom in their experiment.

The abuses of state and municipal governments in the South remain. The misrule of South Carolina, the usurpations of Louisiana, the frauds and anarchy of Arkansas all tell of a condition that imperatively demands a remedy. Several of the southern states have been plunged into huge debts for which they have nothing substantial to show.

Why is all this? It is simply because those who had by education and training most capacity to legislate for those states were bent on avenging the lost cause and cherishing spite toward the freedmen and hatred toward the Union.

Had they been wise they would have hastened to convince the freedmen of their good will and to have established loyalty in the room of the spirit of secession. Their lack of wisdom still remains, and they above all others are reaping its fruits. What they need to do—as some of the wiser of them have discerned—is to obliterate as fast as possible all the animosities engendered by the lost institution, and by the unsuccessful rebellion. What the government needs to do is to see that no state is again ruled by usurpation or fraud, as Louisiana or Arkansas are ruled, but that illegal governments are set aside, and that fair elections are instituted to give legal and honest state governments. Let it also see to it that no government sympathy be shown to corruption in governments like those of South Carolina and several other southern states. Let it wash its hands from all responsibility for state frauds as wicked as those of the Sanborn contracts, or those of the "Credit Mobilier." It is time all the influence of the government were directed to the correction of the misrule of the southern states. Honesty, good feeling, and the public safety require it.

October 21, 1874   The Late Elections

The late elections in Iowa, Nebraska, and Dacotah [Dakota] have resulted altogether favorable to the Republican party. But those of Ohio and Indiana have been the reverse, and have taken both Republicans and Democrats by surprise. Each of those two states has gone Democratic by a majority estimated at fifteen thousand. In Ohio the Democratic party has elected thirteen out of twenty congressmen, and in Indiana it has secured eight out of thirteen. Such results set the politically wise to searching out the reason of this overwhelming defeat of the Republican party in these states, and quite various are their conclusions.

Among the real causes of the Republican defeat in Ohio and Indiana is the depressed financial condition of the country. The party in power is held responsible, however unjustly, by the ignorant class of citizens for any financial embarrassment which the country may suffer.

Another cause undoubtedly was the passage of the civil-rights bill by the Republicans of one house of congress. The negrophobia of former years has not been entirely rooted out of some pretty respectable people, and it is a bugbear to those of low mental and moral endowments.

A cause not less potent than either of those mentioned is the fact that there is in the Republican party a larger portion of radical, earnest temperance men than there is in the other great party. And not only were the "crusaders," who sent such consternation into the ranks of the intemperate and those who encouraged them, more largely composed of persons of Republican sentiment than those which were of Democratic, but the temperance plank in the Ohio Republican platform, though in itself mild, was a cause of alarm to those who love intoxicating drinks, or derive profits from their manufacture and sale.

In some cases, too, very objectionable candidates were by intrigue forced upon the people of the Republican party, and the rebuke given by their defeat was deserved; and it will finally be attended with wholesome results, however mortifying the present Democratic victory may be.

The defeat of the Republicans in these states will still leave them a majority in both houses of congress, but will doubtless teach the party greater care to rid itself of responsibility of corrupt men and measures. A dominant party with an overwhelming majority has strong temptation to such confidence as to its lease of power as to render it rather reckless of its measures, and as to the character of prominent men in its fellowship.

But this defeat will, in all probability, work disaster in the southern states where the "white leagues" prevail. These will undoubtedly triumph; and it is to be feared that they will be encouraged to further deeds of bloodshed, oppression, and cruelty. Yet we trust in the right, and hope our government will have the energy to put them down promptly; though it is also to be hoped that the Government will feel the necessity of seeing that honest elections are held, and that only legal governments are allowed. The want of setting these things right is one of the very causes that has brought this signal defeat of the Republican party in those great states.

January 13, 1875   Affairs in Louisiana

There are questions connected with the condition of southern affairs that may involve some difficulty of solution. And first of all comes the almost impossibility of getting the facts in the case. The telegraph sends out dispatches quite dissimilar to each other; newspaper correspondents contradict each other's statements; and witnesses of apparent credibility testify directly opposite to one another. One is almost compelled to discard the testimony of the present and fall back on known facts, and philosophize from such data as can be relied upon. Instead of this, many will only consult party prejudice and regard evidence according to the bias which this may give. A few startling facts, however, are past all dispute.

The first fact is that the "White Leagues" (political secret societies) have done all they could to prevent the late state election in Louisiana from being a fair expression of the choice of the majority of lawful voters in that state. Fraud and intimidation by these organizations and those they could influence have prevailed extensively and systematically. Whether this has been equal to the estimate of the Returning Board or not it is hard to decide. According to the election returns seventy Democrats and forty Republicans were elected to the House of Representatives. The Returning Board, authorized by law to examine and correct those returns, decided that fifty-two Democrats and fifty-four Republicans were legally elected. Owing to menaces, it was supposed that a sufficient number of Republican members would be deterred from taking their seats at the opening of the legislature to enable the Democrats to command a majority in the organization of the House, and hence give them the offices, as that of speaker and clerk, which is considered a great advantage, especially when strategy is to be the resort.

That the Democrats had not full confidence in being able to command a majority in the organization, most clearly appears from the fact that on the assembling of the members of the House, January 4th, to open the session, they did not allow the clerk of the previous House, Mr. Vigers, to proceed, as the law now provides, to the completion of the regular organization. But after he had called the roll, according to the list made out by the Returning Board, and had declared one hundred and two members (a quorum) present, instead of allowing him to complete the regular organization, a Democratic member arose and moved that L. A. Wiltz, ex-mayor of New Orleans, be chosen as temporary speaker. This member, ignoring the temporary chairmanship of Mr. Vigers, put the affirmative of the motion amid the greatest confusion, occasioned by such an unwarranted method, and declared Mr. Wiltz elected, who, occupying a chosen position according to the programme of usurpation, sprung into the speaker's chair, seized the gavel and began rapping vigorously for order. The usurping speaker proceeded, amid much confusion, to the election of a temporary clerk, to the admission of several Democratic members whose right to seats were in question, and afterwards proceeded to the "election" of a permanent speaker and clerk of the House. All this was done in defiance of even the decencies of parliamentary rules. The Republicans refused to vote on the so-called election of a permanent speaker and clerk, and afterward, attempting to leave the hall, which would have endangered the very pretense of a quorum, the "permanent" speaker, Mr. Wiltz, ordered the sergeant-at-arms (who had been elected in the same revolutionary way) to prevent the members from so doing. Amid great excitement and the flourish of revolvers and knives (Louisiana style), the Republican members, aided by policemen outside the railing dividing the floor of the House from the lobby, and retarded by the "sergeants-at-arms" within, succeeded—all but about a dozen—in escaping.

The "speaker" then, on motion, appointed a committee of three to ask General De Trobriand, the commander of the United States troops stationed near by, to come to the hall and preserve order. General De Trobriand soon came, with clanking sword, up the aisle, and used his influence to aid the "speaker" and "sergeants-at-arms" in clearing the lobby and settling the members into their seats.

Now it is necessary to notice particularly that the state authorities, being apprised of danger of violent or revolutionary intentions on the part of those who perpetrated the legislative farce, briefly sketched in the foregoing, had requested General Emory to station United States troops around the legislative building. The event proved—though a deplorable necessity—the wisdom of such a measure, to check high-handed revolution.

Governor Kellogg, learning of what was going on in the House, sent a request to General Emory to send troops to restore the House to legal authority and eject the members claiming contested seats who had been admitted by the usurping, factionary, Wiltz House. General De Trobriand came, and, after his orders had been read by his adjutant, requested that Mr. Vigers should be allowed to organize the House according to law, which Mr. Wiltz positively refused, and ordered Mr. Vigers put out of the hall by the sergeants-at-arms; but Mr. Vigers appealed to the general for protection. Soldiers, to the number of perhaps fifteen, came in, and the necessary protection was given the clerk. The usurping speaker was compelled to leave his seat, which he did, protesting eloquently, and he also left the hall, attended by nearly all the Democratic members.

After Mr. Wiltz and his supporters had left the hall, Mr. Vigers proceeded to organize the House, it being claimed that fifty-five members (a quorum) had answered to their names. Ex-governor Hahn was then elected speaker by the remaining members. Oaths were administered to the members, and several contestants for seats were admitted, after which a message from Governor Kellogg was received. After the reading of the message, the House adjourned.

The Democratic members, the next night, held a caucus, but did not venture to assume for it the functions of a legislature. The general policy seems to be that of playing the part of martyrs, under the impression that it will gain for them national sympathy. Some leading Republican journals assume that it was the design of the Democratic members, in their revolutionary proceedings, to throw themselves into conflict with the authorities purposely to provoke force that would give them the prestige of martyrdom. This is too theatrical a part, however, to attribute to politicians as terribly in earnest as the Democratic members of the Louisiana legislature are. It is true, however, as the Chicago *Times*, a sympathizer with them, says that they "*made a mistake in attempting a revolutionary seating of their speaker.*" Yes, that is the right name,— "*revolutionary*,"—and it was a great "*mistake*," especially as they had it in their power to have organized the House legally in a way that would not have been unfavorable to their cause.

After the violent proceedings of the day, Lieutenant-general Sheridan assumed command of the Department of the Gulf; and his plain utterances about the condition of the affairs in the state has given great offense, as it is well known that the word of a man of his position and popularity will be received generally at home and abroad as containing the real truth in the case.

What will be the result of all this remains to be seen. It is a bad case, at the very best, when it becomes necessary to call in the United States soldiers repeatedly to suppress revolution in any of the states of the Union. It is now clear that either the state government will have to be still maintained by national military power or that the state will be reduced to the condition of a territorial government. The alternatives in either case are too bad to be contemplated with complacency. It is clear that the old spirit of pro-slavery rebellion is at the bottom of all this difficulty, and that those secret societies, which are the bane of good government, and ought to be put down by law, as Daniel Webster said of the mother of them all in this country, have been the chief means by which a minority by clandestine (and of course unfair) methods have operated to deprive the colored people of their rights as citizens.

October 6, 1875   Currency Inflation

Conversing with a very intelligent and candid member of the Detroit bar a few days since, we received from him a decided expression of opinion that those political leaders who advocate the inflation of our currency know that their theory is ruinous to the country. So clearly is inflation condemned by all reliable writers on political economy, and by the demonstration of all history, that we should be compelled to arrive at the same conclusion had we not long since observed that men of eminent talent, and even of profound erudition, are almost as liable as men of little genius and of limited observation to fall into fallacious methods of reasoning, and to arrive, as a consequence, at the most eroneous [sic] conclusions. Hence our charity for inflation leaders.

Gold and silver, by the common consent of mankind, are regarded as the representatives of value. There are two qualities which especially adapt them to such use. These are purity and beauty. If gold and silver were as abundant as rocks and wood, they would be worth nothing as money. Like the Spartan iron-money, it would then require a wagon-load of gold or silver to purchase a horse, and our cars and vessels of burden would be as much loaded down with the precious metals as a circulating medium, as they now are with produce and articles of merchandise. In a word, gold and silver as a circulating medium would be useless. There was a time in primitive English history when cattle were regarded as money. Such would be a great deal better currency than gold and silver, if these were as plenty as rock in the quarry and sand on the sea-shore, the foot and mouth disease prevailing in England to the contrary notwithstanding.

Paper money is promises [sic] to pay gold and silver. If paper money were wholly irredeemable it would be worth no more than the paper before it received the impression from the engraver's plates. If it is irredeemable till a long period of time shall have expired, it is like a note, without interest, due many years hence. It is, in its purchasing value, very heavily discounted. While it calls for one dollar it is really worth in commerce only thirty, fifty, or seventy cents.

Illustrative of the results of the issue of irredeemable currency, there may be mentioned the "bills of credit" issued by the colonies in the early history of our country, the continental scrip of the Revolution, and the confederate notes issued during the late rebellion. All these systems of currency have involved many in severe loss, and others in total bankruptcy.

Nothing tends more to interrupt trade and repress industry and enterprise than an uncertain currency. If our Government has the power and right to issue legal tenders when it pleases, and in such quantities as it pleases, it possesses a very dangerous power, a power that may enable it to bankrupt multitudes at its pleasure. Indeed, it may continually hold a rod of terror over all enterprise; for who wishes to sell property when he knows not how much the dollars which his debtors' obligations call for may be worth at the next revolution of the great financial wheel of state? To increase the volume of currency ever reduces the value of each paper dollar.

It was held during the war by some that the legal-tender act was unconstitutional. There were few that claimed it would be otherwise except as a measure, justified by the exigency of the times. To hold the right to make a governmental promise-to-pay, issued in time of peace, a legal-tender for debts and to fulfill contracts made in times when such tenders were not as plenty as blackberries, nor as cheap, and then flood the country with them, is a most dangerous power. It is almost as bad as it would be to deliver the people over to the tender mercies of the Wall Street stock-gamblers.

After all, gold and silver are the representatives of value; and all attempts to make money at once plenty and valuable by paper-money schemes are just as sensible and philosophical as the attempts of an idiot to lift himself to the stars by taking hold of his boot-straps. All professions of politicians to the discovery of a currency-cure for financial ills are of the same order as the announcements of methods discovered to generate power by taking advantage of the fundamental laws of mechanics. The perpetual motion humbugs and the currency-generating of wealth are after the same order.

It is true that few wish to handle gold in large business transactions, and that paper notes of the same value as gold on deposit are a great convenience in trade, and tend to business prosperity though nine tenths of the business of the country is said to be transacted without the direct use even of currency. But he who thinks of giving intrinsic value to a piece of paper money is just as foolish as he who would attempt to make the carpenter's shavings nutritious by putting green spectacles on the horses which he desires to feed upon them. Surely the inflationists of our country are trying the use of green spectacles.

November 17, 1875   Why Exclude the Bible?

The congress of the Protestant Episcopal Church held its session, last week, in Philadelphia. Rev. Clement Butler spoke in the convention advocating the abandonment of the reading of the Bible in the public schools.

The Holy Scriptures are an object of peculiar aversion to many who do not like to own the real animus of their opposition. Many oppose the use of the Bible in the public schools who are ready to go into ecstacies [sic] over the Greek and Latin classics, though much in these last are fabulous, obscene, or philosophically false. Many a theory, plausible on its face, is quite sophistical. This theory which argues the justice and expediency of the exclusion of the Bible from the public schools may be of this sort.

Those who seek to exclude the Bible from the public schools on the ground of right, as Mr. Butler does, maintain, first, that all theories of religion should stand equal before the law, just as other rights. Well, so far as a man's own practice is concerned this is granted, provided this does not conflict with the rights of others or with the public good. If some parents should attempt to offer his child in sacrifice to an idol, his practice would justly be interfered with; first, because the natural rights of the child would be involved; second, because the good of society in general would be invaded, and the rights of the state to the life and service of every child born within its realm would be interfered with. It is also true that the will of God, on whose pleasure states exist, is involved. If this last were the only reason for the law forbidding the crime it would be reason enough for a statute forbidding his rights being thus violated. God can not be disregarded by his creatures with impunity.

But some may say that there are those who either do not believe in any God or who question his having such rights. Well, there may be those who deny the natural right of the child to its life, or the right of the state to the services of its citizens, or who may believe that moloch worship is not injurious to society in general. It is a fact that men (a few) may be found who believe any one particular measure of government is wrong. Shall we therefore have no law and no government at all? Shall we allow self-penance, involving crippling for life or death itself, just because some Hindoos [sic], immigrating to our shores, believe in it? If men have equal rights to command others to abstain from all governmental discrimination on religion, have they not equal rights as to any disputed question of political economy or morals? There is a true and there is a false in all these cases, and these may be no more evident in morals and economy than in religion.

The truth is this: The Bible contains the very essence of our moral system and of our laws. It is also true that from it all that is good in morals and laws have their origin. It is the foundation of our civilization. All Christians must admit these truths; and if they do they must admit that a book which teaches all this should not be banished from our schools while books that may, in many respects, be at variance with the best principles of doctrine and morality may have security there. Must the most ancient of all histories be banished? Must the very essence of all good laws be driven from the schools? Must the most sublime of poetry be excluded? Must the most excellent of all maxims of life be driven away from the place where morals and practical life are to be promoted? Without this volume we should lack the key to the history of modern Europe and to every department of government, education, and science. Bible theories have entered into all of these. Shall the Bible be excluded though it is essential to a knowledge of the very principles which influence not only our nation but also a large portion of our race?

Some have adopted the theory—which atheists have assiduously labored to promulgate—that all law must proceed on the theory that there is no God—must entirely ignore deity and religion. This is simply making our government atheistic; and atheism must be admitted to be the most unreasonable, as it is also the most venomous, of all theories of religion. Why this deference to atheism? Will it please Jehovah that we ignore him, that we cast out his word, to please the diversified theories of error and infidelity? Why treat his word with a contempt not shown to the mushroom theories of those who assume to be wiser than the book of eternal truth? Would its banishment be a wise thing for a Christian nation to do? Would it either be a Christian act or consistent with Christianity? If Jehovah is God, his approbation or displeasure ought not to be a matter of indifference to us. It might please atheists to have us adopt the atheistic theory and act in governmental affairs as if there were no God. But would God approbate such a course? Does the Bible teach that Jehovah is indifferent to the attitude of nations toward him? Do not Christians stultify themselves when they adopt the atheistic theory in their national or local governments? Shall atheists have their way though least of all theorists worthy of respect? Shall the blindness of some require all others to suspend a good thing to please them? A nation or state is a commonwealth. We are in one ship's company, and common objects essential to our interests and safety must be subserved even if some are so blind as to object.

There are many considerations bearing on this subject that can not be treated in this article; but what we have attempted to show is the folly of planting ourselves, as a nation, on atheistic ground, the folly of ignoring or casting out the very foundation of our civilization and of our free government simply because some hate the Bible without any just cause, and the wickedness of ignoring Him who is the source of all blessings, the author of all good government, whose providence has built up our nation and preserved our free institutions. We owe gratitude to him and respect to his word; and we would be wholly unjustifiable in taking atheistic ground to please any or all classes of errorists and of irreligion.

February 9, 1876   Our Centennial Celebration

The observation of a centennial is quite natural, and by no means unprecedented. Even the law of God for the Israelites gave them jubilees—semi-centennials. The national centennial is not, of course, obligatory on our people to observe; yet, if rightly observed, there is no just occasion to object to its celebration.

The centennial as a year was in a measure observed last year—grandly, too, at Lexington, Concord, and at other places of patriotic interest. Local celebrations in great number will doubtless take place this year; nor may we suppose the centennial celebration will even cease with the year 1876, but beam anew as the centennial of important revolutionary events may arrive.

Different classes of people have their several ways of celebrating important events. Some celebrate Christmas as if they had not a wish nor thought for the salvation which Christ brought into the world; but others celebrate it as if they rejoiced in the deliverance of their souls from folly and sin, through his merits and grace. So we presume it will be in the celebration of our national centennial. But of the commendable features which it is hoped the celebration will assume, even among people not religious, is that of the industrial, of art, of the educational, and of other commendable interests. These, if wisely conducted, may prove an honor and a blessing to our country. Assemblages with orations, poems, and addresses may also be good. No doubt many ways will be devised to celebrate—some of them good, others innocent, and still others discreditable and deleterious.

Christians should also have their way of celebrating our national centennial. It would be indeed a poor Christianity that should wait to follow only in the plans laid down by the worldly. One of the methods which Christians should adopt is that of celebrating the goodness of God in making us a nation, and in the great blessings conferred upon us during the past one hundred years. For this, why should not special services be held in all the churches sometime during the centennial year? Then there ought to be a great humbling of the churches on account of evil practices which have crept in among their people and into the families of Christians. How much of spiritual death or declension might many individuals and many churches lament in themselves. How many reforms ought to be pushed forward in our nation, and if possible accomplished. How many reforms, too, are needed in the churches, and should be consummated—not more latitude in tolerating sin and folly, but more conscience in rebuking sin and banishing it from the congregations of God's people.

Especially should the work of evangelization go forward. There ought to be a general revival, a great harvest of souls to Christ. What could be more glorious as a national centennial celebration than a revival unprecedented in its magnitude and in its power? Nothing, except a higher moral and spiritual stand on the part of the church, could compare with it in appropriateness and glory.

There should be an individual searching of hearts throughout the churches of Christ in America. Golden wedges, Babylonish garments, spiritual fornication—marriage of the churches to the world—should be put away. In many things a return to the simplicity and Holy-Ghost methods of other days is the very thing that needs to be done. There is enough formality, frippery, and Satan-hatched methods now current to ruin a multitude of souls. Oh, for genuine reform, for more of "old-fashioned" religion.

May 3, 1876   Investigation of Corruption

The events of the times justify investigations. So many have proved reckless of trusts committed to them that it seems as if deception and fraud threaten to overwhelm the land. Agitation and exposure are necessary to abate the evil. But there are features in these investigations which call for serious consideration. The first is the motives which seem to animate investigation. It ought to be patent to all in this country that the absorbing object of the Democratic party in prosecuting investigations is to discredit President Grant's administration and the Republican party. The motive of the Republican party, on the other hand, in pushing investigation, seems, in a measure, to be to make a virtue out of necessity—to show that the Republican party is able to reform itself. Nor are charges and investigation confined to the Republican party, as to their objects. Democratic statesmen and citizens come in for their full share of suspicion and the ordeal of investigation. Especially are the candidates of both parties for nomination for the presidency subjects for charges and investigation, and these apparently in proportion to their prominence and popularity. Blaine, Morton, and Bristow among the Republicans, and Pendleton, Thurman, and Hendricks among the Democrats have been passing through a severe ordeal; and we doubt not every one of them is among the freest from just suspicion, as far as anything corrupt in public life is concerned. But the object now seems to be to put them down to defeat their aspirations for the presidency.

Another feature of the "mania" for investigations is the disreputable character of the witnesses who are called upon to testify. One day the telegraph lines will teem with the statements of some astounding revelator, and almost overwhelm the minds of the reading public with conviction of the guilt of men prominent in official life; then next they teem with exposure of the worthless character of the revelator; and perhaps in a few weeks the revelations which have startled the whole country, and produced impressions, concerning public servants, which are well-nigh ineffaceable, are wholly exploded by the real facts of the case. Such aspersions of character are as detrimental to the public good as they are unjust. They subject good men to incessant suits before the great court of public opinion to maintain their good name, and thus greatly diminish their legitimate labor in the public service, and otherwise deteriorate it. When professional rogues and adventurers in the great field of deception and peculation can at pleasure get the ear of the nation, summon good men to the bar of public censure, and dim the brightness of long lives of eminent public service, it is time for a whole nation to awaken and frown upon the system of investigation in vogue, and the manner of conducting the vehicles of public information. If we as a nation are in danger from the corruption of public servants, we are in far more imminent danger of being ruined by the wide-spread and appalling magnitude of irresponsible lying. The latter is now shaking the very foundations of public confidence, threatening to drive all good men from the public service, and to make the very transactions of official business in our nation perilous, if not entirely impracticable. Investigations and revelators now begin to need investigation, exposure, and punishment quite as much as the persons and combinations against which they are directed. Perdition is likely to reap a far greater harvest from the public lying of the hundredth year of American independence than from other forms of dishonesty.

That we as a nation now especially need able and reliable public men at the front can not be questioned. The present system of defamation and slander is very unfavorable to this. We want able men because our national affairs are of such magnitude and so complicated as to require large, discerning minds to comprehend them and bring forward and decide the best measures for the public. We want men of the most reliable integrity and best moral principles, not only because public confidence needs to be restored and established, but because in a country so widely extended, and in public affairs of so great magnitude, rigid honesty and inflexible straightforwardness can only be maintained by the greatest care and conscientiousness in those managing national affairs. We now especially want *great* men, and *good* men. Small men and men of obscure or uncertain record ought not to be thought of for the presidency, for cabinet officers, or for congress. We need in the public service of the nation the finest minds and purest hearts the country can afford. It is time that political adventurers and intellectual pigmies [*sic*] were placed at a heavy discount.

July 19, 1876   Proscription of Races

Had some modern specimen of civilized perfection lived in the days of the ancient Britons, Anglo-Saxons, or Normans (who are traditionally regarded as the foreparents of the American people), and had he looked in upon some of the finest specimens of those noble fathers, it is quite likely that he would have concluded they were very unpromising subjects for civilization and refinement.

Probably the Romans did take such observations and shake their philanthropic heads ruefully over the dark prospect. The cry against barbarians is not new; the conceits of the favored sons of civilization are by no means of modern origin. As generation after generation, and age after age, goes on repeating the trite sayings transmitted from the past, on other things, perhaps thinking themselves the authors of the sagely utterances which they give, so people are doing from age to age concerning the nations which do not come up to their standard of civilization. Such are the unfavorable comments of people in these times on the mental characteristics, peculiarities, and practices of the African, the Indian, the Frenchman, the Spaniard, the Chinese, and the Japanese.

We were startled, the other day, by the utterance of Hon. Charles Francis Adams, in a centennial oration of rare power and beauty, by his informing us that the Indians had demonstrated by centuries of resistance to civilized influences their incapability to rise to any high degree in the scale of civilization. It may be doubtful to what degree of civilization and refinement even the illustrious Adams family would have attained if only such civilizing influences as have been the staple of that brought to bear upon the red men of the wilderness had been all furnished them from the first moment of their opening their eyes upon the earth. With all the native endowments, which have furnished us four generations of orators and statesmen under the genial influences of education and refinement, it is not certain that under all the influences current among the native race of this country, the Adams family should not have given us, instead of what we have seen, a King Philip, a Tecumseh, a Black Hawk, and a Sitting Bull. Men of noble birth and superior education are not entirely exempt from the whimseys [sic] which ascribe great qualities to some races and deny their existence in others.

The truth is, God has made of one blood all nations to dwell upon the face of the earth. History has demonstrated that men of every race whose opportunity for a few generations have been good, are capable of a high degree of civilization. It has been further demonstrated that men of races which have since been advanced to the highest degree of civilization have, when under uncivilized and degrading influences, remained low intellectually and otherwise. While literature was almost a stranger to Carthage, still a Carthagenian [sic] of fine opportunities was noted as one of the most brilliant literary men of his age. We do not have to travel far to find it demonstrated that the African, who has been supposed to be of a race the lowest of all in capacity, is capable of becoming with fair opportunities the peer of white men as divines, statesmen, and scholars. We have seen demonstrated in our personal knowledge the capacity of the Indian of the lowest tribe and of the native African to attain to ranks of scholarship which proves that the cry against these races as to capacity is unjust. Indeed, as wicked and brazen and foolish as that cry has been in this country, it has probably come far short of that raised ten or fifteen centuries ago against the Angles, the Britons, the Gauls, and the Teutons. The cry against the Indian, the negro, and the

Chinaman may originate in lack of capacity in some cases, and in foolish prejudice in others, but we do hope it is not always to be ascribed to essential little-
ness or wickedness. We plead for a little mercy in judging those who show the
Indian, the negro, or the Chinese judgment without mercy. But men of noble
minds, and especially of Christian hearts, ought to lift themselves against those
prejudices of race and nationality which have been among the blemishes and
follies of many an age, many a nation, and many a race. Shall Christian civilization never bring us up to the recognition of the native endowments and common
brotherhood of all nations and all races?

July 26, 1876   Animosities of Race

The British, a generation since, were regarded by the average American youth as
cruel and tyrannical characters; but it is so no longer. The average Irishman,
even to-day, looks upon "the Dutch" with profound disgust, if not actual enmity;
and many of them feel scarce more kindly toward the Englishman. Most of the
Germans regard the scourging of the French nation in the late war, resulting in
and following the downfall of Napoleon, as only half satisfying to justifiable
Germanic revenge. And all this is but the history of ancient times repeating itself. Such was the spirit of the Romans and Carthagenians [sic], the Persians and
Greeks, the Jews and Samaritans, and even the states of Greece toward each
other. There are whimsies about the inherent qualities of nations,—and even
clans and families, as among the Scottish people of yore, —as well as antago-
nisms of races. In support of such whimsies, some theological philosophers have
attributed the Jewish sharp bargaining of this age to a hereditary bias derived
from Jacob, the supplanter—the pottage-purchaser—of one hundred generations
since! And others refer the cold, cruel character of the Herods back to Esau,
their forty-ninth great-grandfather! If these nice distinctions, ignoring, in the
case of the Israelites at least, less remote parentage of more guileless and magnanimous character than the slandered Jacob or Rebecca are represented to have
been—if, we say, such nice distinctions are made by the nestors of the press and
pulpit, in the land where emigration and transfusion of peoples have so broken
upon the ideas of national superiorities, what should we expect from the common class of thinkers?—or rather of those who scarcely think at all?

But there is such a thing as real enmity of races. Such has existed to too
great an extent between the whites and the Indians, the cisatlantic European and
the African, the American and the Chinese. In this the better class of people too
often take their "cue" from roughs—among whom feuds and hates and antagonistic encounters are indigenous to the dark soil of their souls.

At this time the "sunny South"—nor is the North wholly exempt—is sadly afflicted, disgraced, and degraded by race enmity toward the colored people. This has been induced by long years of contempt toward a servile, degraded race, by the sweat of whose faces their lords have lived in luxury; by long years of angry strife over the question of their liberation; by occasional escapes of these once human chattles [sic] from the house of bondage; by occasional real or threatened insurrections; and, above all, by the deep enmity engendered in a strife to plant a separate republic on the corner-stone of human bondage. Now to have been conquered,—and in part by the arms of their own liberated bond-men,—to be compelled to vote side by side with ex-chattels, is too much for southern "bloods." Smothered hate and revenge can hardly succumb to the bayonets of a government whose faith is pledged to the maintenance of that freedom which the martyred Lincoln proclaimed—and the cry of "bloody shirt" has so affected politicians and the Government as to almost cause the victims of the accumulated vengeance of years to be abandoned to their fate. This cruel, heartless ridicule affects the masses, sways politicians, and palsies the strong arm of paternal government.

The cry of the expiring victims of a massacre comes to us from South Carolina in tones more worthy of commiseration than that of the perishing Custer and his brave comrades; for these are murdered in cold blood when unarmed and unresisting, while Custer fell in actual war by the hand of those who had been taught even massacre by his example and that of other American officers. The story of this foul massacre, as derived from official sources, confirmed by the southern press, is this: On the Fourth of July a company of colored militia, lawfully armed by the State of South Carolina, were marching through one of the streets of the town of Hamburg,—which were over one hundred feet wide,—when they were met by two young "bloods," who insisted on the militia giving way to their horse and buggy, which, after some parleying, they actually did, opening their ranks for that purpose.

These "bloods" instituted suit the next day against the officers of the militia and brought them before a justice, but the trial was adjourned till Saturday, July 8th. On Saturday, before the hour of trial arrived, armed men from the surrounding country began to gather in town, and the officers, through fear, failing to appear before the justice for trial, the armed whites, numbering two or three hundred, demanded of the militia, who were in their armory-building, the surrender of their arms, threatening that if the demand was not complied with in a given time they would open fire on the building. The militia replied, after due consideration, that the demand was unwarranted and illegal, and that they had reason to fear for their lives if they should surrender their arms—as truly they had. The armed whites then opened fire on the building, and soon after one of their number was shot down by the militia, in self-defense. Thereupon a cannon was brought across the river from Augusta, Georgia, loaded with canister, and discharged several times upon the building. The militia endeavored to escape from the rear of the building. The town marshal of Hamburg—a colored man—was instantly shot down, and about twenty-five of the escaping militia were captured and kept till two o'clock Sabbath morning, when, after consultation among their captors, five of them were marched out, one by one deliberately, and shot down in cold blood, in the presence of a large company of their captors! The rest of the captives, being either turned loose or breaking loose, fled, and three of them were severely wounded—one of them mortally, it was supposed. The begging cries of the poor captives, who were so deliberately shot down—and in one case, that of an aged mother, also, for her son,—were of no avail before General M. C. Butler and his fiendish band! General M. C. Butler, the hero of the Hamburg war, may soon be elected to congress; for M. C.—as well as the results in many southern elections—seems quite ominous. The violation of all the laws of humanity and all the laws of honorable conflict, so flagrant, had a special fitness for association with the horrid desecration of the day held sacred by all christendom [sic] in commemoration of the resurrection of the Prince of Peace and Savior of Adam's common race.

What a massacre! And this in America!—and from mere race animosity, and revenge! It shows the spirit of the South; but not of all the whites of the South. No, no! It no more reflects the sentiments of the better class of southern people than the cry of extermination, attributed to Gen. Sherman (falsely, we faintly hope,)—reflecting the spirit of the roughs on the Indian borders—represents the sentiments of the Christian people and Christian press of this country. But it shows the necessity of keeping reliable antislavery men at the head of our general Government. It demands a more vigorous policy in the protection of the emancipated wards of the general Government, who are in the midst of many who feel like tigers robbed of their prey. While forgiveness of the repentant and reconciliation with the alienated are good, the existence of the smoldering embers of hate and revenge in the bosom of the South can not be safely ignored by the humane and patriotic people of the nation. There is a just call for one general voice of righteous indignation from the people of America. Shame on such congressmen as S. S. Cox and others, who sneered and cried "bloody shirt," when Hon. Mr. Small, of South Carolina, a colored member, brought the matter up in the House of Representatives! How low the standard of an Alabama member who could claim that General M. C. Butler is a *"chevalier sans peur et sans reproche!"* What less could that able ex-rebel from Mississippi, Hon. Mr. Lamar, do than characterize the Hamburg massacre as "disgraceful and terrible," and declare that there can be "no excuse or palliation for that outrage and barbarism?" What has been thus perpetrated in South Carolina, by the aid of Georgia cannon, is more flagrant than most cases of southern outrage, but it is otherwise representative of not very uncommon barbarisms perpetrated in Mississippi, Louisiana, and other southern states. It is time for our people to demand that murder rivaling the slaughter at Wyoming and the Black

Hole of Calcutta, should cease to relieve, as a dark background in a picture, Herod's slaughter of the innocents at Bethlehem.

August 30, 1876   Executive Vengeance

The action of President Grant the past few months has left us as one that dreams. Who could have even imagined that a president of the United States would so absolutely defy the better public sentiment of the country? In so doing he has shown greater courage than at Vicksburg, in the Wilderness, or before Richmond. In the midst of an important trial he required the dismissal of Senator Henderson, the chief counsel in the prosecution of the whisky-ring conspirators. The country bore it even too meekly. He held on to intimate friends, who are believed to have abused his confidence in the interests of the whisky frauds, till public sentiment fairly execrated their continuance. Want of sympathy, if not downright enmity to Secretary Bristow, compelled the resignation of that able and upright cabinet officer. Yaryan and Pratt, chief helpers in the great work of exposing fraud, were soon forced to leave their important posts of public service. Bluford Wilson was cast out. Postmaster-general Jewell, second only to General Bristow in the reform of abuses, was most unceremoniously dismissed. The President evidently fancied that he had arisen in his executive might to strike down in his own political household the enemies of himself, his family, and his favorites. The stroke swept a phalanx of the ablest, most faithful, and most loved and trusted servants of the people. His independent, intrepid course we might greatly admire if devoted to a better cause.

Some may indorse his course as sycophants indorse the moods or follies of a tyrant; but to our mind the conduct of the President is that of one rendered desperate by disappointed ambition. The third-term mania could not subside without some signal stroke of spite against those who had exposed the wrongs which reflected discredit on his administration, and caused the total abandonment of the third-term scheme. It verily looks as if the President were reckless of the success of the Republican party, if not seeking its defeat in the next presidential election. The way to the success of that party is to repudiate his conduct in these removals. His action has been wholly foreign to the spirit of civil-service reform, to which his party is pledged.

We could have wished that the President, whose services in war and in peace have been eminent, could have saved himself from the discredit of his recent course, and our nation from the chagrin. We have felt disposed to ignore or cover the shame of our chief magistrate; but we know this is not best. It would be injustice to the noble men whom he has officially slaughtered. It would be connivance at and tacit indorsement of a great wrong. We do not believe our President to be a partaker with iniquities; but when for imagined personal affront he strikes down the heroes who have fought one or another of the major financial powers of this country with its more than human wiles, he commits a public offense against which American citizens have a right to earnestly protest.

November 15, 1876   The Great Political Struggle

The American people have just passed through a great and exciting political struggle. The great body of them are patriotic, but many of them still more partisan, it is to be feared. It may be doubted whether many have at all realized the real issue at stake, and hence the great importance of the struggle. It was so in Polk's election, which involved a great foreign war, and in that of Buchanan, which eventuated in the Kansas struggle and paved the way for the great civil conflict. Yet Providence brought good out of the evil; extended the area of human freedom in the territory acquired by a pro-slavery war, though the enlargement of the dominion of human bondage was intended; and finally overthrew slavery in its old domain. Many things are providentially right, which in themselves are very wrong. So it may be now, whoever the victor, God reigns.

Some think this the most heated of all political struggles, just as some regard the latest cold day as the coldest ever known or the most recent drought as the severest known to history. Such are mistaken, though two or three states regarded as doubtful have hardly ever seen such a contest. Other presidential candidates have been just as much abused as those of this campaign, and with just as little conscience and as little credit. The suspense over some other elections has perhaps equaled if not surpassed that of the present. At the time of this writing both parties claim the victory. It may require several days to decide the question.

Some states have been carried, we doubt not, by intimidation by either threats of violence or want of employment or tenure of homes. Others would doubtless have been lost to the Republicans from the same cause but for the presence or fear of federal troops. And it is a little startling just to think how near (or quite) the foreign population of New York and Brooklyn came to turning the scale in the presidential election and controlling the whole nation as it did the great state of New York. But for an enormous majority given in those cities by ignorant foreigners, General Dix and not Samuel J. Tilden would be governor of New York, and Governor Hayes would be elected president by a decided majority. Some of the foregoing facts are not very comforting.

Each party had its weakness in the recent campaign. Both, but especially the Democratic party, were divided on the "greenback" or inflation question. But the Cooper ticket kept many Democrats from joining the Republicans, and secured the support of still more Republicans; so it was Tilden's ally, after all. The record of the Democratic party, which these many years has been bad, was a source of much weakness. The demonstrations of the late Confederate officers in the last congress was great weakness to the party. Mr. Blaine, by provoking them into exhibition, last winter, probably saved the country from an overwhelming Democratic victory. Violence to the freedmen in the late rebel states was another source of weakness to the party in the North—not as much so as it ought to have been, because so many, after the colored man has helped conquer the Confederacy and preserve the Union, little further care as to what may become of him. Mr. Tilden's great wealth was also a source of weakness, though Governor Hayes' similar endowment saved Mr. Tilden from great disadvantage. Either candidate might have been easily defeated by one having an estate of but a few thousands. Popular sympathy would have prevailed.

The Republicans were weakened first by bitter division on candidates, and then by the nomination of a second choice, who though of high character carried little genuine enthusiasm among the people. He was one who had never trod the paths of the lowly, and who could not easily strike the chord of sympathy in the popular heart. But again: Grant's third-term aspirations, and their symptoms, his extraordinary selfishness, his connivance with rascals if not with rascality, his persecution of those who braved all for reform,—and whom the people loved,—was enough, with the corruptions exposed and the extreme partyism displayed by Republican leaders, to have sunk any party save the Republican. If the Republicans are about even, or a little ahead, it is a marvel; and one or the other they appear to be.

But whatever betide, let us submit to the results of the legitimate decision of the nation's will as shown by the ballot. Let us have peace. Let us not think all is lost if the election should prove to be averse to our judgment. We may despite all have good government and national prosperity. Let us make the best of what must be. This will give good results.

January 10, 1877   Railroad Laws

A number of years ago, in conversation with a friend of some distinction in his own state, we suggested the necessity, in the years to come, of putting railroads under United States law. To this our friend readily assented; and probably many others entertained similar views of the subject, though it was years since that we saw any public proposition to bring about such railroad regulation.

It seems now to be almost a necessity that United States laws should regulate the railroad systems of this vast country. The capital invested in railroads is very great, amounting to almost innumerable millions of dollars. Railroad kings are increased by mammoth combinations; and never did emperor or hierarch plan and labor more assiduously than do the railroad kings and princes to overthrow each other. And as yet we have seen only the beginning of what may assume greatly increased and even multiplied proportions. It is not uncommon for one railroad combination to buy up the roads of one of less proportions, or rent or lease lines to cripple other combinations and increase its own power and profits. This sometimes almost completely deranges the freight or travel of the lines reached by such action, to the great inconvenience and financial injury of cities, towns, and farming communities. We have a case in mind where a large railroad combination, having leased a certain line and rented another at a certain per cent of profits, determined to almost sweep business from the one line—except that which is merely local—that it might carry the principal freight and travel over the leased line, which it could do without increased cost on its lease. Here are hundreds of millions of property in one of the finest sections of the Union affected by the greed or caprice of a railroad combination. The interests of farmers, merchants, manufacturers, holders of real estate—almost every financial interest of the country—are to be despised by railroad kings, who plan and fight and gamble for the ascendency, often expending their strength, enterprise, and means in tilts and pitched battles, in which the courage and perseverance of rams in their combats with each other are almost put to shame.

These railroad combinations have it in their power to levy, virtually, on cities and farming communities—involving a large extent of territory,—and on commercial and manufacturing interests, for such concessions, favors, or boons as they may crave. They can bring down the value of real estate in city or country ten or twenty per cent at pleasure, thus inflicting an injury of many thousands and even millions of dollars by their control of great thoroughfares. These roads, in many cases, the people have contributed to build, and ought to be regarded, by rights, inalienable interests of the commonwealth. Railroad managers may even seek to vent spite or wreak vengeance on communities which are not as subservient as desired to personal or corporate interests. Wall-street stock gamblers are not less scrupulous or less crushing in their deals than are some railroad combinations.

Railroads now surpass our navigable rivers—and we had almost said the high seas—in the extent and value of freights and travel. On account of the conflicts and complications and abuses which are common to them, they need regulation fully as much as our large rivers and the high seas do. The power of congress to regulate commerce ought surely to be conceded to extend to our railroad system. If it is not so, let us have a constitutional amendment placing the question of control beyond dispute.

As it now is, a small part of the line or lines of one railroad combination may be under the laws of one state and another portion under those of another. So railroad employees may be under the laws of one state one hour and those of another an hour later. We need uniform railroad laws. We need, too, such laws as will convince railroad companies and combinations that capital, commerce, manufacturing interests, agriculture, and travel have some rights which these great combinations are bound to respect. It must be apparent to every one that state laws which vary and even conflict with each other are inadequate to reach the evil and to promote the good contained in our railroad system. We need national laws to govern railroads, and national inspection of them, that they may have more of unity, have better regulations, and that they may better promote the interest of labor and capital in general, and even the best interests of railroad companies themselves. It is strange that congress has so long delayed a system of national laws for the regulation of railroads throughout the United States.

January 17, 1877   The National Controversy

The prospects are not the best for a satisfactory adjustment of the controversy about the presidency. Probably the majority of the people of both great political parties believe the candidate of their choice legally entitled the presidential office, so that either party, if denied the gratification of their wishes, will regard itself as defrauded of its just rights. Viewed in this aspect alone, the situation is a grave one, involving injury to our country. While we doubt not that there was intimidation in Louisiana seriously affecting the presidential vote, there are, no doubt, many who believe that there was no more intimidation and coercion there than in the northern states. It matters little that it is most apparent that reports about intimidation and coercion in any northern state would, if untrue, obtain no credence; men will continue to deny that there were fraud and violence in Louisiana, Florida, South Carolina, and Mississippi, just as the same was disbelieved and denied with regard to Kansas during the reigning days of border-ruffianism. Many will sincerely believe what they wish to believe, whatever evidence there be to the contrary.

When we see Mexico, San Domingo, and some of the South American states at war over elections, and consider that threats of civil war are indulged by some of the political leaders of this country, there is some reason for serious apprehension. Especially is this true when we see two state governments contending for power in Louisiana, and witness the fact that last week New Orleans was in a state of insurrection, the insurgents having the ground, and that the state-house was in a state of siege, which was raised only by the interference of United States troops. It has been only a little better in South Carolina, and, in Mississippi, peace only prevails because violence has subdued the freedmen and crushed out their hope and spirit.

That the great body of the American people have any idea of getting into civil war, or that the political leaders of the country intend such a thing, is wholly improbable. We do not expect to see civil war. But that we should avoid all resort to violence, it behooves every intelligent American citizen to be temperate himself on the subject of the controversy, and most determinedly frown down all threats of violence.

The eighth of January was chosen by the violent of the Democratic party to hold indignation meetings in various places throughout the country. That these meetings were comparatively a failure admits of little doubt, though probably far less so than represented, generally, by the reporters of the Republican papers. The tone of some of the speakers was not creditable to their patriotism; but they find response in too many hearts, and add so much to the seriousness of the situation; for it is evident that menaces are not the best way to carry measures among intelligent American citizens.

That the counting of the electoral vote is surrounded with peculiar difficulties is quite certain. The Senate will doubtless insist on counting the regular electoral vote of Louisiana, while the House will certainly seek to throw it out, and perhaps also the electoral votes of Florida and South Carolina. It is probable also that the House will seek the admission of the votes of the irregular electors of those states. Perhaps it will be claimed that the two houses of congress form a joint convention to count the electoral vote, and that a majority of the members composing the joint convention must decide the question. This is of course contrary to all former theories and precedents, and would be resisted by the Senate, which would under this arrangement be outvoted by the Democratic House. It is claimed by some that if the count can be defeated it will throw the choice of president into the House of Representatives. But the Constitution provides for election by the House only in the event that after the count it shall appear that neither of the candidates has received the majority of electoral votes, which would not be the present case. Others hold that a failure to count the electoral votes would make the the [sic] president of the Senate after the fourth of March president of the United States. This has strong claim to be the legal statement of the case. Whatever may be the result of the effort to count the electoral vote the 12th of February, it is to be hoped that enough of our congressmen of all parties will subordinate their party feelings to the truth, to the right, and to patriotism, to prevent revolutionary measures which might bring confusion and involve our nation in strife—possibly in civil war. Christians are praying that God will guide and save our country.

January 24, 1877   The Compromise Muddle

The committee appointed by the Senate and House of Representatives to consider and report a plan best calculated to accomplish the lawful counting of the electoral votes for president and vice-president have prepared a bill which they, irrespective of party, almost unanimously regard as containing the best provisions that could be submitted. This bill was reported in each house of congress January 18th, and will probably be acted upon the 21st, the day our paper goes to press. The following, slightly modified, from an editorial statement in one of the leading dailies of the West, is a synopsis of the chief provisions of the bill: First, the president of the Senate is to open all the certificates—the true and the sham—from the states in alphabetical order, and tellers are to count the votes so far as not objected to. Second, when an objection is made to the counting of any vote, the two houses shall separate and take a vote on it. If they concur, that settles it. If the [sic] do not concur, the whole question of fact and law is to be referred to a commission, to be constituted as follows: 1. Four assorted justices of the Supreme Court, namely, Clifford and Strong, chosen as Democrats, and Miller and Field, chosen as Republicans, are to choose one other justice, making five justices, whose preponderance of party color will depend on the choice which the four shall make of the fifth. 2. The House of Representatives is to choose five members, and the Senate a like number. These deputations from each branch of congress are, with the aforesaid five justices, to constitute the board of arbitration, to decide all questions. In other words, it is the grand returning board, the decision of which is not to need the approval of congress, but is to stand, unless both houses concur in rejecting it.

When the dispatches from Washington announced that the committees of both houses of congress had almost unanimously agreed upon a method of proceedure [sic] in counting the electoral vote, a sense of relief gladdened thousands of hearts. Patriots were anxious for almost any legal, peaceful solution, provided it should not involve future trouble to the nation. But upon considering the measures proposed in the bill, we do not see that it promises much as to an impartial decision of the controverted questions involved nor as to a satisfactory settlement of the main question for which it aims to provide.

Of whom is the commission to be composed? Of fifteen commissioners, ten of whom are to be congressmen, five elected by the Republican Senate and five by the Democratic House. The Republican Senate will most likely choose Republicans supposed to be firm in the conviction that Messrs. Hayes and Wheeler are legally elected president and vice-president; and the democratic House will choose Democrats of like devotion to Messrs. Tilden and Hendricks. If each House should choose part of its commissioners from the party opposed to the majority of its members, it would be likely to choose such as it supposes could be most easily changed—we say not bribed. Then ten members of the commission are likely to be all strong, stubborn partisans, or part of them doubtful men, in an unfavorable sense.

The remaining third of the commission are to be two Democratic and two Republican judges of the Supreme Court,—as named in the foregoing synopsis,—and a fifth is to be chosen by the four. So we shall have seven Republicans and seven Democrats on the commission, and one—we do not know what. Will these, as in disputed elections of members of congress, vote according to party ties and prejudices? "But," says one, "they are to take an oath to decide according to the Constitution and the laws." True; but are not congressmen equally bound by oath as to their action in congress in disputed elections of members? If we are to expect impartiality mainly from the five members of the Supreme Court, why not let them alone be the commission? If that impartiality is to be found in the fifth justice, chosen by the other four, why not refer the question to him alone? He is likely to be the real umpire in the proposed commission.

To be sure, the commission *might* be composed exclusively of those distinguished for candor, impartiality, and sound judgment; and in such case the plan might work most admirably. But will it be so? We would hope that it might be so, if there were reasonable ground for so doing. But the probabilities are that the commission, composed largely of strong party men, will decide most questions referred to them by a bare majority,—a strictly party vote,—after party feelings have been intensified by discussions.

Is there one congressman, who cares for anything of patriotic concern, who is not committed in advance on questions to be decided by the commission? And how many are there who have not a heart for a cabinet appointment or hope of a foreign mission under the administration of their choice? How impartial are such commissioners likely to be, if ever so honest?

Will decisions rendered by the proposed commission be likely to allay irritation in congress and in the public mind? Is it not probable that suspicion and charges of fraud in the composition of the commission, and of bribery and treachery in its members, will add to the existing irritation?

After decisions are rendered by the commission, they are likely to be concurred in by the majority of only one angry house of congress. The compromise plan is likely to embroil the nation, instead of soothing public feeling. Further, it encourages fraud, intimidation, violence, tricks, and bribery in elections, by enabling them to compel a "new deal," instead of an honest election, to secure the president and vice-president. It establishes a precedent which may enable a future congress, on pretexts, to override an election and trick a candidate into the presidential chair. It is of doubtful constitutionality. It taints the Supreme Court by taking some of its judges, as men of party bias, out of their really exalted positions, to assist in deciding questions raised by partisan feelings and prejudices.

The indications are that the bill will be adopted by both houses of congress. We can not believe it will pass without essential modifications. It may be so modified as to become as worthy of commendation as it now is of disapproval.

March 7, 1877   The Electoral Count

The electoral votes for president and vice-president of the United States have been counted. The struggle terminated last Friday morning about four o'clock, after a very stormy day and night in the House of Representatives. Mr. Rutherford B. Hayes and George A. Wheeler have been declared elected president and vice-president by a vote of 185 for them to 184 for Samuel J. Tilden and Thomas A. Hendricks. The count had consumed over three weeks. Part of the time the work was very stirring. Toward the last it was almost anarchy. The commission appointed to decide questions of dispute between the two houses of congress was as good as could have been constituted according to the terms of the electoral bill. But all voted as party men. The fifteenth man was a Republican, and that fact decided the result, rather than argument or deliberation; for the vote was uniformly *eight to seven* on all the essential questions. If Judge Davis, of Illinois, had not been elected United States senator just at the time the commission was to be constituted, it is quite certain that he would have been one of the commissioners. Whether he would have voted with the Republicans or Democrats on the commission is a question; but it is probable he would have voted with the Democratic party. So his election as United States senator by the Democrats and liberals of the Illinois legislature was probably a Democratic defeat.

The great struggles were on Florida, Louisiana, South Carolina, and Oregon. Each occupied several days. One Cronin, an Oregon electoral candidate, had set up an electoral college of his own, had chosen two accomplices to help him fill it, and had cast his vote for Mr. Tilden. All the commission concurred in repudiating his college; but the seven Democrats on the commission voted against counting one of the regular votes for Hayes on account of the alleged ineligibility of the elector. Not a little time was consumed in scenting up ineligible electors in other states; but only the Democratic commissioners could be convinced of their irregularity.

When it was found that the count must inevitably result in placing Mr. Hayes in the presidential chair, about one half of the Democratic congressmen favored breaking up the commission or in some way preventing the consummation of its work. But to the honor of the other half be it said, the proposition of bad faith, tending to anarchy and civil war, was rejected.

Failing in their first move, the minority resorted to various expedients to prevent the completion of the count till the session of this congress would expire. Dilatory motions were resorted to, showing the ingenuity of seventy or eighty conspirators who wished to defeat the count. Part of the time the rulings of the Speaker of the House, Mr. Randall, were worthy of all praise, though at other times he most plainly evinced the desire to serve two masters, a thing which the Savior teaches is not a success—certainly it was not in this case.

One of the strange things was that in the effort to defeat filibustering, Fernando Wood, of New York, a noted party Democrat, became for a time the leader of the Republicans.

The honor and patriotism displayed by something like one half of the Democratic members in keeping the contract under which the count was entered into is deserving of all praise. It is also notably true that the southern Democratic members showed their honor and patriotism in larger proportions than did those of the North, though there were diverse exceptions from both sections. Some fell into distinguished dishonor. The last day, when the House was considering one of the questions involved, the legislative hall was turned for hours into comparative anarchy—sometimes bordering on the superlative. One representative leaped upon the desks and gesticulated wildly. Others talked and acted as if demented.

What bad faith would have been exhibited if all efforts to complete the count of the electoral vote had been defeated. It would have covered the Democratic party with infamy.

The bearing and rulings of Vice-president Ferry are worthy of much praise. He showed that of the high estimate heretofore placed on him as a presiding officer he was well worthy.

The whole affair has turned out as we anticipated. All the commissioners were most faithful to their party convictions. The whole thing really turned on the choice of the fifteenth man. It was Bradley, a Republican, instead of a Democrat; therefore Hayes, and not Tilden, is President. It wrought up the defeated party to the highest possible pitch of dissatisfaction with the result of the count. But it is said all is well that ends well; and we hope that the saying may be true in this case at least. We further hope that the whole machinery of an electoral college will be done away with before another presidential election.

March 28, 1877   The New Administration Policy

When any great conflict terminates in clear victory to either side, it is wise policy in the conquerors to reconcile, at the earliest practicable moment, those defeated. It is no less good policy in the vanquished to accept the situation and harmonize with the new order of things, unless some moral principle or sacred right is thereby sacrificed. Our Government has been for twelve years laboring to reconstruct and rebuild what the rebellion had rent and torn to pieces. A conviction has been for some years increasing that twelve years after the close of the war reconciliation ought to be more nearly effected between the once contending parties. Perhaps some have been unreasonably sanguine of speedy reconciliation. All have a right to long for it.

With the incoming of the present administration there has been an unusual effort to reach at once this desirable object. The key-note of President Hayes' letter of acceptance, of his inaugural address, and of his first weeks of administration has been the pacification of the South, or rather of the discordant elements of American politics, as existing between the two chief sections and races. He proposes the most friendly and liberal policy toward the South, provided the legal rights of all—freedmen and late confederate—shall be unmistakably assured. His appointments to cabinet positions have been the clearest proofs that his proposition was not for the ear only, but also in deed. Nor is his appointment of Frederick Douglass, the great ex-slave orator, as marshal of the District of Columbia less in harmony with his policy, which had for one of its chief conditions the recognition of the colored people as American citizens, with all the rights and consideration which the Constitution and laws guaranty and imply as theirs.

President Hayes proposes the withdrawal of national troops from those southern states—where their presence was deemed necessary to repress violence and bloodshed—but only on condition of the fullest assurance and adequate guaranties that henceforth the lives and legal rights of all southern citizens, black and white, shall be maintained in good faith by the strong arm of state authorities. Until the real situation has been duly investigated by a first-class, non-partisan commission, to be appointed by the President in the spirit in which he chose his cabinet, and until full assurance and ample guaranties can be secured for the maintenance of peace and the rights of all, the President's policy is to maintain the *statu* [*sic*] *quo* as to the presence of United States troops. This policy appeals for favor to the reason of all, whatever their convictions or party predilections.

The President's utterances and administrative acts, thus far, have harmonized well with civil-service reform, which has been for years establishing itself in the minds and hearts of the great body of honest, intelligent American citizens. In this, as also in the other measures referred to, he has been as consistent as he has been firm and conciliatory.

In several respects his administration began under favorable auspices for the success of the policy it is pursuing. Mr. Hayes was barely elected by the Republican party, and that without a popular majority. Party claims on him seem to be confessedly slight. In his acceptance as a candidate, he had fore-shadowed his present reform policy; and the platforms of both of the great political parties had favored the same. The popular heart demanded civil service reform. It demanded also an honest, independent administration. It inclined, too, to regard the spirit and measures growing out of the war as something that ought to be of the past. Mr. Hayes' administration is likely to have the sympathy and support of the real friends of reform, of which we may hope the number is great. Those in the South who are tired of continued conflict will also wish it the completest [*sic*] success. All everywhere who regard strife as hateful, impoverishing and dangerous will hail all sincere and hopeful signs of progress in pacification. None will regard it with more favor than the freedmen, if they can be assured that their lives, liberties, and rights as citizens will not be sacrificed. The President may possibly secure much support from white citizens of the South who have been for years compelled to choose between incompetent or designing rulers and those cherishing the memory of slavery and hating the liberated race.

The President will be openly or secretly opposed by patronage princes who have thought to secure or continue to maintain seats in the Senate or House of Representatives by dispensing executive patronage—hitherto placed at their disposal—to reward those who work most successfully for their election. Those who claim executive reward for distinguished party services will also feel sore from disappointment. Those, too, who count it patriotism to hate anything not Bourbon in its Democratic degree must needs oppose the President—the more if his policy promises popular success. Those also who suspect that the President's policy either intends or will eventuate in the triumph of southern intimidation and the sacrifice of the freedmen will be slow to fall in with the bold measures of pacification which have signalized his administration thus far. Those who doubt the practicability of the pacification policy of the President will also be slow to give it effectual support.

The President will have powerful and hitherto effective rings and combinations to fight. It may also be difficult to strike the line of safety between that *rigor* necessary to restrain a still existing disloyalty, which once sought the destruction of our Government, and that *license* which would renew the southern massacres of the past, and turn elections into struggles of mob violence against the real choice of voters. Mr. Hayes has begun well, and will, we trust, prove true and victorious. The approval of the American people is with him thus far, and there now seems to be good ground to hope that his administration will receive the favor of the best class of white citizens in the South—who perceive that anarchy means evil and ruin—and continue to have that of the American people generally.

Portrait of Bishop Milton Wright. Photograph by S. P. Tresize, Dayton, Ohio, 1883. Image courtesy of Special Collections and Archives, Wright State University, Dayton, Ohio.

RELIGIOUS
TELESCOPE
CHURCH OF THE UNITED BRETHREN IN CHRIST

Vol. 100   Dayton, Ohio, December 29, 1934   No. 52

Our Editors of Other Years

William Hanby	David Edwards	John Lawrence
Daniel Berger	William R. Rhinehart	Milton Wright
J. W. Hott	I. L. Kephart	J. M. Phillippi

1834 CENTENNIAL NUMBER 1934

Editors of the Religious Telescope, 1834-1934. Image courtesy of the Center for the Evangelical United Brethren Heritage, United Theological Seminary, Dayton, Ohio.

Epilogue

After two terms of service in the position to which the General Conference called us eight years ago, we now retire from editorial duties and responsibilities. We do this grateful to our people for the confidence and support which they have given us, and with gratitude to God for his grace and providence which have sustained us in our arduous labors and brought us to the present day with health unimpaired, though severely tried, and sometimes crying for respite from long-protracted toil and care.

We entered upon editorial duties at a peculiarly critical period of our church history, and have passed through these years, meeting the responsibilities attaching to our position with sincere purpose best to serve the true interests of the Church and promote the cause of our Master.

Inexperienced in editorial work, we entered upon our responsible labors only confident that we should have the prayers of the Church in an unusual degree, and that the Lord would not withhold his grace nor fail in his good providence if we put our trust in him. Our own failure and resultant disesteem in the public mind seemed not at all improbable; yet we doubted not that God would be glorified, in his own way, by our feeble but sincere efforts to promote the truth. No doubt we have often erred in judgment, but our labors and record have had strict regard to that which we would be willing to meet in future years, and to answer for in the final day.

In the exercise of our best judgment we have sometimes been compelled not to gratify the wishes of some of our warmest friends, as well as those having less sympathy with us in our work; but we are conscious that our course has been free from captiousness and partiality, and we are thankful for the degree of forbearance and good-will generally shown us in those inevitable differences of

247

opinion which arise between an editor and that most helpful and highly-valued class of co-laborers who furnish correspondence. Who could please all if he were never to err in judgment? But who is it that never errs?

We enter upon a more sacred and honored office, but one not presenting greater opportunities for usefulness, nor involving greater responsibility. While the confidence and good-will expressed in our election to a new position is fully appreciated, we trust that in our heart we accept it with humility, feeling our own unworthiness and insufficiency.

In closing our present relations to the office, we can not forbear acknowledging our obligations to our co-laborers in the publishing house, including the foreman and others of the composing-room. We part with them all with the kindliest feelings.

Toward our associates in editorial work on the paper we are sure kind feelings and esteem have not suffered but increased with these years. Both remain to serve the Church in the editorial relations for which their talents and taste eminently fit them. With these years our love and esteem have grown toward our now immediate associate, with whom we part with the utmost confidence in his learning, ability, piety, and devotion to God, and his faithfulness to the best interests of the Church.

Our successor in editorial labors is no stranger in Zion, but one whose praise is in all the churches. As a man of God and as a servant of the Church he is as true as he is facile with the pen and brilliant in speech. In our heart's affection and confidence he is among the nearest of our co-laborers. We confidently anticipate increased interest and success to our dear church paper under his labors and management. For him—as also for his worthy associate—we bespeak the prayers and sympathies of our people; for to him these labors will be new and trying.

Our direct relations with the editorial fraternity now terminate. Members of this honored brotherhood have shown us—almost without exception—nothing but good-will and courtesy. We have loved them as brethren, and shall henceforth miss the periodical return of their many fair faced journals, containing news, instruction, and cheer. We, not missed, shall greatly miss their choice words.

But our most tender feelings of farewell are toward our many readers and correspondents. To the latter, we and our people are under lasting obligations. The Lord reward them. To our readers we say *farewell,* feeling that of our selections and of our own words they have partaken, and hoping that some have been warned against error and led into the right path by our feeble efforts, with the divine blessing. Others have been brought to Christ, and others still have been built up in the faith, comforted, and cheered by the columns with which we have been connected. We will never fully know what the harvest shall be till the reaping-time shall come. Then we hope to greet many loving and beloved readers whose faces we have never seen on earth. Warm greetings, the past few years, from previously unseen friends, cause us to think of the "harvest-home" when we shall all greet our Savior as all in all, and greet each other as his servants and friends, and as joint-heirs with him in his Father's kingdom.

MILTON WRIGHT

June 20, 1877 · **Bishop Milton Wright**
A Tribute by W. O. Tobey

"The proper character, the sign, of a great man is, that he succeeds. Whoever does not succeed is of no use in the world, leaves no great result, and passes away as if he had never been." Such is the language of Victor Cousin in his History of Modern Philosophy. By this standard we judge churchmen as well as artists, philosphers [sic], legislators, and warriors. We have men in our denomination who are entitled to the name of great men estimated by this true and modest test.

As a preacher, presiding elder, educator, and editor, Rev. Milton Wright has been eminently successful. His eight years of journalism at the head of the RELIGIOUS TELESCOPE have given him the best opportunity to prove his activity, versatility, and strength of thought. He stands entitled to-day to rank among the ablest of the religious journalists of the American churches. Not only we, his recent associate in editorial work, say so, but his impartial contemporaries throughout the country have held him in no lower estimation than ours. Those who look not beyond the subscription list of the paper he edited may not fully coincide with our view. Editor Wright must be judged by a higher principle. He is in everything much the turn of the great Dr. Arnold, of Rugby, who, while exercising the strictest discipline in that noted institution, said: "It is *not* necessary that this should be a school of three hundred, or one hundred, or fifty boys; but it *is* necessary that it should be a school of Christian gentlemen." In Editor Wright's mind it was not necessary that the TELESCOPE should have ten thousand, or forty thousand, subscribers; but it was necessary that it should be an able and correct exponent of our Church principles. He succeeded according to the highest test of church journalism. We never expect to look with more satisfaction upon any years of our life than those four in which we were associated with him in working out that ideal of journalism in our Church. We are not aware that those four years of associate editorship have proved the failure of the plan. In all essentials our views and work were the most harmonious, especially after they had fully ripened into a reliable adjustment. Our high appreciation of him as one whom close intimacy has helped us to love not less but more delays us in proceeding to a more general sketch of his life and labors.

Bishop Wright was born in Rush County, Indiana, November 17th, 1828. He
is, therefore, now nearly forty-nine years old. His parents, by example and precept, gave him an early bias toward true piety, as well as industry, study, and
other useful habits. We have seen how he enshrines his pious and sainted mother
in his affections. Both parents died happily, at a ripe old age. He was converted
at the age of fourteen years, and at once began preparation for a life of usefulness. He has never lost sight of this idea of usefulness. Four years after conversion, he first entered into church relationship, deliberately choosing the United
Brethren in Christ, not on account of its popularity, but as the best in doctrine,
discipline, and purity of membership. On his twenty-second birthday he
preached his first sermon. He joined White River Conference in 1853, and is
still one of its foremost members. For two years he preached in a local capacity
while engaged in hard study. Indianapolis was his first charge, where he was
very successful. The next year he was assigned to Andersonville Circuit, his
home charge. Before the close of the year he was appointed by the Board a missionary to Oregon. He sailed *via* the isthmus, and reached Oregon in August,
1857. He was prostrated by Panama fever, and barely recovered. He was employed as principal of Sublimity College, then just opened in Oregon, and taught
two years, also preaching much. He voluntarily ceased teaching to preach as a
missionary. In 1859 he returned to Indiana, and was married to Miss Susan C.
Koerner, an accomplished Christian lady, who has since been a devoted companion in all his labors. After his return he traveled circuit three years and districts eight years in his conference, and saw many conversions, especially on
Williamsburg Circuit, where in one year two hundred and twenty were added to
the Church. He was next elected to a theological chair in Hartsville University,
where he taught and served as pastor nearly a year, when he was appointed editor of the RELIGIOUS TELESCOPE by the General Conference of 1869. He
served in that trust for four years, and was re-elected for another term of the
same length. At the recent General Conference he was honored with election to
the office of bishop, and was assigned to the West Mississippi District.

Bishop Wright was early indoctrinated with opposition to slavery, organized secrecy, and intemperance. He has long been a recognized leader in the
reforms dear to our Church. Many who have been reading his writings have
never seen him, and he has not been before this sketched in any of our papers.
Hence this attempt may deserve a little indulgence for length. He is five feet
eight inches in hight [*sic*], solidly formed, and weights about one hundred and
eighty pounds. His appearance is pleasant, with the attraction of dark hair, dark-
grey eyes, and full face. His voice is round and forcible. He is commanding as a
speaker, and always says things that are worth hearing. His labors have been
highly beneficial to the Church; and instead of his work being done, it has been
a serious question whether he was most needed in the immediate future as an
editor or bishop.

Index

Abbott, F. C., 195
Abel, 16
Abraham, 16, 42, 70
Absalom, 37, 112, 164, 165
Adam, 34, 52, 63
Adams, Charles Francis, 229
Adams, John Quincy, 70
Africa, 123, 131, 132, 156, 157,
    158, 168
African Americans, 29, 146, 156,
    157, 179, 183, 190, 216, 217,
    218, 222, 229, 230, 231, 235,
    237, 243, 244
Alleghany Theological Seminary,
    129
Allison, R., 115
Amaziah, 112
Ambition, 24, 53, 63, 64, 106
American Antislavery Society, 1
American Centennial, 226
American Civil War, 5, 29, 138,
    178, 184, 187, 198, 202, 213,
    216, 217, 223
    Andersonville Prison, 29
    Libby Prison, 29
    The Union, 29
American Jurist, 213

American Missionary Association,
    131
American Revolution, 89, 223
American Wesleyan Connection,
    162
Aminadab, 60
Amram, 70
Anabaptism, 3
Angels, 16, 20, 22, 24, 26, 34, 39,
    44, 58, 63, 80, 81, 83
Anna, 104
Anthony, Susan B., 184
Anti-masonic Party, 1
Apelles, 126
Apostles, 16, 18, 38, 39, 40, 42, 44,
    46, 51, 59, 71, 77, 87, 102, 110,
    111
Arkansas, 217, 218
Arnold, Thomas, 249
Ascension, 38, 47
Asia, 123, 172
Associate Reformed Church, 162
Atheists, 212, 225
Atonement, 23, 24, 28, 54
Aydellott, Dr., 195

Babylon, 47

Wilberforce, Daniel F., 130, 131
Wilberforce, William, 214
Willdenow, Carl Ludwig, 171
Wilson, Bluford, 233
Wilson, Henry, 198, 204
Wiltz, Louis Alfred, 220, 221
Winnipeg war, 68
Wisconsin
  Madison, 95
Wisdom, 23, 28, 35, 43, 51, 55, 71,
  77, 78, 83, 106
Wishart, George, 25, 44
Wolsey, Thomas, 176
Woman's Advocate, 184
Woman's Journal, 184
Woman's Suffrage, 184, 185
Women, 3, 4, 7, 19, 38, 45, 94, 95,
  176, 184, 186
Wood, Fernando, 242
Woodland Cemetery, 161, 188
Wooster University, 195
Work, 4, 21, 24, 31, 39, 41, 51, 55,
  56, 57, 58, 60, 72, 75, 76, 81,
  94, 95, 103, 109, 110, 247, 248,
  249, 250
Worship, 16, 20, 24, 28, 43, 46, 50,
  58, 60, 63, 72, 74, 75, 78, 79,
  81, 86, 87, 93, 96, 101, 105,
  109, 110, 112
Wright, Milton, 1, 2, 3, 5, 6, 7, 120,
  249, 250
Wright, Orville, 5, 7
Wright, Susan Koerner, 4, 250
Wright, Wilbur, 5, 7
Wyoming, 182, 185, 186, 232
  Cheyenne, 186

Xerxes, 69

Yaryan, H. T., 233
Young, Brigham, 181

Zacharias, 71
Zadok, 164
Zinzendorf, Nicholas von, 26

About the Editor

Timothy S. G. Binkley is a graduate of The Defiance College, Bethany Theological Seminary, and Wright State University. An ordained minister in the Church of the Brethren, Tim served as Pastor of the Onekama (Michigan) Church of the Brethren from 1994 to 2003. He has worked as a museum professional in Ohio, Michigan, and Illinois, and as a graduate assistant in the Wright State University Special Collections and Archives. Since 2005 Tim has served United Theological Seminary as Archivist and Curator of the Center for the Evangelical United Brethren Heritage. His first major exhibit at United was "Milton Wright: Editor Bishop."